PAGE 1: At 8:30 A.M., on February 16, 1945, after a withering aerial and naval bombardment, the first wave of airborne troops from the 503rd Parachute Infantry Regiment made difficult jumps from C-47 transports, aiming for two tiny flat areas on the island of Corregidor.

THIS PAGE: On March 15, 1944, soldiers from the U.S. 1st Cavalry Division land near Lugos Mission on Manus, in the Admiralty Islands, and for three days carry weapons and munitions through waist-deep water as they work towards Japanese-held Lorengau airdrome.

ARMY
An Illustrated History
The U.S. Army from 1775 to the 21st Century

Chester G. Hearn

ZENITH PRESS

Project manager: Ray Bonds
Design: Ian Hughes/Compendium Design
Editors: Ray Bonds and Don Gulbrandsen
Maps: Mike Marino

ISBN-13: 978-0-7603-2680-0
ISBN-10: 0-7603-2680-0

Printed in China

Acknowledgments
Thanks to all those who helped with photographs including Mindy Day, Simon Dunstan, George Forty, Katie Johnston, Marc Seigerman. Most of the images in this book come from National Archives, Department of Defense, or U.S. Army sources except the following: Compendium 76 (T&C), 96(T), 100. Corbis 21(B), 24(R), 45(R), 60, 92(L), 97(L); Bettmann/Corbis 23, 25, 26(L), 108; Dave G. Houser/Corbis 12(L); Ink 2, LLC/Corbis 48(BR&TR), 53(TR), 55(B), 64(TR, CR, BR), 73(R), 116(L); KT Historical/Corbis 94 Jeremy Flack 38(both), 42(TL), 54(T). Getty Images 10, 11, 12(C), 15(B), 20(B), 22(B), 24(L), 26–27, 52(T), 92(R), 114, 142; AFP/Getty Images 91, 128; Time Life Pictures/Getty Images 7, 52(BR), 93, 119, 125(R), 126(L), 129, 131(both)132, 147 Library of Congress 6, 12(R), 13, 14(both), 15(T), 16(both), 18(all), 19, 20(A), 22(B), 24(T), 44(all), 45(L), 47(both), 48(T), 49(both), 50, 51(all), 52(BL), 53(T&BL), 64(R), 78, 115

Weary soldiers slug through the Italian mud, casting an occasional look at the M8 HMCs alongside. These vehicles were equipped with a 75mm howitzer in an open-topped turret mounted on an M5 light tank chassis.

CONTENTS

INTRODUCTION

The United States Army is and always has been a work in progress. Ever since the formation of the Continental Army on June 15, 1775, the soldier has always been the protector of American democracy. Those men were a special breed of patriots willing to sacrifice their lives so that others may enjoy life, liberty, and the pursuit of happiness. From a rabble in homespun rags fighting under George Washington in 1775, the American soldier has transformed through the centuries into "An Army of One," which is actually much more than a slogan. The army is a team of professionals interacting together as one, but the soldier of today is a highly capable individual fitted out to fight as an army of one. The U.S. Army was not always the best equipped, the best trained, the best led, and the most respected and highly motivated volunteer military organization on earth, but it is today, and the soldier makes it so.

The transform-ation did not come easily, nor will it stop. As technology advances, so will the doctrine of warfighting. The days when masses of troops were thrown at each other to gain a slice of battlefield are ending. So are the traditional demands for "uncondit-ional surrender"—the last world power to fall under this blood-spattered doctrine of attrition was Japan in August 1945. Today the objective of the army is not to waste men, but to use them purposefully, train them extensively, and provide them with all the means of protection that new, constantly evolving technology makes possible.

Enemies also change. The army fought Great Britain in 1775 and 1812, but the United Kingdom is now our closest ally. During the Civil War the army separated into two adversarial forces and for four years clashed in a politically and economically induced rebellion supported by Americans of two conflicting cultures. The U.S. Army fought Germany, Italy, and Japan in World War II. Today they are our allies, standing beside the United States through forty years of political turmoil in a joint effort that brought

RIGHT: On September 13, 1847, Americans storm the fortified rocky slopes leading to Chapultepec, the last major obstacle outside Mexico City. On that day a pair of young lieutenants, Ulysses S. Grant and Thomas J. Jackson, won brevets for heroism.

an end to the Cold War. As Russian president Vladimir Putin grudgingly admitted in April 2005, "The collapse of the Soviet Union was the greatest geopolitical catastrophe of the century." The armed forces have made it possible for enemies to become friends, and no service branch has more direct and ongoing contact with friends and enemies than the U.S. Army.

In a world governed by geopolitical and economic interests, enemies change. The war on terror and insurgency added another dimension to warfighting doctrine. Terrorists and insurgents have no national standing, no government, no uniformed army, no allegiance to international law, no interest in humanity, and no restrictions on the weapons they are willing to use to achieve economic, political, and theocratic domination of the world. The role of the U.S. Army constantly changes to meet new threats and challenges. The army must remain flexible, agile, technologically superior, and project military power abroad while dividing the soldiers time between missions of warfighting, peacekeeping, and nation building wherever such duty calls.

The one million men and women serving in the army, the reserves, and the National Guard cost a great deal of money, more than $100 billion per year. Politicians and the public alike expect something in return for the expenditure. Today the public is getting the best standing all-volunteer army in the world. There will always be budgetary restraints, and there will always be political changes in government where civilian authorities hold conflicting views about

BELOW: On the night of December 25, 1776, with his little army disintegrating as enlistments expired, General George Washington took a desperate chance. Using small boats loaded with 2,400 men, he crossed the ice-caked waters of the Delaware River during a snowstorm and early in the morning defeated the British at the Battle of Trenton.

applying military restraints to world and national threats. It has happened through the centuries, and in all likelihood it will happen again.

Today's army is one with a trail-blazing history. It is a fascinating study of change and technology, evolving through 230 years of trial and error. The transformation began the day soldiers of the Continental Army, whose officers were influenced by eighteenth-century European military theory, decided that fighting "Indian-style" made more sense than fighting "Redcoat-style." Colonists also discovered that accurate hunting weapons with rifled barrels were far more lethal than flintlock muskets carried by British regiments. The failure to adapt to changing weapons

technology as it applied to warfighting doctrine trickled through the years and caused enormous casualties in America's Civil War. More than 600,000 men lost their lives because generals had not adjusted obsolete European field tactics to improvements in rifled and rapid-fire weapons.

And so the transformation began, erratic for the most part, sometimes leaping ahead and sometimes falling behind, but always evolving. To understand the great changes in the army today is to understand the successes and mistakes of the past. The AirLand Battle doctrine adopted by the army in the late 1970s—a doctrine that became so successful in the Persian Gulf Wars—is the net result of warfighting adjustments to the technology of today. The emerging strategy for fighting terrorism and insurgency is the net result of experiences in places like Vietnam, Lebanon, Bosnia, Kosovo, Somalia, Afghanistan, and Iraq.

New warfighting tools are coming on line everyday. They cost a great deal of money, but they will save soldier's lives. Even in Operation Iraqi Freedom there were failures in communication that are being corrected today. A corps commander could not always keep track of his army on the move. Today an individual soldier using a Navstar Global Positioning System, which connects him to an overhead satellite in orbit, knows exacting where he is and can communicate accurately his position up the chain of command. In the war against insurgency there will be weapons that can shoot around corners, locate and eliminate targets beyond the line of sight, and distinguish friendlies from unfriendlies. A new series of weapons for Future Combat Systems are already in the works and on schedule for 2008. Nanotechnology, with massive communications potential, will be sown into soldiers' uniforms or implanted in his goggles. The future soldier is rapidly becoming part of a "system of systems" that

BELOW: In July 1967, men of the 4th Battalion, 60th Artillery, stand guard on the perimeter of a Fire Support Base in Dek, Vietnam. Although the M42A1 self-propelled antiaircraft gun was obsolete by the time of the Vietnam War, the twin 40mm Bofors nonetheless could lay down a withering fire against ground troops.

encompasses, monitors, targets, and controls a defined tactical area. Nor are tactical areas exclusively massive battlefields. They are becoming insurgent safe houses, unseen tunnels, and improvised explosive devices capable of releasing chemical and biological substances.

What the army has done over the centuries speaks of the progression into what the army is doing today and planning to do tomorrow. Together, the transformation provides a remarkable trip from the past into the future.

BELOW: When NKA forces invaded South Korea on June 25, 1950, the only tanks available were relics from WWII. MacArthur sent all the M4A3 Shermans available in Japan, but they were poorly matched against the T-34/85s furnished by the Soviets.

THE FORMATIVE YEARS 1620–1814

The Colonial Militia

No establishment in the United States has a longer or more fascinating past than the army. In 1620 the Pilgrims initiated the military process by hiring Captain Miles Standish, a professional English soldier, to form and train a band of part-time warriors to protect the colony from Indians. As immigration increased, enrollment became a local matter and soon every township in New England had its own organized militia. During 1636–1637 the colonies of Plymouth, Massachusetts Bay, and Connecticut

banded together, incorporated their local units for the first time into regiments, and virtually annihilated the Pequot Indians. A generation later levies from those same colonies massed again in 1675 and during King Philip's War brought an end to Indian resistance in all of New England.

Like Standish, former British soldiers became the drillmasters, bringing with them the warfighting doctrine of Europe. Old World tactics did not work so well in the virgin forests of America, but the training, organization, and discipline bonded fighting units

BELOW: One of the first altercations between the colonists and the Wampanoag Indians occurred during King Philip's War, which began on June 20, 1675, in southern New England and lasted three years.

together. By the eighteenth century every colony in America had a number of militia companies structured along the lines of a British fighting unit, but with the Indians neutralized in coastal areas, the militias became fraternal organizations rather than fighting units. They were officered by incompetent political appointees, favorites of colonial governors, or popular appointees entirely unfit for military leadership. The frivolity ended when the fighting began.

The French and Indian War

Colonists-in-arms learned bitter lessons about fighting during the mid-1700s when Pennsylvanians and Virginians began drifting into the Ohio Valley and clashing with the French-Canadians who were exploiting the area. In 1755, the second year of the seven-year French and Indian War, England sent General Edward Braddock to North America with two regiments (1,000 men) of British regulars. Reinforced by four hundred colonials, mostly Virginians, Braddock's men marched in fine military order westward. Braddock followed a trail along the banks of Monongahela River, his men ready for battle European style. Young Colonel George Washington accompanied the expedition as a volunteer advisor, but Braddock did not want advice. Eight miles from Fort Duquesne (later Pittsburgh, Pennsylvania) an unseen enemy attacked from the front and flank. Braddock's well-appointed regulars, their red coats making bright, distinguishable targets in the forests, fled in panic. Washington had clashed with the enemy in 1754 and learned the hard way of how the

BELOW: On July 9, 1755, General Edward Braddock learned a bloody lesson about wilderness fighting when the French and Indians, led by Charles Langlade, fired from the woods and ambushed 1,500 British regulars near Fort Duquesne.

French and Indians fought. He reformed the scattered elements, led them into the brush, and saved the survivors from losing their scalps.

Braddock lost his life and so did many of his men, and this gave birth to a fallacious tradition that American frontiersmen and militiamen were somehow superior to the British regular. Braddock's defeat clearly demonstrated that eighteenth-century battle tactics—precise linear masses of musketmen fighting shoulder-to-shoulder—did not work in the wilderness. What did work was the carefully aimed fire of a marksman disciplined to make every shot count. The best-trained marksman could not make many shots count firing a smoothbore flintlock musket, the most popular British infantry weapon in the eighteenth century, because the discharged ball never went straight. Robert Rogers of New Hampshire filled the gap by gathering together a band of trained hunter-woodsmen and formed them into Rogers' Rangers. He armed the unit with Kentucky (actually Pennsylvania-made) rifles, which enabled a marksman to knock the head off a turkey at two hundred yards. In Rogers' Rangers, every shot counted.

The British recognized that fighting tactics in the colonies required adjustment and in 1756 formed the Royal Americans (Sixtieth Foot). Composed of

Americans, Germans, and British regulars, the regiment received training in an entirely new technique called open-order fighting. With better muskets and Kentucky rifles, the new tactic proved immensely effective during General James Wolfe's successful assault on Quebec during the French and Indian War. The same tactics are used today, though they are constantly modified to keep pace with improvements in weapon technology.

With the close of the French and Indian War, the martial spirit ebbed but the militias survived, becoming much as they were before the war. They consisted of two types—the "minutemen" who turned out like a volunteer fire company when the alarm bell tolled, and the "regular" militia, which

ABOVE: A reenactor wears the uniform of an early Virginia militia company. Each wooden flask draped around his torso contains a single ball and gunpowder to fire it. The flask contains powder to prime the pan.

RIGHT: One of the recruiting posters used to attract young men into the Continental Army showed the ten steps required for loading a flintlock musket.

FAR RIGHT: Robert Rogers (1731–1795), a daring, able, and resourceful leader of scouts and rangers, fought for the British in both the French and Indian War and in the American Revolution.

lapsed back to the old habit of assembling once a year for a beer party and a venison roast on the village green. In the towns of New England, however, minutemen took their responsibilities seriously.

The Shot Heard Round the World

On April 19, 1775, British General Thomas Gage decided to teach a lesson to the disobedient Massachusetts rabble resisting the king's punitive tax measures, and sent 700 men from his Boston garrison into Lexington and Concord—where Massachusetts had established a revolutionary government—to "seize and destroy all the Artillery, Ammunition, provisions, Tents & all other military stores you can find." When the British column stopped at Lexington, someone fired a single shot that led to the killing of eight minutemen and ushered in the Revolution. A verbal skirmish later ensued over who fired the first shot. Angry militia from surrounding towns converged on the redcoats. Using Indian-style hit-and-run tactics, the minutemen fired from cover, killing seventy-three and wounding 174, and drove the British back to Boston. On May 9, while General Gage paused to assess what had happened at Lexington and Concord, Ethan Allen's Vermont irregulars, the "Green Mountain Boys," aided by Colonel Benedict Arnold's Connecticut militia, attacked and seized the British garrison at Fort Ticonderoga, New York, on the western shore of Lake Champlain.

BELOW: On April 19, 1775, British regulars ran into a hornet's nest at Lexington and Concord and were chased back to Boston by colonial Minutemen, losing 73 killed, 174 wounded, and 26 missing during the retreat.

The Continental Congress, formed in September 1774 at Philadelphia, Pennsylvania, now had something to do, and after much debate decided on May 25, 1775, to put the colonies in a state of military readiness. On June 14 the legislators adopted a general plan for the Continental Army and authorized several companies of regular riflemen; that date is now recognized as the birth of the United States Army. European-style seniority played a role on June 17 when Congress named General George Washington commander-in-chief, because he had been America's ranking officer during the French and Indian War. While Washington was receiving handshakes from the legislature, the bloody Battle of Breed's (Bunker) Hill raged on the peninsula of Charlestown opposite Boston.

Congress also adopted a code to govern the armed forces. As might be expected, the Continental code of conduct came directly from British regulations. It imposed a higher standard on officers, and read, "Whatsoever commissioned officer shall be convicted, before a general court martial, of behaving in a scandalous, infamous manner, such as unbecoming an officer and a gentleman, shall be discharged from the service." The code of honor became the cornerstone that governed the conduct of officers for decades to come and gave Washington the authority he needed to trim from the army the pilferers and incompetent philanderers who held lofty commissions in the militia.

On July 3 Congress sent Washington to the Boston area, where almost all the colonial forces were massed. The headcounts showed 16,770 militiamen on the rolls, but nearly 20 percent of the men were either absent or on the sick list. Enlistments for most of the men, already homesick, were scheduled to expire in December. When asked to reenlist under the new Continental regulations, only one man in six agreed.

> I found a mixed multitude of People here, under very little discipline, order, or Government….Confusion and disorder reigned in every Department. The men regarded their officers no more than broomsticks.
> *George Washington at Boston.*

No wonder—one man could barely be

distinguished from another. There were no uniforms, except the few variegated and tattered rags worn by some volunteer militia companies. Continental infantry units arrived in civilian clothes, usually brown, frock-like hunting shirts, which soon became the most common pattern for the army. Extemporized ribbons and cockades of various colors served as insignia of rank. Congress ordered that army uniforms were to include brown coats with different colored facings to distinguish the regiments—a system borrowed from the British army—but the legislature never produced the funds to clothe the men. Sometimes the only part of the uniform that distinguished a soldier from a civilian was the headwear, a prized "cocked hat," provided that a soldier could find or afford one.

Volunteers provided their own weapons, usually muskets or fowling pieces of different calibers. They had to melt and make their own lead bullets and

RIGHT: On May 10, 1775, while his Green Mountain Boys wait below, Ethan Allen (1738–1789) ascends stairs with sword raised to tell the commandant that he has taken command of Fort Ticonderoga.

LEFT: On April 19, 1775, somebody fired the "shot heard 'round the world," and though William Barnes Wallen painted a masterwork of the battle on Lexington Green, the skirmish actually took place at Concord.

THE BATTLE OF BREED'S (BUNKER) HILL

During the first months of the war, neither side occupied Charlestown's peninsula, which lay across the river from Boston. On June 13, 1775, General Israel Putnam of the Connecticut militia and Colonel William Prescott of the Massachusetts militia decided that the colonists had better take control of Charlestown before the redcoats did. Two days later, with permission from the Committee of Safety, colonial militia began moving into the area. Putnam brought carts filled with entrenching tools and, after a two-hour discussion of where best to dig, made the mistake of putting the main fortification on sixty-two-foot-high Breed's Hill instead of on 110-foot-high Bunker Hill.

The British General Gage could not allow the colonists to move artillery capable of bombarding Boston onto Charlestown's hills. He agreed to a pair of amphibious landings along Mystic River, one to attack the colonists on Breed's Hill and the other to land in the rear and cut off the enemy's retreat. The strategy made sense, but the execution proved sloppy. At noon on June 17, preceded by a Royal Navy bombardment, Brigadier General Robert Pigot's fifteen hundred redcoats crossed the river and landed unopposed at Moulton's Hill. There they formed three lines and moved on Breed's Hill. Another one thousand men under Sir William Howe enveloped the American left to execute a classic pincer's movement.

British tactics did not work as planned. Firing from behind fences, Colonel John Stark's New Hampshire militia, all good marksmen, held their fire until the British came in close range and tore the head of Howe's column apart. Howe attacked again, but Stark had arranged his riflemen in three rows, one firing while the other two reloaded. He instructed his men to aim low and shoot the British officers.

Howe and Pigot regrouped and together sent their infantry against the redoubt on Breed's Hill and the rail fence below the hill. The second attack failed as dismally as the first and for the very same reasons, but some of the colonials had now exhausted their ammunition and were falling back to Bunker Hill.

Reinforced by four hundred fresh troops, Howe organized a third assault. He ordered his men to drop their knapsacks and charge with bayonets. British artillery opened fire on the redoubt to cover the assault. At some point Putnam was quoted as yelling, "Don't fire until you see the whites of their eyes," but that order probably came from Prescott. The colonials opened fire at ten yards and discharged most of their remaining ammunition, repelling the assault. The next British column to storm the redoubt was met with rocks and clubbed muskets. Most of the colonists fought their way out of the redoubt and took refuge on Bunker Hill.

The British sustained 1,150 casualties, the colonials 441. No action did more to rally the colonies and spur the Continental Congress into action than the fight on Breed's Hill.

RIGHT: On June 17, 1775, the British attempted to break the siege of Boston by driving the Continentals off Charleston Neck. The battle resulted in two phases, the first against Breed's Hill: the second against Bunker Hill. The Battle of Bunker Hill rallied the colonies.

LEFT: On June 17, 1775, the British crossed from Boston to Charlestown in ships in an effort to break the siege. E. Percy Moran's painting depicts the bloody British charge up Bunker Hill.

LEFT: English ships and artillery attempt to soften up the Continental's position on Breed's Hill as the British form to launch the first of several attacks against the colonial redoubt.

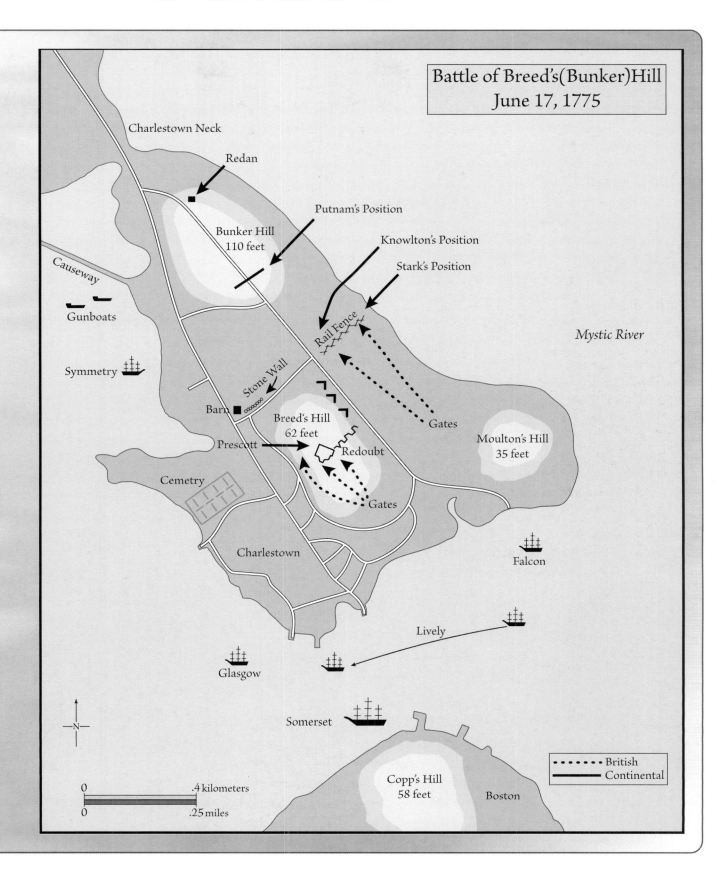

Battle of Breed's(Bunker)Hill
June 17, 1775

Charlestown Neck

Redan

Putnam's Position

Knowlton's Position

Stark's Position

Bunker Hill
110 feet

Mystic River

Causeway

Gunboats

Rail Fence

Symmetry

Stone Wall

Barn

Breed's Hill
62 feet

Gates

Moulton's Hill
35 feet

Prescott

Redoubt

Cemetery

Gates

Charlestown

Falcon

Lively

Glasgow

Somerset

British
Continental

Copp's Hill
58 feet

Boston

0   .4 kilometers
0   .25 miles

—N—

ABOVE: General Horatio Gates (1728–1806) performed valuable service organizing the Continental Army around Boston, but he is best known as the general commanding Continental forces during the Battle of Saratoga (June–October 1777).

BELOW: Anthony "Mad Anthony" Wayne (1745–1796) probably fought in as many Revolution War battles as any general in the Continental army and commanded the Pennsylvania line at Brandywine.

buckshot. There was no system of supply, no commissariat or quartermaster, and no transportation system to support one. There were few cannon aside from fifty-eight guns dragged over the mountains from Fort Ticonderoga by Henry Knox, and very little powder and shot available to fire them.

A congressional committee visited General Washington at Boston to determine what he needed. The general asked for 20,370 men organized into twenty-six battalions of eight companies each, exclusive of artillery and riflemen. Washington saw no immediate need for cavalry at Boston, or the means of providing for them, so he temporarily asked for none. Congress apportioned the battalions among Massachusetts (sixteen); Connecticut (five); Rhode Island (two); and New Hampshire (three). When fewer than one thousand enlisted, Washington had to invest the British at Boston with militia.

Continental Pay per Month in 1775	
Privates, Infantry	$ 6.67
Privates, Artillery, Cavalry	$ 8.33
Ensigns	$10.00
Lieutenants	$13.33
Captains	$20.00

A few kernels of wheat managed to fall from the chaff. Along with George Washington there were men like Henry Knox, a Boston bookseller who acquainted himself with artillery, and John Stark, second-in-command of Rogers' Rangers. There were three ex-British regular officers who took a liking to life in the colonies, Arthur St. Clair, who had fought at Quebec; Horatio Gates, a major in the Royal Americans, and Charles Lee, also a veteran of the recent war. And there were other men with leadership ability: "Mad Anthony" Wayne, "Light

Horse Harry" Lee, Nathaniel Greene of the Rhode Island militia, and Daniel Morgan, a backwoods' rifleman who had fought under Braddock. Out of the rabble came perhaps the most gifted general of all, Benedict Arnold, the despised traitor who, had he died at Saratoga, may have been carried on a roster of America's greatest heroes. Of the thirteen general officers appointed by the Continental Congress in 1775, all but two had fighting experience.

Washington wanted men enlisted for the duration of the war, but the states prevailed upon their congressional representatives to prevent this. The general had to settle for mainly one-year enlistments.

ABOVE: The collage titled "Independence Declared" depicts bust portraits of the first eight presidents, along with the statues of Liberty (left) and Hope (right), and with thirteen soldiers representing the thirteen colonies.

GEORGE WASHINGTON

Born on February 22, 1732, George Washington was the great grandson of an Englishman who settled in Virginia in 1658. He had an undistinguished and uneventful youth despite the fanciful legends others attributed to him. His formal education ended at age fifteen—his ample estates came by inheritance—and he became a wealthy planter. Like men of means, he joined a militia company, fought the French, and in April 1854 became lieutenant colonel of Virginia's militia. This appointment gave impetus to Washington's military career.

While Washington may not have been a military genius, for seven years his true character and fortitude showed through. At any one time his Continental Army seldom numbered more than thirty-five thousand men and some of his biggest battles were little more than skirmishes. He faced one of his greatest strategic challenges during the New York campaign where his army was in danger of being trapped on Manhattan and annihilated by the British army. Yet he made a masterful escape to White Plains and saved his Continentals from annihilation. A true flash of strategic genius came during the winter campaign at Trenton and Princeton, during which he used about three thousand hardy souls to rout the British.

Washington practiced a simple strategy. He did not expect to win in a struggle against the better-trained, better-equipped British army, so he worked diligently not to lose.

Without Washington it would have been difficult to shape America's military future. Few commanders could have held together half-starved, demoralized, and almost naked troops, in the dead of winter, who were paid irregularly in depreciated Continental dollars backed only by the printing on its paper.

George Washington became a respected general and the first president of the United States not because he was gifted with brilliance, but because he knew how to lead men.

RIGHT: On Christmas night, 1776, General George Washington leads his small flotilla of boats through loose ice on the Delaware River, the prelude to his brilliant surprise attack on Trenton in the morning.

Henry Mosler.
1912

Despite half-measures, on January 1, 1776, he succeeded in forming the Continental Line, a corps of longer-term soldiers into which short-term militia could be blended. On that day, in front of Boston, Washington raised the first flag of the united colonies—thirteen red and white stripes with the crosses of St. George and St. Andrew in the canton. On March 17 the Continental Line registered its first major victory when the British occupying Boston admitted defeat, evacuated the city, and sailed for Halifax, Nova Scotia, only to return to Staten Island, New York, a few weeks later.

Silas Deane of Connecticut, American commissioner and purchasing agent in Paris, perhaps unwittingly solved one of Washington's greatest problems. He recruited some of Europe's finest professional field and staff officers and sent them to

America: men like Johann de Kalb (infantry), Friedrich W. A. Steuben (general staff), Casimir Pulaski (cavalry), "Thaddeus" Kosciuszko (artillery), and the Marquis de Lafayette of France. Instead of shunning this collection of foreigners, as a British general might have done, Washington used the experienced veterans to train his infantry, cavalry, and artillery. Von Steuben wrote a manual of regulations and framed a system of tactical discipline. In 1778, at Valley Forge, he learned what Washington already knew about the colonial volunteers—what made them tick. Steuben called it the key to opening the door to the military education of American soldiers,

BELOW: Baron Friedrich Wilhelm von Steuben (1730–1794) came to the United States during the autumn of 1777. He offered to serve as a volunteer Continental officer, met George Washington at Valley Forge, and established training procedures for American soldiers.

BELOW: On June 14, 1777, Congress passed the Flag Resolution, specifying thirteen stripes, red and white alternately, and a union of thirteen stars in a blue field. Many patterns were proposed, but seamstress Betsy Ross won the honors.

Betsy Ross Flag 1777

men who usually balked at discipline and were uncomfortable being away from their homes and farms for extended periods of time. "The genius of this nation," wrote von Steuben, "is not in the least to be compared with that of the Prussians, Austrians, or French. You say to your [European] soldier, 'Do this,' and he doeth it; but [in America] I am obliged to say, 'This is the reason why you ought to do that,' and then he does it."

While Washington held the army together, von Steuben trained it. An astounding transformation to professionalism occurred within the Continental Army, a blending of the British military system commingled with German military discipline and tactical training bolstered by an individual autonomy typically American.

About two hundred and thirty thousand soldiers served in the Continental Army, but never at the same time. State militias provided another one hundred and sixty-five thousand. Of nearly four hundred thousand men serving in the army, seldom were there more than twenty thousand on the battlefield at any

BELOW: General Banastre Tarleton's cavalry attack American dragoons during the January 17, 1781, Battle of Cowpens. Tarleton was disastrously defeated by Continental General Daniel Morgan's double envelopment.

RIGHT: On October 7, 1781, British Colonel Patrick Ferguson's corps of 1,100 Tory riflemen was demolished by 1,400 sharpshooting Carolinian "mountain men" and Virginia militia led by colonels Isaac Shelby and Richard Campbell.

BELOW: On October 17, 1781, General Charles Cornwallis opened negotiations with General Washington and offered to surrender the British army. Two days later Yorktown's garrison marched out and laid down their arms.

one time. The British fielded a force of forty-two thousand professional soldiers, the best trained in the world, and augmented that force with thirty thousand German (Hessian) mercenaries.

The fighting ended on October 19, 1781, when Lord Charles Cornwallis surrendered at Yorktown, Virginia. With the considerable aid of French army forces commanded by the Comte de Rochambeau and a French fleet under Admiral de Grasse, Washington had trapped Cornwallis. It was a defeat from which the British could not recover.

It had been a war of opposites. The colonists fought in unorthodox ways, not because of superior training, but because they were unfettered by traditional European warfighting doctrine. The

British brought a completely orthodox army to America and fought in conventional and predictable ways. There were times when the colonists came close to giving up, but never did. There were also times when the British came close to winning the war, but never capitalized on opportunities. The formal end came on September 3, 1783, when the Paris Peace Treaty became final. The British were not particularly elated by the outcome. Most of them were related in some way to their pugnacious cousins.

The Question of National Defense

During the Revolution, Washington built an army complete with the combat elements of infantry, artillery, and dragoons (cavalry). He also provided all the supporting elements of a professional army and drafted a blueprint for national defense, the principles of which exist in modern form today. He also asked for a navy, without which the United States could not protect its maritime commerce or its seaports. Congress ignored his suggestions and disbanded the officers and men who Washington had forged into soldiers to create a new republic.

Such shortsightedness led to consequences. The British still manned forts on the frontier, and Indian massacres of settlers were again on the increase. Indian trouble would last a hundred years, but in 1784 Congress possessed no such vision. On June 3 the legislature authorized a single Regular Army unit and named it the First American Regiment. Revolutionary War veteran Lieutenant Colonel Josiah Harmar mustered the men at Fort Pitt (later Pittsburgh). The regiment was never disbanded and survived through the decades to become the Third Infantry Division.

During a winter accident in Harmar's district, a soldier fell overboard during a winter ration trip. With legs and feet frozen, he was pulled from the water and taken to Fort McIntosh for treatment.

Three people attended the sick soldier: Sergeant Major Duffy, his wife, and a corporal, but Mrs. Harmar was also there. The colonel's wife pitched in with Judy O'Grady and saved the man's life. The incident marked the first recorded appearance of the American Regular Army woman on the frontier.

In 1789 George Washington became president and Henry Knox of Massachusetts, the general's wartime chief of artillery, officially became the first secretary of war. Section 2, Article II of the Constitution designated Washington as "the Commander-in-Chief of the Army and the Navy…and of the militia of the several states when called into actual service." He immediately instructed Knox to rebuild the army. Not much happened because Congress, instead of passing an act to increase the Regular Army, passed the Militia Act, which threw the responsibility and cost for protection back upon the respective states. When in 1812 President

LEFT: On March 15, 1781, American mounted militia skirmished with British cavalry at Guilford Courthouse and withdrew to the Carolinas.

RIGHT: General Zebulon M. Pike (1779–1813) led an expedition through the southwest (1806–1807) into Colorado, where he sighted a peak that bears his name.

James Madison went to war with Great Britain, the small Regular Army occupied frontier outposts and little or no cohesion or cooperation existed among the inadequately trained state militias.

Western Expansion

Several remarkable actions occurred between the Revolution and the War of 1812. In 1802 President Thomas Jefferson of Virginia, though an opponent of a standing army, signed an act establishing the army on a permanent basis. He also authorized the formation of the United States Military Academy at West Point, New York, and appointed twelve cadets. A year later he obtained $2 million from Congress and purchased Louisiana from France, a territory that stretched from the Gulf of Mexico to Canada, and from the valley of the Mississippi to the Rocky Mountains.

Now that Jefferson had an army, he began using it. In 1804 he sent Captain Meriwether Lewis and Lieutenant William Clark with thirty regulars and twelve guides and interpreters on a two-year epoch-making expedition across the unexplored West to the Pacific coast. In 1805 General James Wilkinson, the ranking officer in the army, dispatched Lieutenant Zebulon Pike on another exploration into the Southwest. Wilkinson, however, had been cozy with Spain, and his actions may not have been as altruistic as Jefferson's.

Military intrusions into the West came with a cost. Although Plains Indians did not react immediately,

RIGHT: Early explorers of the West, like Lewis Meriwether and William Clark, depended heavily upon the Indians to show them the route to the Pacific.

ABOVE: The bronze statutes give tribute to Weriwether Lewis (1774–1809) and William Clark (1770–1838), who together in 1804–1806 blazed a trail from St. Louis to the Pacific Ocean.

tribal unrest spread rapidly into the Midwest. When in 1811 Shawnee chieftain Tecumseh formed an Indian confederacy and made alliances with the British, General William Henry Harrison, governor of Indiana, mobilized his militia and called for reinforcements from the government. James Madison, a far a more militant president than Jefferson, dispatched the 4th U.S. Infantry Regiment. Harrison personally trained the combined force and routed the Shawnees at Tippecanoe. Indian disturbances, however, continued.

1812—The Impetuous War

On June 18, 1812, the United States declared war on Great Britain over mainly naval and maritime issues. Among other notions, President Madison thought America's problems could be solved by taking control of Canada and driving the British from the continent. Madison endured his first setback when two months later General William Hull, a regular with a well-equipped force, shamefully surrendered without a fight to a much weaker British-Canadian force at Detroit, Michigan.

ABOVE: On October 5, 1813, during the Battle of the Thames, William Henry "Old Tippecanoe" Harrison (1773–1841), riding a white horse, kills Tecumseh, the powerful Shawnee chief allied to the British.

FAR RIGHT: Standing among bales of cotton thrown up as breastworks, the American troops fire down on the British during the Battle of New Orleans.

BELOW: General Andrew Jackson (1767–1845) rides among his batteries, urging them to fire rapidly into the British ranks advancing through the fog.

BELOW RIGHT: Hyacinth Ladotte, one of General Jackson's engineers, attempts to represent visually the supreme moment when the American army vanquished the resplendent British army.

The small Regular Army, now more than twenty-five years old, suffered from inefficiency and incompetence in the high command, and in many cases, plain stupidity. In the early stages of the conflict Secretary of War John Armstrong relocated the war department to the front and, in the years before telegraphic communication, wasted any opportunity to coordinate the movements of the army. If nothing else, Armstrong created a model for the future by providing the army with the first comprehensive set of regulations.

The young regulars from West Point had built their commands on several decades of tradition, and among the militia were volunteer officers who took their responsibilities seriously and studied tactics. Together they began to emerge out of the fog of inefficiency because they believed in professionalism.

The few disastrous defeats suffered along the Canadian border convinced the British that no good would come from continuing the war, but the greatest defeat of all was yet to come. On Christmas Eve 1814, the signing of the Treaty of Ghent brought the war to an end and established a clear border between the United States and Canada, but not quite soon enough. Two weeks later at New Orleans, Louisiana, having no knowledge of the peace settlement, General Andrew Jackson's motley army of a few thousand poorly equipped soldiers (though some carried Kentucky rifles) whipped eight thousand British regulars under the command of Major General Sir Edward Pakenham, brother-in-law to the great Duke of Wellington. Jackson did this by declaring martial law, fortifying the approaches to the city, and assembling his troops behind a natural bottleneck formed by the Mississippi River on one side and the Rodriquez Canal on the other. He called for volunteers, though having no congressional authority to do so, and inducted free blacks, convicts, privateers, and a band of Jean Laffite's smugglers. Pakenham advanced through a shroud of fog and into volleys of American fire. He pushed forward and lost 1,971 men trying to break through the neatly set trap. Jackson reported only seventy-one casualties. Pakenham withdrew to the Gulf of Mexico and sailed away. Nobody criticized Jackson because the Ghent treaty explicitly required ratification, which did not occur until February 1815.

For the United States, the army fought the War of 1812 mainly with militia and volunteers. The army raised 528,274 men, but only 56,652 were regulars. There were barely any casualties: nineteen hundred killed and four thousand wounded. As in most early wars, disease probably killed more men than any other cause, but nobody kept count.

The mix of regulars to volunteers did not go unnoticed by Congress, and all the forces except those required to contain Indians were quickly disbanded. From the earliest times in America, and through its wars against the French and the British, the Indians never stopped defending what they viewed as their rightful tribal lands.

THE BATTLE OF CHIPPEWA

New faces brought new beginnings. Twenty-seven-year-old Winfield Scott, a young lieutenant colonel of artillery from Virginia, came from civilian life and earned his commission by recruiting a volunteer company. General Jacob Brown, a New York militiaman and wealthy landowner on Lake Ontario, joined the Regular Army and replaced James Wilkinson, who in 1813 led an unsuccessful campaign into Montreal and was rewarded with a dishonorable discharge. Brown took command of western New York, recognized that his men needed training, and turned them over to Scott.

In the spirit of von Steuben, Scott found a textbook of instructions written by Napoleon and for three months trained Brown's militia. He taught officers how to march and wheel, handle muskets, and use the bayonet, and then he watched and advised as the officers trained four regiments of infantry and two companies of artillery. "If, of such materials I do not make the best army now in the service," Scott told Brown, "I will agree to be dismissed from the service."

In July 1814 Brown sent one of his brigades against Fort Erie, located on the Canadian side of the Niagara River, and captured the works without firing a shot. Scott went into Ontario with his own brigade of thirteen hundred men. Fifteen miles north of Lake Erie he encountered a British force of four thousand men, mostly regulars, near the Chippewa River. Scott's well-trained troops broke the enemy line with a skillfully executed charge. Early in the fight, British Major General Phineas Riall noticed that the Americans were dressed in gray instead of regulation blue and swore they were militia out for a frolic. When he saw them charging with bayonets fixed for business, he said, "These, by gad…are regulars!" and fled with his battered and bleeding survivors across the river. To honor this victory, in 1816 the gray uniform was formally approved for use by the cadets at West Point, which provides the sartorial basis for the Long Gray Line, as the graduates of the United States Military Academy are known.

ABOVE: General Jacob J. Brown (1775–1828) organized the American army on the eastern Great Lakes and on July 3, 1814, captured Fort Erie, Ontario

CENTURY OF DEVELOPMENT 1814–1898

The Regular Army

The years following the War of 1812 and the onset of the Mexican War became a defining period for the U.S. Army. Major changes began in 1817 when President James Monroe, during the first year of his administration, visited West Point, discharged the superintendent, and replaced him with Brevet Major Sylvanus Thayer, an 1808 product of the academy. Monroe then named John C. Calhoun of South Carolina secretary of war and instructed him to give Thayer full support. Calhoun thought of war as an art;: Thayer viewed war as a profession. The new superintendent intended to prove his point. He went abroad, studied military schools in Europe, and came back to West Point determined to concentrate on engineering, artillery, and tactics. He also established specialist schools. In 1824 Fort Monroe, Virginia, at the mouth of Chesapeake Bay, became an artillery school. In 1827 Jefferson Barracks, at St. Louis, became a one-year specialized infantry school.

Thayer remained superintendent for sixteen years and advanced the academy from a school of basic infantry training to the first American technological school. After 1824 the Army Corps of Engineers took the leading role in building and expanding the nation's roads, seaports, railroads, and canals, but the academy also laid the cornerstone for introducing scientific education to colleges across America. By the outbreak of the Mexican War in 1846, the academy had graduated one thousand cadets. Although West Point had been in business since 1802 under different

superintendents, Thayer remains the father of what the academy is today.

> War is not, as some seem to suppose, a mere game of chance. Its principles constitute one of the most intricate of modern sciences.
> *Major General Henry W. Halleck*

After completing a tour of duty, a West Point graduate had choices in life. He could remain a professional soldier, teach science in a civilian college, or use his civil engineering skills to expand the nation's infrastructure. Whatever pursuit a West Point graduate chose, civilian or military, he would always be a soldier.

Opening the West

In 1829 General Andrew "Old Hickory" Jackson became the seventh president of the United States. His nickname stemmed from hickory ramrods used to load

RIGHT: In December 1835, Seminole Indians attack an army fort on the Withlacoochee River, which necessitated a rescue effort by Major General Winfield Scott to save his rival, Major General Edmund P. Gaines, from extermination.

the standard-issue flintlock rifle. A ramrod never bent and neither did Jackson. The general launched his political career in 1815 by defeating the British at New Orleans. Jackson was also a shameless expansionist. Congress obliged him by passing the Indian Removal Act of 1830, which called for the relocation of five tribes—Cherokee, Chickasaw, Choctaw, Creek, and Seminole—from the fertile tobacco and cotton growing lands of the southeastern states to the dusty plains of Oklahoma. While some tribes went peacefully, the Seminoles resisted and took refuge in the Florida Everglades. Sending southern tribes to the Oklahoma Territory put pressure on the Plains Indians who occupied and hunted the land.

What the government regarded as "Thirty Years' Peace" after the War of 1812 never existed. Settlers and soldiers began to clash with a new foe—the Plains Indians of the West, the best irregular light horse soldier ever produced. Infantry could not constrain the wild bareback-riding Native Americans. On May 23, 1833, Congress authorized the Regiment of Dragoons, giving birth to the First U.S. Cavalry. There had not been a regular regiment of dragoons since the dissolution of the Continental Army, mainly because Congress did not want to shoulder the expense. Although several militia and volunteer cavalry companies came and went through the decades, their members, like traditional English militias, provided their own weapons, mounts, and accouterments. When in 1836 the army formed the Second Dragoons, it appeared that cavalry was here to stay.

The dragoons naturally appealed to men of the South who owned plantations, needed horses for transportation, and had leisure time available for militia activities. Many West Point graduates from the South, being skilled horsemen, readily joined the cavalry service.

Pioneers settled the West, but cavalry and infantry opened and protected the open spaces by building a

LEFT: The Second Seminole War (1835–1842) became a series of deep penetrations into the swamps and backwaters of Florida. On one of these expeditions, General Eustis burned the town of Pilak-li-ka-ha.

SEMINOLE WARS

Over a span of forty years, more than ten thousand troops became involved in two Seminole wars. In 1817 Major General Andrew Jackson, commanding the Southern Department, initiated the First Seminole War by invading Spain's Florida because of Indian raids into Georgia. While chasing Indians, Jackson captured several Spanish posts. He created a diplomatic mess for the state department but achieved one of his purposes by inducing Spain to cede Florida.

In 1835 the Seminoles revolted when the army attempted to move them to Oklahoma. Brigadier General Zachary Taylor drew the assignment of tracking through alligator-infested swamps searching for bands of Seminole guerillas led by their leader, Chief Osceola. Taylor used flat-bottomed boats, canoes, and bloodhounds, and after five years of limited success, turned the work over to others. The war ended in 1842 when Brigadier General William Worth, after destroying the Indian's means of subsistence, captured what he believed to be the last forty Seminoles near Lake Ahapopka. There were still a few Seminoles hiding in the everglades, but Congress regarded Worth's pacification complete and on August 23, 1842, reduced the Regular Army to 8,613 officers and men.

More than ten thousand regulars and thirty thousand militia served in the Seminole Wars (1817–1818, 1835–1842), which some viewed as one continuous conflict. Disease claimed 1,138 soldiers, combat accounted for 328. For Taylor and Worth, there would be one more war to fight, but not in Florida.

LEFT: During the campaigns and battles of the Second Seminole War, federal troops wade Lake Ocklawaha in central Florida in an effort to flush out bands of Seminoles.

string of forts from Jefferson Barracks in St. Louis (1826) westward to the Platte River. In 1829 four companies of the Sixth Infantry blazed the Santa Fe Trail to New Mexico. In 1830 seven Army posts occupied the west bank of the Mississippi from Fort Snelling, Minnesota, to Fort Gibson, Oklahoma, on the Arkansas River. In 1835 Captain Benjamin L. E. Bonneville, after a three-year exploration, returned with the first authentic maps of the far Northwest. All this activity did not go unnoticed by Native Americans, and Indian uprisings in territories west of the Mississippi increased.

> I start this morning with the dragoons for the Pawnee Country, but God only knows where that is.
> *George Catlin, artist*

Congress took very poor care of its newly created Regular Army. Regimental promotions came so slowly that a lieutenant had little chance of ever becoming a captain. A second lieutenant received $63.91 a month, a colonel $172.66. Brigadier and major generals received $257.75 to $401.50. Uniform expenses came from officer's pay. Hardships increased in the 1830s when the army began sprucing up, adding costly changes to the standard blues. Brevets awarded for heroism augmented an officer's pay, but fighting Indians did not result in many handouts. Buffalo steaks came cheap, but poor pay in the lower ranks and harsh duty, coupled with no prospect of retirement, discouraged many of the best-trained and eager young officers from planning careers in the army. In 1836, 117 officers resigned to take jobs in the civilian sector.

In 1842 Lieutenant John C. "The Pathfinder" Fremont set out on another expedition to explore the

RIGHT: During the Second Seminole War, a company of South Carolina dragoons arrives at the Withlacoochee River to replace a large number of troopers felled by malaria and other diseases.

West. He used knowledge acquired from Bonneville and followed many of the same tracks. He discovered new routes and laid out the Oregon Trail, which soon put more pressure on the Indians as long columns of canvas-covered Conestoga wagons rumbled across the prairie. Fremont probed the Rocky Mountains and followed the Columbia River to its mouth. He struck a path south through Oregon and in 1845 entered California, a territory claimed and mainly populated by Mexicans. The fortunes of war found Fremont at Monterrey at a time when American settlers were in open revolt with Mexicans. Fremont assumed command of the so-called "Bear Flag Revolt," defeated the Mexicans, and became governor of the "Bear Flag Republic" on the eve of the Mexican War.

Fremont's activities, coupled with trouble in Texas, temporarily shifted attention away from Indians and focused it on Mexico, which had become increasingly antagonistic over American intrusions.

The Mexican War

In 1835 more than thirty-five thousand Americans made their homes in the Mexican territory of Texas. The Mexican government, though tolerant at first, soon disapproved of the settlers' independent behavior and barred further immigration. In 1836 American Texans rebelled and declared their independence from Mexico. Before the year ended, General Sam Houston defeated the Mexican forces in Texas and applied for admission to the United States. Most Americans agreed with Houston. The holdouts included Congress, which debated for ten years whether it would be proper for the United States, without risking war, to annex a territory still claimed by Mexico. Public pressure for annexation could only lead to one outcome.

In November 1844 James K. Polk of North Carolina, a man without military knowledge or experience, won the presidential election partly because he accepted a

mandate from the people to annex Texas. On March 1, 1845, when Polk took office, Congress passed a resolution admitting Texas to the Union. Mexico broke off diplomatic relations and prepared for war.

Without waiting for ratification by Texas voters, Polk ordered Brevet Brigadier General Zachary Taylor to move his forces from Louisiana to the Rio Grande, which served as the border between Mexico and Texas. Taylor collected a force of thirty-five hundred regulars, volunteers, and Texas Rangers and marched deep into an area controlled by Mexicans and never claimed by Texas. He then encamped at the mouth of the Rio Grande, built Fort Texas across the river from the Mexican town of Matamoros, and spread cavalry patrols along the river. On April 25, 1846, a Mexican detachment crossed the Rio Grande, attacked a reconnaissance force of 69 dragoons, and killed 16 men. Taylor informed Polk that war had commenced and prepared for a fight.

BELOW: On February 22–23, 1847, General Zachary "Old Rough and Ready" Taylor (1784–1850) overlooks the crucial Battle of Buena Vista, during which he supposedly and historically said, "A little more grape, Captain [Braxton] Bragg." He more likely and less gently said, "Double shot your guns and give 'em hell!"

On May 8, while returning to Fort Texas from Point Isabel with supplies, Taylor encountered General Mariano Arista's six thousand-man army arrayed in battle formation at Palo Alto, Texas. Taylor's "flying artillery" opened with six-, twelve-, and eighteen-pounders charged with canister and solid shot and inflicted more than five hundred casualties. Young Lieutenant Ulysses S. Grant witnessed the artillery battle, noting that he and his fellow infantrymen were mainly spectators.

On May 9 Taylor found Arista's army in a strong defensive position blocking the road at Resaca de la Palma. He attacked boldly, broke through Arista's line, and after a brief but intense fight, drove the Mexicans back across the Rio Grande. This time the infantry became heavily engaged. During the two-day battle

Arista lost 1,100 men, as opposed to American casualties of 170 killed and wounded. Taylor could not cross the river and pursue without a pontoon bridge.

Four days later, on May 13, Congress declared war on Mexico and authorized the expansion of the army to 15,540 regulars and 50,000 volunteers. The standing army, though small, was better prepared for war than ever before. There were eight 10-company regiments of infantry, four of artillery (including Taylor's "flying artillery"), and two of dragoons, totaling about 7,200 regulars. There was also a corps of engineers with forty-five officers, including captains Robert E. Lee, George B. McClellan, and George G. Meade. The Mexican War would be the first conflict in which a volunteer army rather than militia played a major role. It would also be the first

RIGHT: During the Mexican War (1846–1848), Lieutenant Ulysses S. Grant (1822–1885) was better known as Sam, although his real name was Hiram Ulysses. Grant served under both General Taylor and General Scott.

FAR RIGHT: Lieutenant Grant commanded an infantry platoon during the Mexican War and served with distinction, earning two brevets from General Winfield Scott, one for storming Molino del Rey (September 8) and another to captain for storming the Mexican fortress at Chapultepec five days later, which is pictured in a contemporary illustration of Grant at the capture of Mexico City.

time that every soldier wore the standard uniform of his particular service.

Mexico, a nation of 8 million people, already had a standing army of forty-four thousand men, but with bizarre ratios. There was one general for every 220 men, and one officer for every enlisted man, usually an Indian or poor laborer. Mexico had recently won its independence from Spain and many of its men were veterans, but most of the infantry carried secondhand muskets purchased from the British army. The artillery guns were inefficient relics provided by France, and most of the twelve regiments of Mexican cavalry carried only lances.

After the War of 1812 the U.S. Army changed from flintlock muskets to percussion-lock weapons, which eliminated the problem of worn flints, damp priming powder in the flashpan, and hangfire—a delayed discharge after pulling the trigger. Percussion-lock muskets also shortened reloading time. Breech-loaded .54 caliber carbines also became available and proved to be a handy weapon for the cavalry. The artillery also improved its mobility by adopting light horse-drawn six-pounders, which proved of immense value during the Mexican War.

Winfield Scott, now a major general and commander in chief of the U. S. Army, decided with President Polk upon a three-prong attack into northern Mexico. While General Taylor crossed the Rio Grande and moved on Monterrey, Brigadier General John E. Wool's three thousand-man army would move 600 miles overland from San Antonio to Saltillo. Brigadier General Stephen Watts Kearny would move west from Fort Leavenworth with seventeen hundred men and occupy New Mexico and California. The strategy worked with very few hitches, one of them being Polk's efforts to control the war from Washington.

By the end of 1846 Taylor controlled northern Mexico and the main road leading from Saltillo to Mexico City. There he fell out of favor with Polk,

LEFT: On March 27, 1847, after a five-day bombardment, General Winfield Scott sent 10,000 U.S. soldiers ashore at Veracruz, forcing a massive surrender of the 5,000 Mexicans garrisoning the city. Scott disarmed the Mexicans and moved quickly inland to avoid yellow fever.

disobeyed Scott's instructions to fall back to Monterrey, and came under attack by General Santa Anna's fifteen thousand-man army at Buena Vista. With only 4,650 troops, Taylor fought and eventually out-maneuvered Santa Anna. Colonel Jefferson Davis' Mississippi Rifles distinguished themselves by repulsing repeated charges by the Mexican cavalry. Santa Anna retired, ending the northern campaign and leaving behind fifteen hundred casualties. Taylor lost 267 killed and 456 wounded.

BELOW: On February 23, 1847, General Zachary Taylor fought and won the decisive battle of Buena Vista against superior forces. Mexican General Antonio Lopez de Santa Anna retreated to Mexico City, where he would soon face another American army under General Scott.

WINFIELD SCOTT

Born in 1786, a year before the passage of the American Constitution, Winfield Scott became general-in-chief of the Regular Army in 1841. Having made his mark in the War of 1812, he now had an opportunity win another laurel, this time in Mexico. Polk feared Scott as a future presidential candidate, causing much delay in making military arrangements, but he finally agreed to the general's proposal to land an expedition at Veracruz as a preparatory step to capturing Mexico City.

On March 9, 1847, while Taylor held northern Mexico, Scott executed the first amphibious landing in American history and landed a force of ten thousand men at Veracruz. On April 18, after marching several days, he paused at a fortified defile at Cerro Gordo where he found Santa Anna waiting with twelve thousand men. Scott put his engineers to work to get at the Mexicans. Captains Robert E. Lee, George B. McClellan, Joseph E. Johnston, and Pierre G.T. Beauregard discovered a flanking mountain trail. Scott turned the infantry and artillery loose, enveloped most of Santa Anna's army, took three thousand prisoners, and inflicted one thousand casualties, losing only 64 killed and 353 wounded.

On August 7 Scott cut his communications and advanced with eleven thousand men on Mexico City. He had been forced to stop for three months at Puebla for reinforcements to replace four thousand men whose one-year enlistments had expired. Santa Anna waited with thirty thousand men to pounce on Scott. The Duke of Wellington, viewing the news from England, said, "Scott is lost. He has been carried away by successes. He cannot capture the city, and he cannot fall back on his base."

Scott proved all the strategists wrong. He knew he had a professional army and Santa Anna did not. On August 20 he stormed Contreras at dawn and routed the defenders. Another column struck the fortified convent at Churubusco and after a stubborn fight drove the Mexicans into the capital city. An armistice followed, and when peace proposals failed Scott resumed the offensive and on September 8 routed twlve thousand Mexicans at Molino del Rey. Five days later Lieutenant Ulysses S. Grant and Thomas J. Jackson's artillerymen distinguished themselves during the Battle of Chapultepec, thus opening the way into Mexico City.

Scott accomplished what few believed possible, and with fewer than seventy-five hundred effectives, occupied the surrendered city.

LEFT: On September 14, 1847, after working through the night to clear the streets of Santa Anna's troops, General Winfield Scott made his grand entry into Mexico City astride his white horse.

LEFT: On March 25, 1847, during the five-day bombardment of Veracruz, many of the shells from the U.S. Navy flew over the main fort and landed in the city.

LEFT: On September 13, 1847, American infantry stormed up the rocky slopes, and using scaling ladders, swarmed the fortified citadel of Chapultepec. Two lieutenants earned brevets for heroism, Ulysses S. Grant and Thomas J. Jackson.

The war with Mexico officially ended on February 2, 1848, with the signing of the Treaty of Guadalupe Hidalgo. American troops came home to country increased by more than one million square miles. The United States paid Mexico $15 million for title to Texas and a huge tract of land that eventually became New Mexico, Arizona, California, Nevada, Utah, and parts of Colorado and Wyoming. The other cost came in American lives. Disease took a huge toll. Of thirteen thousand deaths, only seventeen hundred were attributed to battle.

A Disquieting Interlude

After the Mexican War, the army resumed its duties on the frontier, now greatly expanded to include former Mexican lands. Despite thirty separate major conflicts with Indians, army strength fell back to sixteen thousand regulars, and nine-tenths of them were spread over areas west of the Mississippi. They were constantly on patrol or fighting, and there were times when territory militias, some authorized and some not, caused more trouble than the Indians.

Civil war broke out in Kansas between proslavery and free-soil men. On May 21, 1856, a proslavery band from Missouri crossed into Kansas and burned Lawrence. John Brown, a fanatic abolitionist, sought revenge and murdered five proslavery farmers near Pottawatomie. Chased out of Kansas by Lieutenant James E.B. "Jeb" Stuart's cavalry, Brown recruited a force of followers in 1859 and raided the federal armory and arsenal at Harpers Ferry, Virginia. Lieutenant Colonel Robert E. Lee captured Brown and turned him with his band over to Virginia authorities for trial and execution. By then the nation had become politically split by abolitionism in the North and a southern agricultural economy based on slave labor in the South.

On November 6, 1860, the election of a Republican president, Abraham Lincoln of Illinois,

precipitated the succession of seven southern states. James Buchanan of Pennsylvania, the nation's "lame duck" president, did nothing to stop it. On March 4, 1861, the day of Lincoln's inauguration, the Confederate States of America had already been established. Jefferson Davis of Mississippi, a West Point man, became the elected president of the Confederacy, formed a cabinet, and called for one hundred thousand volunteers.

Civil War—The Army in Rebellion

At the beginning of the Civil War, the Regular Army numbered 1,108 officers and 15,259 enlisted men. Three hundred and thirteen officers, most of them West Point graduates, resigned their commissions and joined the Confederacy. After Fort Sumter surrendered to South Carolina's militia, Lincoln called for seventy-five thousand volunteers and began looking for someone other than Winfield Scott, enfeebled by old age and gout, to command the Union army. Scott called sixty-one-year-old Robert E. Lee "the best soldier I ever saw in the field." Lincoln

ABOVE: On the night of October 16, 1859, rabid abolitionist John Brown raided the Federal Armory at Harpers Ferry, Virginia. On the morning of October 18, Colonel Robert E. Lee arrived with a force of marines who broke into the fire-engine house, and captured Brown and his men. The scene depicts the aftermath of the assault that wounded Brown and killed several of his men.

ROBERT EDWARD LEE

Born on January 19, 1807 in Stratford, Westmoreland County, Virginia Robert E. Lee kept the Southern cause afloat when faced by better-equipped, better-fed, better-trained, and usually better-disciplined troops—and often when heavily outnumbered.

Remarkably, when he took command of the Army of Northern Virginia on June 1, 1862, he was almost a complete novice. He had never commanded a sizeable body of troops in battle—indeed, he had never commanded more than a regiment. He graduated from West Point second in his class in 1829, made a name for himself in the Mexican War impressing Winfield Scott, and returning to the United States to become a brevet colonel. In 1852 he became Superintendent of West Point, in 1855 lieutenant-colonel of the 2nd Cavalry in Texas, and between February 1860 and February 1861, he commanded of the Department of Texas. Destined for greater things, as Civil War loomed Winfield Scott brought him to Washington where, in April 1861, he was offered command in the field of the United States Army.

Lee was not a secessionist himself but he was a loyal man—to his family, his friends, and his state. When Virginia seceded in April 1861 this honorable man was left with no choice: he resigned his commission with the U. S. Army. He was immediately given the command the Virginia State forces, and in August 1861 he was made a general and a military adviser to President Davis—and when the South's military commander, Joseph E. Johnston, was wounded in May 1862, Lee took over.

He fought valiantly for three years and when the Army of Northern Virginia surrendered at Appomattox on April 9, 1865, the Southern cause was lost. In those years he and his men had accounted for themselves with great strength of character and often brilliance: from the Seven Days' Battle in 1862, through the Second Battle of Bull Run, Antietam, and Chancellorsville to Gettysburg he kept on the offensive, but the Confederates could ill afford the losses of July 1–3, 1863, and were forced to retreat to Virginia. On the defense, Lee performed magnificently at the battles of the Wilderness, Spotsylvania, and Cold Harbor, but he had to protect the administrative heart of the South and once tied down on the Petersburg– Richmond line the end was in sight. In February 1865, Lee was named general-in-chief of the Confederate armies, and tried to break out to link up with Johnston's army in North Carolina, but Grant was tenacious and Lee was forced to surrender.

His treatment by the Union showed the esteem in which he was held by friend and foe alike. Paroled, he returned to Richmond and in September 1865 became president of the Washington College at Lexington, Virginia, where he died on October 12, 1870.

RIGHT: General Robert Edward Lee (1807–1870) as he appeared after the Civil War and at a time when he was serving as president of Washington College (later Washington and Lee) in Lexington, Virginia.

ULYSSES S. GRANT

Born in Ohio on April 27, 1822, Grant grew up "quiet, introspective, and seemingly lazy." His father sent him to West Point, where young "Sam Grant" earned the reputation of being an abysmal student, preferring romance novels to tactics. Pegged as a person "least likely to succeed," Grant nonetheless managed to graduate in the middle of the class of 1843 and exit the Mexican War as a captain with two citations for gallantry and one for meritorious conduct.

Grant could not bear the monotony of postwar military service. He resigned to avoid a court martial for drunkenness and became personally destitute until Lincoln called for volunteers in 1861. Congressman Eli Washburne of Illinois managed to get Grant a brigadier general's commission, and slowly everything began to change. Lincoln took notice when Grant captured Fort Henry and Fort Donelson and pugnaciously demanded "unconditional surrender." The press liked the term, and U. S. Grant became "Unconditional Surrender" Grant. It worked again on July 4, 1863, when Vicksburg surrendered to Grant. In fact, unconditional surrender was precisely what Lincoln and Congress wanted the South to do.

During the autumn of 1863 Lincoln transferred Grant to the Chattanooga area, where Major General William S. Rosecrans had allowed his army to become bottled-up by a weaker Confederate force. Grant brought Major General William T. Sherman's corps from Mississippi and drove the Confederates out of Tennessee. On March 9 Lincoln promoted Grant to lieutenant general and made him commander-in-chief of the Union armies, the highest rank awarded any army officer since George Washington. Though some members of the war department questioned the appointment, Lincoln replied, "He fights," and that ended the debate.

Grant avoided Washington, where everyone could look over his shoulder, and established his headquarters with the Army of the Potomac. There he could direct Meade in the final operations against Lee's masterfully commanded Army of Northern Virginia. Grant and Lee knew each other, but not well. They had not met for many years. Nor would they meet again until April 9, 1865, at Appomattox Courthouse, Virginia, where General Lee solemnly accepted Grant's usual terms: unconditional surrender.

RIGHT: General Ulysses Simpson Grant (1822–1885) as he appeared in the February 1864 as lieutenant general after being appointed by the president commander-in-chief of all the Union armies.

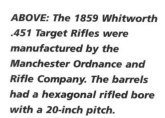

ABOVE: The 1859 Whitworth .451 Target Rifles were manufactured by the Manchester Ordnance and Rifle Company. The barrels had a hexagonal rifled bore with a 20-inch pitch.

knew absolutely nothing about military matters, but he took Scott's advice and offered Lee command of the field armies of the Union. Lee considered duty "the most sublime word in the English language," but he chose loyalty to his beloved state of Virginia and resigned his commission, although he personally opposed secession and slavery.

Defections from the Regular Army provided the Confederacy with some of the very best men of West Point. Lee graduated second in his class at West Point and during 1852–1855 served as the academy's superintendent. Joseph E. Johnston of Virginia graduated thirteenth in the class of 1829, suffered five wounds in Mexico, and won three brevets for bravery. Albert Sidney Johnston of Kentucky graduated eighth in the class of 1826. The federal government offered him a general's commission as second-in-command to General Scott, but he turned it down. Pierre G. T. Beauregard of Louisiana graduated second in the class of 1838. He served as Scott's staff engineer during the Mexican War, suffered two wounds, and won two brevets. Thomas J. "Stonewall" Jackson of Virginia went to West Point with virtually no formal education, graduated seventeenth in the class of 1846, and won two brevets during the Mexican War as an artillery officer. James E. B. "Jeb" Stuart of Virginia frolicked his way through West Point and graduated thirteenth in the class of 1854. One might note that Jefferson Davis, a product of West Point

BELOW: The .53-inch Sharps Breech-Loading Carbine became an early favorite of the Union cavalry. During the Civil War, the federal government purchased 80,512 Sharps carbines.

class of 1828, graduated twenty-third in a class of thirty-three. These men, and dozens of others who were trained at West Point in warfare and leadership, kept the Confederacy alive on Civil War battlefields for four torturous years.

President Lincoln agonized for most of the war searching for someone to lead the Union armies. His ranking generals were all West Point graduates. With few exceptions they moved slowly and gave the president constant grief. Not until July 1863, when Major General George G. Meade turned back Lee at Gettysburg and Major General Ulysses S. Grant captured Vicksburg, did the tide change. Meade graduated nineteenth in the West Point class of 1835, served in Mexico as an engineer, commanded a corps in the Army of the Potomac, but had done nothing in particular to distinguish himself other than to demonstrate a willingness to fight hard in battle.

Organization of Armies

At the outset of the Civil War, after eleven states seceded from the Union, there were 18,936,579 whites in the North compared with 5,449,646 whites and 3,521,111 slaves in the South. The slave-laboring class contributed heavily to the Confederacy's ability to wage war. Militias played a small role in the early months of the war but were quickly assimilated into regiments of volunteers. Both sides eventually resorted to conscription, and during the latter months of 1862 the Union began forming regiments of black infantry.

The basic unit of the U.S. Regular Army was the company (nominally 100 men). Ten companies formed a regiment, five regiments a brigade, three brigades a division, and three divisions a corps. At the beginning of the war the Regular Army had 198 line companies (16,367 men) distributed among ten regiments of infantry, five of cavalry, and four of artillery. Volunteer units were formed the same way

FIRST BULL RUN

The great opening battle of the Civil War—First Bull Run, also called First Manassas—set the stage for a four-year struggle to reunify the nation and abolish slavery.

In July 1861 President Lincoln wanted to end the war quickly. Every newspaper in the North ranted "On to Richmond." The president also had another problem: After calling for 75,000 ninety-day volunteers in April, enlistments were about to expire, and the rush to war gathered speed.

Either side could have won the First Battle of Bull Run. Both came to the battlefield with armies of equal strength and inadequately trained soldiers. Brigadier General Irvin McDowell, a graduate of West Point, commanded the Union's thirty-five thousand-man army. General Pierre G.T. Beauregard commanded twenty-two thousand Confederates near the vital railroad intersection of Manassas Junction, thirty miles west of Washington. General Joseph E. Johnston also had twelve thousand Confederates at Winchester, Virginia, all within supporting distance of Beauregard.

McDowell expected Major General Robert Patterson, with eighteen thousand Pennsylvanians, to hold Johnston's force in the Shenandoah Valley, which would have given the Union army a numerical advantage at Bull Run. McDowell also intended to launch a complicated flanking movement on Johnston's defensive position with troops unfamiliar with tactics and with brigade commanders unfamiliar with roads and topography. Like many movements during the Civil War, McDowell expected the Confederates to hold a position while Union troops maneuvered over bridges, streams, and hills unimpeded and unchallenged.

McDowell created the first tactical error by bringing his force to Centreville, the launching point, and then waiting several days to review his plans. The second problem occurred when General Patterson refused to move from Harpers Ferry and failed to hold Johnston's army in check at Winchester. While McDowell dallied at Centreville, Johnston began shuttling his army to Manassas by rail, thus setting the stage for the Union's first major military disaster.

On July 21 McDowell put the Union army into motion. The main attack concentrated on the Confederate left flank. A secondary attack attempted to breach the Confederate center while two regiments feinted on the rebels' right. Beauregard and Johnston controlled the interior lines while McDowell spread his forces over six miles of outer lines. McDowell attacked and Beauregard and Johnston defended. Three years would pass before Union commanders discovered that with near equal forces face-to-face on the battlefield, a well-organized defense always won. There were moments when the battle might have swung in favor of the Union if McDowell could have seen what was happening on the field.

At 4:00 P.M. the Union army began an orderly withdrawal that soon became a stampede. Hundreds of Washington spectators who had come to see McDowell whip the rebels panicked and joined the race back to the capital. Notably, Thomas Jackson and his Confederate infantry brigade gained everlasting fame as they were observed to be "standing like a stone wall" in the face of attacking Union forces that threatened to carry the day as the main attack met with initial success.

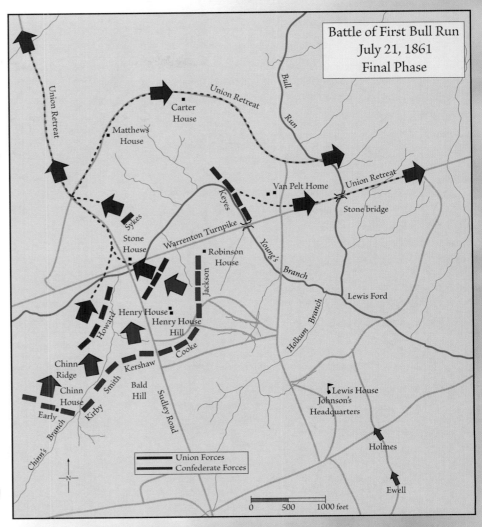

Battle of First Bull Run July 21, 1861 Final Phase

***ABOVE:** The map of the Battle of First Bull Run shows the positions of the Confederate and Union armies as they engaged during the afternoon. The Confederate counterattack crumbled sections of the Union line that ended in a rout.*

***BELOW:** Dedication of a battlefield memorial at Bull Run, 1865.*

COLD HARBOR
—A LESSON LEARNED

Since the opening of the spring campaign in May 1864, General Grant had been pushing Meade's 115,000-man Army of the Potomac hard against General Lee's 60,000-man Army of Northern Virginia. Meade suffered serious casualties because Lee always managed to take strong defensive measures.

On June 1 Grant began to lose patience as the Army of the Potomac approached Cold Harbor, where good roads led directly into Richmond. Having been recently reinforced by sixteen thousand men, he decided to contain the Confederate right flank with cavalry, break through the enemy's long line of breastworks, and force Lee to fight in the open. For two days, while Grant maneuvered for position, Lee emplaced his artillery, strengthened his defenses, and brought up reinforcements. Lee's position at Cold Harbor was among the best he ever defended.

At 4:30 A.M. on June 3, the Army of the Potomac, on double lines along a 6-mile front, charged the virtually impregnable Confederate defensive positions. Expecting to be slaughtered, Union soldiers in the forty thousand-man attack force pinned their names to their shirts. As the blue lines moved across open farmland, concealed Confederate veterans opened with a thunderous volley of thousands of rifles. As one rebel recalled, an "inexplicable and incredible butchery" began. The entire Union line crumpled with men stacked one upon the other. In less than 30 minutes the attack dissolved, leaving seven thousand Union soldiers killed and wounded.

Grant always regretted the assault. He seemed to have forgotten what had happened on so many other battlefields where generals incautiously threw assaulting forces against prepared defensive positions. He also seemed to have forgotten that Civil War weapons were no longer inaccurate muskets but weapons with rifled barrels loaded with minie bullets that went where they were aimed. Cold Harbor would be remembered as Grant's greatest mistake. For the remaining months of the war he focused on outmaneuvering Lee, ultimately succeeding ten months later.

RIGHT: The map of Cold Harbor shows the setup of Union and Confederate forces before the battle. Though the battle would be regarded as General Grant's greatest mistake, he consistently focused on his goal of engaging the enemy and destroying its army.

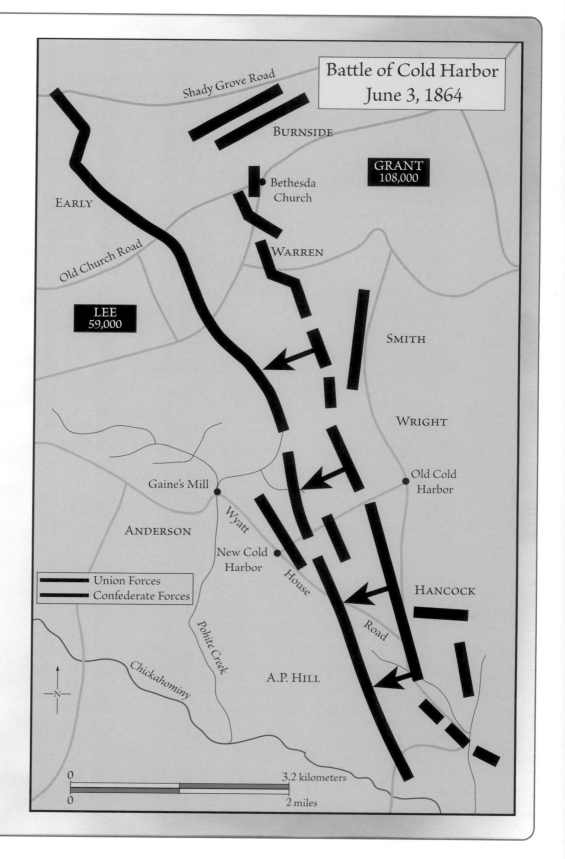

Battle of Cold Harbor
June 3, 1864

Shady Grove Road

BURNSIDE

GRANT
108,000

EARLY

Bethesda
Church

Old Church Road

WARREN

LEE
59,000

SMITH

WRIGHT

Old Cold
Harbor

Gaine's Mill

Wyatt

ANDERSON

New Cold
Harbor

House

HANCOCK

Road

Pohite Creek

Chickahominy

A.P. HILL

—N—

Union Forces
Confederate Forces

0   3.2 kilometers
0   2 miles

but not always with 100 men to a company or exactly ten companies to a regiment. Regular Army regiments retained their identity throughout the war and were never melded into volunteer regiments. Battle losses destroyed units, and often a brigade contained fewer men than a regiment. When losses decimated a regiment, it would usually be dissolved and a new unit formed.

The Confederate Army closely followed the organization of the Regular Army.

Armies were the largest component of each government and were named for the area where they served, such as Lee's Army of Northern Virginia, Jackson's Army of the Shenandoah, and Meade's Army of the Potomac. There were sixteen named Union armies and twenty-three Confederate armies. The North raised 2,040 regiments, of which 1,696 were infantry, 272 cavalry, and 72 artillery. Southern records are incomplete. At least six hundred thousand men served in the Confederate Army, and possibly twice as many more.

The Regular Army contained eight staff bureaus: the adjutant general's, inspector general's, judge advocate general's, quartermaster general's, subsistence, medical, and pay, plus a corps of engineers and a corps of topographical engineers. A Signal Corps came later. The Confederate Army had four staff bureaus; the adjutant and inspector general's, the quartermaster general's, the commissary generals, and the medical department. The bureaus of both governments were organized under the secretary of war and later the commander-in-chief of the army, but for most of the war Lincoln and Davis guided the strategic decisions.

On May 1, 1865, the Union Army numbered 1,000,000 men. During the span of the war 2.3 million men enlisted for three-year terms. One of the most hotly debated subjects has been the size of the "Army of the Confederate States of America," the

ABOVE: Mathew Brady's late spring 1861 photograph of the officers of the 69th New York State Militia at Fort Corcoran, Virginia, one of the ring of forts that protected the capital.

Southern army's proper name. Figures range from six hundred thousand to 1.5 million, and the actual number is probably somewhere in between. At the close of the war only 174,223 Confederates surrendered. From a Regular Army of 16,367 men in 1860, the Union and the Confederacy mustered nearly 4 million men. For four years brother fought brother, father fought son, and friends fought friends. After relentlessly killing each other, the United States repaired itself and finally abolished slavery.

Losses	Battle Losses	Disease	Total
Union	110,542	249,458	360,000
Confederate	198,703	59,297	258,000

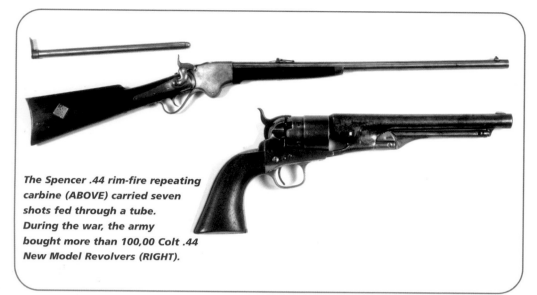

The Spencer .44 rim-fire repeating carbine (ABOVE) carried seven shots fed through a tube. During the war, the army bought more than 100,00 Colt .44 New Model Revolvers (RIGHT).

the Thirty-eighth, Thirty-ninth, Fortieth, and Forty-first Infantry became the first African-American regiments to serve in the Regular Army. The "Buffalo Soldiers," and they were called, retained their regimental designations until desegregation in 1950. Also entered on the army list were one thousand Indian scouts, whose duties involved chasing other Native Americans. On such a beginning was the West pacified.

Between 1865 and 1898 the Regular Army fought 943 actions in twelve separate Indian campaigns, all because of an unremitting national expansion westward.

ABOVE: Taking a well-earned rest, these 21st Michigan infantrymen certainly look as if they've been through the wars. Formed in Iona and Grand Rapids, the regiment spent most of their thirty-two-month service in the western theater, where they took part in most major battles.

War with the Indians (1865–1898)

During America's Civil War, the Indians enjoyed a short reprieve from the constant emigration of settlers. General Stand Watie, a Cherokee transplanted from Georgia to Oklahoma, raised a regiment of mounted rifles and fought for the South. Other members of the tribe repudiated Watie and fought for the North. Even the Indians took sides.

In 1866 Congress cut the line strength of the Regular Army to 54,600 enlisted men and 3,036 officers, spread among forty-five regiments of infantry, ten of cavalry, and five of artillery. The Ninth and Tenth Cavalry, and

RIGHT: Company E, 4th U.S. Colored Infantry, was stationed at Fort Lincoln, located east of Washington near the Maryland line. Most African American companies performed garrison duty in forts.

On December 21, 1866, the army became sensitive to the beginning of a new war when two thousand Sioux led by Crazy Horse and Red Cloud massacred Captain William Fetterman's eighty-two-man detachment near Fort Kearny, Wyoming.

In 1868 Major General Philip Sheridan, commanding the Department of the Missouri, launched a winter campaign. The cavalry carried Spencer repeating rifles, a late Civil War carbine loaded by a tubular magazine that passed through the butt of the stock and held seven copper rimfire .52-caliber cartridges. Some troops carried .50-caliber Springfield breech-loaded rifles that were even more lethal.

Sheridan's campaign expanded into a decade of fighting. In September 1868 Major George A. Forsyth fought a nine-day defensive action against Indians led by

LEFT: After the Civil War, Congress reduced the cavalry to ten regiments. The 9th and 10th became the first African American cavalry units in the Regular Army. Led by a white officer, the 10th heads west, where the men became known as "Buffalo Soldiers."

BELOW: Buffalo Soldiers of the 25th Infantry, some wearing buffalo–hide coats

In 1876 the war shifted to the northern plains, where the Sioux and the northern Cheyenne joined forces with Sitting Bull and Crazy Horse to resist the containment of their tribes on reservations. Five battles took place in the area of the Big Horn Mountains in the Dakotas and southern Montana. The greatest disaster occurred on June 25, 1876, when Colonel Custer's Seventh Cavalry caught up with Crazy Horse at Little Big Horn. Custer divided his command into three columns, led one of them into a carefully laid trap, and lost all 212 men, including his own life.

Such were the wars of the latter 1800s, and if nothing else the activity kept the Regular Army involved in tactics and training through a new generation of men. Until 1898, the wars of the United States had been fought on the continent. The outside world, however, had rapidly changed, and American expansionists began to take notice.

ABOVE: The original caption to this engraving identifies "the massacre of United States troops by the Sioux and Cheyenne Indiand near Fort Philip Kearney, Dakotah Territory, December 22nd, 1866."

Roman Nose at Beecher's Island, Colorado. In November Lieutenant Colonel George A. Custer's Seventh Cavalry defeated Black Kettle in the Oklahoma Panhandle. In May 1869 Major Frank North's cavalry crushed a band of Cheyenne at Summit Spring, Colorado. No year passed without dozens of skirmishes with Indians.

BELOW LEFT: General Crook's battle on the Rosebud River, Montana during the Sioux War—Sioux portrayed charging Colonel Royall's detachment, June 17.

BELOW RIGHT: In 1888, Chiracahua Apache chief Geronimo (1829–1909) "One Who Yawns" (far right) with three of his warriors. Repeatedly sent to a reservation, they always escaped.

CHIEF JOSEPH AND THE NEZ PERCE WAR

On June 17, 1877, young Chief Joseph, leader of a the Nez Perce Indians, resisted being herded onto a reservation so whites could take over his rich homeland in the Wallowa Valley of Oregon. After defeating an army of regulars in White Bird Canyon, Joseph pulled together his tribe of three hundred warriors and four hundred women and children and marched east into Idaho and Montana looking for a new home.

Brigadier General Oliver O. Howard tracked Joseph's band to the Clearwater River, impetuously charged, and suffered an unexpected repulse. Constantly pursued by infantry and cavalry, Joseph and his people crossed the Bitterroot Mountains into Montana, skirmishing in a series of minor engagements as they fled. Howard's troops discovered to their unpleasant surprise that the Nez Perce fought with the same skill and discipline as regular soldiers.

Coming unexpectedly from the east, Colonel John Gibbon surprised Joseph in the Big Hole Basin of Montana. The Nez Perce rallied, surrounded Gibbon's force, but withdrew on August 11 when Howard's battalion arrived.

Joseph tried to take the remnants of his tribe into Canada. In late September the small band, now in desperate condition, reached the Bear Paw Mountains, thirty miles from the Canadian border. After a trek of nearly two thousand miles, the Nez Perce found themselves surrounded by the combined forces of Generals Nelson B. Miles and Howard. On October 5, after fighting against ten-to-one odds for ten days, Joseph surrendered. Casting down his rifle, he said, "I will fight no more forever."

Chief Joseph deserves a place among America's greatest military leaders.

BELOW LEFT: The collage depicts the army's long chase of Chief Joseph and the Nez Perce Indians from the Wallowa Valley in Oregon to Eagle Rock, (near Chinhook), Montana. The portrait is of guide George A. Huston

BELOW: In 1877, Chief Joseph (1840-1904), known as "Thunder Rolling over the Mountains," led his small band of Nez Perce in an epic fighting but losing retreat to reach the Canadian border.

A FLEXING OF POWER 1898–1918

In 1890 America awoke to the realization that it had been living in a provincial backwater when compared with the great powers of Europe. With the West pacified and enjoying the benefits of modern civilization, a growing crop of American empire-builders began looking offshore for opportunities to grab territory but discovered that the Europeans had already staked out most of the world. Americans still perceived war as a glorious undertaking without recognizing that their armed services were poorly prepared for one. Although the army adopted the Krag-Jorgensen rifle as its infantry weapon, most of the men still carried the .45-caliber single-shot Springfield carbine. It would take another war to bring the armed forces up to speed on weapon technology. By 1898 the Regular Army's forty-two regiments had little to do and seemed anxious for a reason to flex their muscle.

Regular Army Regiments (1898)	
Infantry	25
Cavalry	10
Artillery	7

War with Spain

On January 25, 1898, the battleship USS *Maine* pulled into the harbor of Havana for the ostensible purpose of protecting American interests in Cuba. Three weeks later an explosion of undetermined cause killed 266 officers and men and sent the *Maine* to the bottom. American newspapers howled treachery, and the people hollered, "Remember the *Maine!*" Together they set the nation on an irreversible course to world power.

On March 9, Congress appropriated $50 million for war against Spain and spent the next month trying to prod a declaration out of President William McKinley. When McKinley merely asked Congress for authority to intervene in Cuba, the request failed to satisfy congressional imperialists.

On April 25, after a minor incident with a Spanish transport occurred at sea, Congress declared that a state of war existed with Spain and goaded McKinley into calling for 125,000 volunteers. Congress authorized the formation of brigades, divisions, and corps like those of the Civil War, specifying three regiments to a brigade, three brigades to a division, and three divisions to a corps. The army formed seven corps and assigned the regulars to the V Corps.

By the time the rolls filled in late May, Commodore George Dewey had captured Manila Bay, destroyed the Spanish fleet in the Pacific, detached a cruiser to capture Guam, and was waiting impatiently for the army to send troops to occupy the Philippines. Two U.S. based naval squadrons under the commands of Admiral William T. Sampson and Commodore Winfield S. Schley simultaneously pounded through the Atlantic and the Caribbean searching for Spain's Atlantic fleet. For the first time in American history, all army operations were predicated on the actions of a sister service. Thereafter the conflict became a soldiers' war. Major General

William T. Shafter commanded the Cuban expedition, and Major General Wesley Merritt commanded the Philippines expedition. In August Spanish forces in the Philippines surrendered as soon as Merritt landed, but Shafter ran into a hornet's nest in Cuba.

The Rough Riders were one of the few units in the Spanish-American War that carried magazine-loaded, bolt-action Krag-Jorgensen rifles. Most of the volunteers, including Regular Army veterans, still carried single-shot rifled muskets. Spaniards could fire eight rounds from their clip-loaded 7 mm Mauser

The Rough Riders

On April 22, 1898, Congress authorized the formation of the First U.S. Volunteer Cavalry, a rough-and-ready outfit composed of outdoorsmen, cowboys, and Ivy League athletes who were "good shots and good riders." The army offered forty-year-old Assistant Secretary of the Navy Theodore "Teddy" Roosevelt command of the unit, but he considered his friend, Regular Army Colonel Leonard Wood, more experienced in military matters. Roosevelt became the unit's second-in-command with the rank of lieutenant colonel. He immediately resigned his naval post and devoted full time to organizing and training what newsmen nicknamed "Roosevelt's Rough Riders." Roosevelt's attempts to call the regiment "Wood's Rough Riders" failed. He eventually took great pride in having his name associated with the unit.

Wood and Roosevelt organized the regiment at San Antonio, Texas, and managed to get in a few weeks of training before sailing for Cuba. On June 22 more than twenty thousand soldiers, among them the Rough Riders, landed at the fishing village of Daiquiri, east of Santiago de Cuba. General Shafter began an overland march to Santiago with the cavalry and a thousand infantry in the van. At Las Guasimas the Rough Riders encountered a strong Spanish force. War correspondents followed Roosevelt through the ensuing battle, thus giving coverage to the future president's legend as a hero.

On July 1, during the Battle of Santiago Heights, General Shafter encountered unexpectedly stiff Spanish resistance. Americans sustained heavy casualties, losing 400 men at El Caney. When Brigadier General S.B.M. Young fell with a serious wound, Wood replaced him, and Roosevelt assumed command of the Rough Riders. There had been mass confusion when the regiment became pinned to the base of Kettle Hill. Roosevelt quickly reorganized the unit and with army regulars led the assault on Kettle Hill, one of the two hills that flanked the main road to El Caney. Roosevelt then gathered together four or five men, jumped the entanglements holding back the soldiers, led the charge up San Juan Hill, and was first to reach the enemy trenches. After taking the hill, the Rough Riders continued to attack and seized the heights overlooking Santiago. Two weeks later, August 13, the Spanish surrendered.

In 2001 Roosevelt was belatedly awarded the Congressional Medal of Honor for his role on San Juan Heights. The citation read, "His leadership and valor turned the tide." Roosevelt's performance, be it partly legend or all fact, became one of the great epics of American history.

Wood also received the Medal of Honor and eventually became the army's first truly effective chief of staff, serving in that capacity from 1910 to 1914.

LEFT: Theodore "Teddy" Roosevelt (1858–1919), the twenty-sixth president of the United States, gained fame as colonel of the "Rough Riders," the first volunteer cavalry unit in the Spanish-American War.

Right: On July 1, 1898, during the advance on Santiago, Cuba, the all African-American 10th U.S. Cavalry charges up San Juan Hill.

ABOVE: On July 17, 1898, American forces descended on Santiago from the rear. General José Toral surrendered the city, unaware that American ranks had been severely thinned by yellow fever and malaria.

BELOW: In the early 1900s, President Teddy Roosevelt vowed to rebuild the Regular Army, and once again recruiting posters began appearing on the streets of cities

rifles in the same time that Americans armed with Springfields cycled a single shot. The regulars, however, used one weapon that made a difference. Three 40-year-old Gatling guns delivered six thousand rounds in eight minutes during the assault of San Juan Hill, marking one of the first uses of massed machine guns.

The fighting in Cuba unfortunately reinforced the army's doctrine of favoring marksmanship over rapid fire, as well as its parsimonious emphasis on conserving ammunition. Observers noticed that while Spanish soldiers discharged relentless volleys, American soldiers took deliberate aim. Single-shot rifles made a soldier think about the importance of making every shot count. Not until 1903 did the Regular Army begin exchanging its old single-shot weapons for modern Springfield bolt-action rifles.

Consequences of Expansionism

In August 1898, when Spain surrendered to the United States, the Philippines, Puerto Rico, and Guam suddenly became U.S. property. Plans to retain the Philippines as a possession angered nationalist leader Emilio Aguinaldo, a dissident who commanded an army of eighty thousand Filipinos. He had been fighting the Spanish for several years and now turned against the United States. After General Merritt pushed Aquinaldo's forces out of Luzon in the first phase of the Philippine Insurrection, the fiery Filipino began a ragged guerrilla campaign through all the islands of the archipelago. In 1899 Merritt turned the governorship of the Philippines over to Major General Elwell S. Otis, who adopted a policy of "benevolent assimilation" but looked the other way when his soldiers burned and pillaged villages occupied by insurgents.

In May 1900, Lieutenant General Arthur MacArthur replaced Otis and expanded the harsh punitive measures employed by his predecessor. Faced with guerrilla warfare, as opposed to conventional warfare, MacArthur departed from the conventional organization pattern of the army. He decentralized his force, mixing regulars with fifty companies of newly created Philippine Scouts. In 1902 the scouts helped to capture Aguinaldo and brought an end to the insurrection. Guerrilla activity, however, continued in the Muslim-populated areas of the southernmost islands, as it does today.

The Boxer Rebellion

While MacArthur put down the insurrection in the Philippines, the army fought an action in China against a fanatical secret Chinese organization known as the Society of the Righteous Harmonious Fists, or "Boxers." The sect performed depredations against foreign missionaries and Christian converts and enjoyed secret support from the Dowager Empress Tzu Hsi. When a small allied force landed and moved on Peking to protect Christians, thousands of Boxers attacked and drove the relief force back to their ships. The second China Relief Expedition consisted of 4,800 Russian, 3,000 British, and 2,500 American regulars, marines, and bluejackets under the command of Major General Adna R. Chaffee. On August 14, 1900, the allied force fought their way into Peking. When the U.S. Fourteenth Infantry assaulted the northeast corner of outer wall, Bugler

Calvin P. Titus climbed to the top and hoisted the American flag. The Boxer Rebellion spread through China and petered out in September 1902. Had the Chinese been well lead and trained in the use of modern weapons, the China Relief Expedition would have met disaster.

The New Army

After settling the Spanish-American War, President William McKinley put Major General Grenville M. Dodge in charge of an investigating committee to examine the Regular Army. Dodge started with the war department, reported gross inefficiency at all levels, and cited the army's departments as fiefdoms rampant with corruption. The investigation had just gathered momentum when, on September 6, 1901, an assassin shot McKinley. Vice President Teddy Roosevelt took over the administration and told Secretary of War Elihu Root, a brilliant administrator, to clean up the mess and recommend a better way to prepare for war.

FAR LEFT: During the Boxer Rebellion (1900–1901), the U.S. 11th Infantry Regiment on July 23, 1900, joined in a 5,000-man assault that stormed the city walls of Tientsin and captured the fortress.

LEFT: Several months after the capture of Peking on August 14, 1900, the mainly African-American U.S. 9th U.S. Cavalry lined up before the Sacred Gate to honor Count Alfred von Waldersee, who led the German expedition during the Boxer Rebellion.

Deeply conscious of his lack of military knowledge, Root began an extensive study of European military structure. He read British military critic Spenser Wilkinson's *The Brain of an Army*, which extolled the efficiencies of Germany's general staff. He examined the Dodge commission's reform proposals and discovered that the organization of the Regular Army had not changed since the Civil War. Root then investigated the turf fights that existed between the bureaus of his own staff and began making changes. He reduced the power of the bureau chiefs and reverted strictly military matters back to the generals by creating a chief of staff, who superseded the army's commanding general. The chief of staff headed a general staff, thus providing the "brain" that undertook the planning function and prepared war plans for all possible contingencies while ensuring the availability of weapons and equipment. The chief of staff would also act as chief adviser and executive agent of the president on military policy.

Congress adopted Root's proposals and passed the Militia Act of 1903 (called the Dick Act sponsored by Representative Charles W. Dick of Ohio). Root then created the Army War College, enlarged West Point, and converted state militias into what later became the National Guard and the Army Reserves. He also increased the Regular Army to 3,820 officers and 84,799 men. Root's changes were so thorough and modernizing that another revision did not occur until 1947.

On August 15, 1903, Root named Lieutenant General Samuel B. M. Young, a Civil War veteran and a leader in the Battle of Santiago Heights, as the army's first chief of staff. Young's appointment as the nation's top soldier established an organizational structure that still exists. Today the chief of staff is selected by the president from among the generals of the army and with the advice and consent of the Senate.

In 1905 a 28,000-man army division, instead of a corps, became the basic combined arms unit. A division consisted of three brigades, each comprised of two of more infantry regiments, an artillery regiment, a cavalry regiment, an engineer battalion, and other supporting units.

Probably the most important invention in the years prior to World War I was the combustion engine, which made possible motorized tanks, trucks, and airplanes. On August 1, 1907, a few years after aircraft made their first appearance, the army created the Aeronautical Division of the Signal Corps. The impact of the combustion engine on tactics would be revolutionary, but in 1907 nobody could clearly envision the future of air power. The air arm remained a part of the army until 1947, when the government belatedly made the U.S. Air Force an independent service branch.

The first four chiefs of staff muddled about without clear direction, but things changed in 1910 when Major General Leonard Wood, former commander of the Rough Riders and a Medal of Honor winner, took over the post. Wood reached the high office by following an unconventional route. He did not graduate from West Point but from Harvard's medical school. He came into the army through the back door by joining the Medical Corps before becoming a field officer. For four years Wood served as the first truly effective chief of staff.

He believed that an officer could be trained in six months or less and became involved in creating short-term officer-training programs that became absolutely essential throughout the twentieth century.

Although the army restructured its forces, the general staff did little to improve the army's weapons. While the Germans produced thousands of short-recoil machine guns invented by American Hiram Maxim, the Regular Army continued to depend on the less efficient gas-operated designs manufactured by Colt. When Americans went to war in 1917, they were compelled to rely on French aircraft, tanks, and automatic weapons.

Below the Rio Grande

In 1904 the Army Corps of Engineers began construction of a canal across the Isthmus of Panama. It opened ten years later and was 50 miles long, 110 feet wide, and 41 feet deep. Chief engineer Brigadier General George W. Goethals directed the construction, and Colonel William C. Gorgas developed a process for ridding the area of yellow fever, thereby making the work possible. The Federal government operated the canal until December 31, 1999, when it reverted to the Panamanian government by an agreement signed by President Jimmy Carter in 1977.

In 1914 the peaceful opening of the Panama Canal marked the beginning of another conflict with Mexico when Francisco "Pancho" Villa, a bandit and

FAR LEFT: In 1914, the cavalry remained as important as ever, and the drillmaster still had plenty of problems acquainting recruits with their mounts.

self-appointed general, attempted to topple the government. The army sent Brigadier General Frederick Funston's Fifth Brigade to Veracruz to maintain stability, but trouble merely intensified. Captain Douglas MacArthur arrived to assess the situation on behalf of the war department. He conducted an unauthorized reconnaissance into the interior, came under fire, and had to fight his way back to Veracruz.

ABOVE: In 1914, the 8th Cavalry Regiment receives instruction in the positioning and firing of machine guns.

BELOW: In 1916, Brigadier General John J. Pershing launched punitive expeditions into Mexico, using cavalry regiments to hunt down Francisco (Pancho) Villa's raiders.

RIGHT: In March 1916, Francisco (Pancho) Villa (on white horse) led raids across the U. S. border. The guerrillas traveled in small bands. Villa led many of the raids, but was never caught.

On March 9, 1916, Pancho Villa sallied across the Rio Grande and killed fifteen civilians in Columbus, New Mexico. The war department sent Brigadier General John J. "Black Jack" Pershing to capture Villa and put him out of business. Cadets at West Point dubbed Pershing "Black Jack" after they contemptuously discovered that he nourished an overly enthusiastic opinion of black soldiers. Pershing invaded Mexico with three brigades (five thousand men), among them First Lieutenant George S. Patton. He also used Curtiss R-2 airplanes from the First Aero Squadron for scouting and communication. Pershing never captured Villa, but he succeeded in dispersing the bandit's followers. The campaign gave him considerable exposure to mobilizing and sustaining a large force in the field. The experience could not have come at a better time. In January 1917, when it became apparent that the army would be needed in Europe, Pershing returned to the United States.

BELOW: In 1916, General Pershing used Curtiss R-2 airplanes from the army's 1st Aero Squadron to scout and maintain communications over a 140-mile route between Columbus, New Mexico, and El Valle, Mexico.

BELOW: Although Pershing's forces in Mexico succeeded in rounding up many of Pancho Villa's lieutenants, they never captured the elusive leader.

Over There

In 1913 fifty-seven-year-old Woodrow Wilson became the twenty-eighth president of the United States. He entered the White House one year before war erupted in Europe. For three years he espoused neutrality and kept the country out of World War I. During those years he increased the army, but ever so slightly. When Congress declared war against Germany on April 6, 1917, the U.S. Army ranked seventeenth in the world with a uniformed force of 127,588 regulars, 5,000 Filipino Scouts, 15,000 reservists, and a National Guard of 174,000 men, half of whom had been federalized. This whittled down to a combat strength of two hundred thousand for an army that had not conducted military operations above division level since the Civil War.

On May 2, 1917, General Pershing received secret instructions from Secretary of War Newton D. Baker to select five regiments and form an infantry division for service abroad. Pershing melded the Sixteenth, Eighteenth, Twenty-sixth, and Twenty-eighth Infantry Regiments, the Sixth Field Artillery, and two other artillery regiments into the First Expeditionary Division, later designated the First Division, which would become better known as the "Big Red One" from its distinctive shoulder patch. Pershing placed Captain George C. Marshall, the man who would become the army's most gifted staff officer, in charge of division operations.

Although Pershing was not the senior officer in the

army, Wilson named him commander-in-chief of the American Expeditionary Force (AEF), mainly because of the general's performance in restoring order to Mexico. Baker instructed Pershing to cooperate with Allied forces but to keep the identity of American

ABOVE: *Prior to their departure to join General Pershing on the Mexican border, troops are reviewed at the training center at Des Moines, Iowa.*

LEFT: *Brigadier General John J. "Black Jack" Pershing reflects under the shade of a tree beside his headquarters near Columbus, New Mexico.*

BELOW: *As American involvement in World War I approached, army posters became more prevalent.*

ABOVE: *John M. Browning designed many rifles. One of the most popular weapons in World War I became the .30-caliber M1918 Browning Automatic Rifle (BAR) produced by Colt. Note the original production version had no provision for a bipod.*

BELOW: *On June 13, 1917, General John J. Pershing (center) arrives at Boulogne, France, to make arrangements for receiving the 1st Infantry Division of the American Expeditionary Force.*

units distinct and separate from European elements. On May 28 Pershing sailed for France and established general headquarters (GHQ) in Chaumont. Three weeks later advance elements of the First Division sailed for Europe. On July 4, American Independence Day, regulars from the Big Red One bolstered French morale by marching through the streets of Paris. One of Pershing's aides stopped at the tomb of the Marquis de Lafayette to remember the French nobleman's support during the American Revolution and shouted, "Lafayette, we are here!" Although these words are often attributed to General Pershing, they were actually spoken by Lieutenant Colonel Charles Stanton.

The next question involved the mobilization of the National Guard. Major Douglas MacArthur, a member of the general staff, recommended calling up units from different states. The system proved equitable and resulted in the formation of the Forty-second "Rainbow" Division, because, said MacArthur, "[It] stretches like a Rainbow from one end of America to the other." Promoted to colonel, MacArthur became the division's chief of staff and on October 17, 1917, accompanied the unit to France.

President Wilson built the AEF through the Selective Service Act of May 18, 1917, which made males between the ages of 21 and 30 eligible for the draft. He decreed a "mobilization of every resource in the nation," and the government began selling war bonds to raise money. Unlike conscription efforts in the past, which were managed by the war department, Congress authorized local draft boards run by civilians. Twenty-four million men registered at 4,648 draft boards, and over a span of eighteen months more than 2.7 million draftees were inducted into the armed services.

As new combat companies formed, Pershing began blending them into regiments and the training them for combat. He ordered that every inductee receive the same basic training as West Point cadets. The most rigorous combat training began after the officers and soldiers reached France. By December 1917, 9,800 officers and 165,000 doughboys had reached France with thousands more arriving every week. Pershing refused to put the men into battle before they were ready, and despite pressure to integrate American forces into British and French divisions, he refused to deploy the AEF except as an independent entity operating in its own sector of the battlefield. Almost as an afterthought, now with American troops pouring into France, President Wilson asked Congress for a declaration of war on the Austro-Hungarian Empire, the other major player comprising the Axis.

Before the spring campaign, Pershing began integrating his divisions into corps to build the First Army. At the beginning of 1918 he had eight divisions. Only three were in combat, but more were on the way. On January 15 he incorporated four divisions into the I Corps (the First, Second, Twenty-sixth, and Forty-second) and placed the unit under the command of Major General Hunter Liggett. The II Corps was already fighting alongside a French force and never officially became part of Pershing's First Army. As more divisions arrived, he moved them into the III, IV, V, and VI Corps and finally created his army.

On March 21, 1918, Germany launched the spring offensive, a series of five concentrated attacks aimed at winning the war before the AEF mustered the strength to tip the scales in favor of the Allies. The German high command, in particular Field Marshal Paul von Hindenberg and General Erich Ludendorff, launched an assault against the British sector on the Somme, as well as a supporting attack in Flanders. Sir Douglas Haig, commanding the British forces, pleaded for help and Pershing responded, sending AEF forces to wherever they were needed.

After checking the German offensive and striking back, Pershing— now with 260,000 troops— prepared to turn the enemy out of their trenches and drive them from France. The fighting at Château-Thierry had produced a 30-mile-wide bulge in the enemy lines, making them somewhat vulnerable to attack. When the German general staff attempted to mount another offensive to regain the Marne, Pershing decided to wait for the attack, weaken the Germans by attrition, and strike back with the AEF.

On July 15 Ludendorff began the second Marne campaign, once more attempting to drive the British out of Flanders by attacking Champagne and a lightly defended area west of Reims. Fourteen divisions of the German Seventh Army made it across the Marne but were stopped by Dickman's Third Division, gaining it the name "Rock of the Marne." Ludendorff withdrew from the Soissons-Château-Thierry-Reims salient to reduce the front defended by his now depleted forces. In five months the Germans had lost a half-million men, and though Allied losses had been slightly higher, Americans were now arriving in France at a rate of three hundred thousand per month.

ABOVE: Posters begin to change as the Tank Corps compete against other branches for men

LEFT: Men of 107th Infantry Regiment, 27th Division leave their trenches in a September 1918 attack.

The Aisne Offensive – Château-Thierry

On May 27, 1918, General Erich Ludendorff launched the third German offensive. A final blow calculated to drive the British out of Flanders and make a dent in the Allied front, it created a salient thirty miles wide and twenty miles deep. By noon three German armies, the Eighteenth attacking southwesterly and the First and Seventh attacking westerly, began crossing the Aisne. By evening they were across the Vesle, and on May 30 they reached the Marne.

Meanwhile, on May 28, Pershing rushed the Second Division, commanded by Major General Omar Bundy, and the Third Division, commanded by Major General Joseph T. Dickman, to reinforce French forces at Cantigny. Before Bundy and Dickman arrived, Major General Robert L. Bullard's First Division stormed Cantigny's strongly fortified German observation post and repulsed a series of violent counterattacks by Germany's veteran Eighteenth Army. Though only a local operation, the action marked the first American offensive and boosted Allied morale.

The U.S. Second and Third divisions continued on to the Marne and were thrown against the spearhead of the German

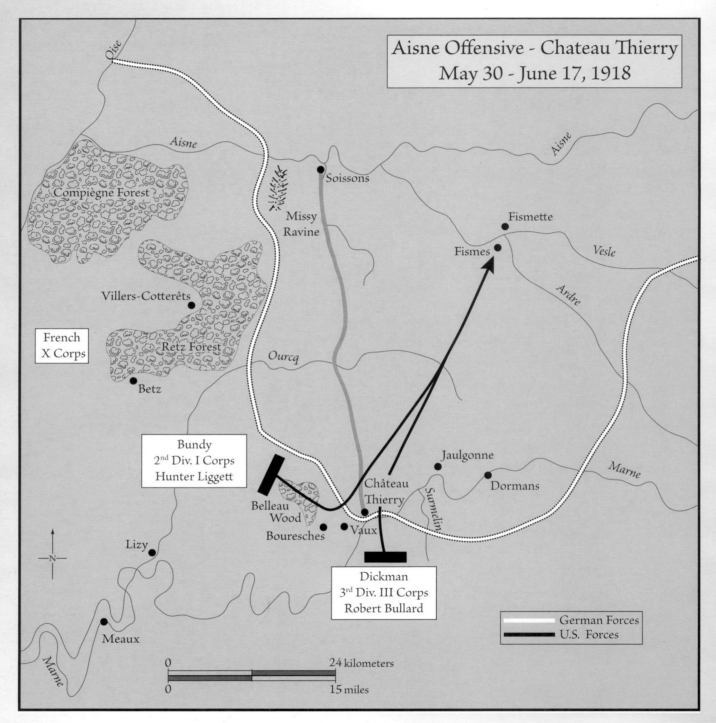

ABOVE: The Chateau-Thierry action shows the relative position of American forces in the early phase of the Ainse offensive.

56

offensive. Dickman's Third Division passed through thousands of retiring troops from the French Sixth Army, filed into vacated positions at Château-Thierry, and held the bridges against German assaults. During a pause, Dickman ordered a counterattack, rallied the French troops, and drove the Germans back across the Marne at Jaulgonne.

In the Battle of Château-Thierry, Dickman's division became involved in unrelenting combat for forty-one days. The action actually encompassed three operations by two divisions sent by Pershing to General Ferdinand Foch, who on April 14 became commander in chief of French, British, and American forces. The three phases included the defense of the line on the Marne River, the battle of Belleau Wood (which was stopped by the Second Division's Fourth Marine Brigade), and the capture of Vaux.

Bundy's Second Division, having taken over the sector of the French XXI Corps west of Château-Thierry and between Vaux and Belleau, checked German efforts to breach the extended line. When Ludendorff called off the assault on June 4, Bundy used his marine brigade to spearhead a counterattack. In six successful attacks on enemy positions, the Germans retired after losing 9,500 men and 1,600 prisoners. During the fighting at Vaux, German chemical warfare (mustard gas) injured 400 Americans.

RIGHT: Men of 77th Division receive instructions on the art of camouflage from a British sniper (foreground, left), May 1918.

BELOW: On May 5, 1918, African-American troops of Company I, 368th Infantry Regiment, 93rd Division, fight from trenches at the western edged of Argonne Forest. The army was still segregated with the exception that white officers mainly commanded.

The Lost Battalion – The Meuse-Argonne Offensive

At 5:25 A.M. on September 26, 1918, Pershing launched the First Army—three corps abreast—down the Meuse Valley. The plan, designed by Colonel George C. Marshall, would be the AEF's largest and most costly battle of the war. Six hundred thousand U.S. troops with 3,900 guns marched down the Meuse River and into the Argonne forest while General H. J. E. Gouraud's French Fourth Army advanced simultaneously on the left. Marshal Foch viewed the operation as the culmination of his summer counteroffensive, but he worried because twenty-two divisions of inexperienced American soldiers would be assaulting the Kriemhilde Line, part of the heavily fortified Hindenberg Line and the enemy's main line of communications through Metz, Sedan, and Mezieres.

The initial American attack overran the German lines, but communication and transportation breakdowns caused delays and confusion. Many troops received no food for four days, German resistance stiffened, and after several days of intense combat, the American attack stalled.

On October 2, while the First Army regrouped, the Seventy-seventh Division sent a battalion composed of elements from the 307th and 308th Infantry Regiments into the Argonne Forest. The battalion slipped through the enemy line, disappeared into the woods, and soon lost contact with headquarters. Major Charles W. Whittlesey, commanding the "Lost Battalion," refused to surrender though repeatedly assaulted by superior forces. For five gloomy and dreadful days the battalion repulsed one attack after another. Thanks to the late arrival at division headquarters of "Cher Ami," Whittlesey's last carrier pigeon, on October 7 a relief column arrived. Of 554 officers and men comprising the "Lost Battalion," only 194 Doughboys walked out of the forest under their own power.

Three days later the AEF drove the Germans out of the Argonne forest. The forty-seven-day Meuse-Argonne offensive lasted from September 26 to November 11, 1918, and led to the final armistice.

The relief of the "Lost Battalion" made epic headlines and gave birth to an AEF's legend. For their stubborn defense against overwhelming odds, Whittlesey and his second-in-command, Major George McMurtry, received the Medal of Honor.

A total of 4,057,101 American soldiers served in World War I, including 545,773 regulars, 728,234 volunteers, and 2,783,094 draftees. At the time of the armistice, the war was costing America $42 million per hour. Only 13 percent of this amount went for soldiers pay.

Killed in combat	37,568
Died of wounds	12,942
Wounded	193,663
Captured	4,416

Ammunition (rounds) expended by AEF	
.30-caliber rifle	181,391,341
.45-caliber pistol	120,901,102
37-mm cannon	2,274,229
77-mm howitzer	7,550,835
Grenades	2,724,067

LEFT: On September 26, 1918, the first phase of the Meuse-Argonne battle was launched. Nine U.S. divisions were involved, along with 142 French and British tanks manned by Americans.

LEFT: The Meuse-Argone campaign became America's costliest. On October 11, 1918, the 18th Regiment, 1st Division, attempts to work through the Argonne Forest near Exermont.

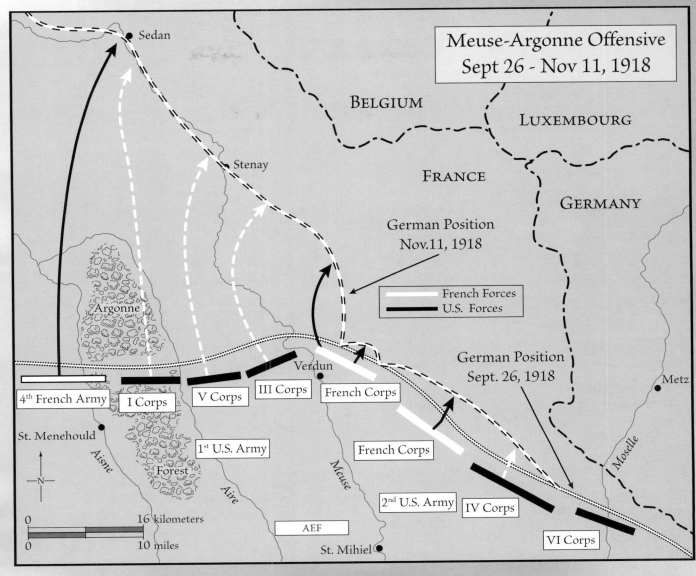

Meuse-Argonne Offensive
Sept 26 - Nov 11, 1918

BELGIUM

LUXEMBOURG

FRANCE

GERMANY

Sedan

Stenay

German Position
Nov.11, 1918

French Forces
U.S. Forces

Argonne

German Position
Sept. 26, 1918

Metz

4th French Army

I Corps

V Corps

III Corps

French Corps

Verdun

St. Menehould

1st U.S. Army

French Corps

Forest

Aisne

Aire

Meuse

2nd U.S. Army

IV Corps

Moselle

0   16 kilometers
0   10 miles

AEF

VI Corps

St. Mihiel

LEFT: At Hoboken, New Jersey, cheering troops with arms waving return from France aboard the troopship SS Agamon.

ABOVE: The map depicts the flow of the AEF's September 26–October 3 phase of the Meuse-Argonne offensive, which ended on November 11 with the German surrender.

WORLD WAR II IN EUROPE 1918–1945

ABOVE: Although in 1918 the cavalry still advertised for troopers, motorized vehicles would soon replace horses.

RIGHT: As America begins to mobilize for another war, thousands of young men join the army, and after training, march in review with bayonets fixed to their rifles.

At the end of the "War to End All Wars," the United States and Europe attempted to achieve disarmament or, at minimum, arms control. On January 8, 1918, President Wilson laid before Congress fourteen points as the "only possible program for peace." He had in mind a League of Nations, which the U.S. Senate later refused to ratify.

On February 6, 1922, in an effort to establish a ten-year moratorium on building capital ships, the United States, Great Britain, Japan, France, and Italy hammered out the Washington Naval Treaty limiting the number of battleships and aircraft carriers, which at first appeared to be a step in the right direction but was eventually ignored by Japan.

On June 17, 1925, the League of Nations met at Geneva and attempted to control international trade in arms and ammunition and prohibit the use of poison gas. The U.S. refused to sign the treaty.

On August 27, 1928, world powers signed the Kellogg-Briand Pact renouncing aggressive war, but made no provisions for sanctions if one of the signatories stepped out of line.

On April 22, 1930, the London Naval Treaty attempted to regulate submarine and cruiser tonnage but inadvertently excluded Germany and did little to curb Japan's shipbuilding aspirations.

In 1932 the powers to be, this time with Germany included, attended a World Disarmament Conference at Geneva to reduce rearmament efforts and provide for inspection and control under the direction of the League of Nations. After Germany and Japan withdrew from the League, the conference adjourned in 1934 without agreement. Japan then denounced the Washington and London naval treaties, and German Chancellor Adolf Hitler repudiated the disarmament clauses in the Versailles Treaty, which had also stripped away Germany's pre-war possessions and levied $56 billion in reparations.

While the world ineffectually negotiated, Germany, Italy, and Japan prepared for war.

Mobilization

Since World War I the U.S. Army, which now included an air corps, had been in military limbo. In 1920 Congress passed the National Defense Act, reduced the Regular Army to 280,000 men, and rejected a request by the chief of staff for universal military training. When Congress placed tanks under the control of the infantry, Major Dwight D. Eisenhower and Major George S. Patton argued that the function of armor was to penetrate and exploit enemy lines and should not be mingled with infantry regiments. They lost the argument until 1928, when the army established an experimental mechanized force at Camp Meade, Maryland, and demonstrated the assault potential of armor.

In 1930 fifty-year-old Lieutenant General Douglas MacArthur became America's youngest chief of staff and as one of his first acts directed that all branches of the army be mechanized. Because the stock market had crashed in 1929, it was not a time for MacArthur to be looking for money. Nevertheless, he lumped the

First and Thirteenth Cavalry regiments into the Seventh Cavalry Brigade (Mechanized) and turned the unit over to Major General Adna R. Chaffee Jr., another proponent of armor, and the cavalry began exchanging their horses for tanks. Chaffee built the brigade at Fort Knox, Kentucky, and soon had his men performing exercises with light tanks, armored cars, infantry-carrying half-tracks, and truck-drawn 75 mm guns. Because of the dearth of funds, the army did not begin to design a medium tank until 1939.

Franklin D. Roosevelt, who in 1933 became the thirty-second president of the United States, confronted too many depression-related economic issues to worry much about the military preparedness of the nation. He called upon the army to assist in the administration of the Civilian Conservation Corps (CCC), which generated some good publicity but detracted from the army's primary mission of preparing for war. The lack of funds affected all branches of the service, but especially the infantry. While the armies of the world developed automatic rifles, the U.S. soldier still lugged cumbersome bolt-action 1903 Springfield rifles. MacArthur became disgusted, retired from the U.S. Army, and in 1935 went to Manila to take command of the Philippine army.

ABOVE: Dressed in full tank gear, Major General George S. "Old Blood and Guts" Patton (1885–1945) stands in front his command vehicle while training the 2nd Armored Division in Louisiana.

RIGHT: The M3 light tank was a development of the M2A4 and was armed with a turret-mounted main 37mm gun and three 30-cal machine guns, two of which were in sponsons. It became an important recon vehicle until declared obsolete in July 1943.

ABOVE: U.S. FT17 tanks leave Rock Island, Illinois to go to Canada where they will be used for training.

On October 2, 1935, General Malin Craig, a hardheaded realist and Pershing protégé, became the army's new chief of staff. His first shock occurred when he found the general staff engaged in highly theoretical military planning having no practical relationship to the feeble condition of the army. The weapons employed during the Spanish Civil War (1936–1939) demonstrated the horrible condition of America's weapon technology. Craig accomplished more than MacArthur in preparing the nation for war, but he failed to grasp the growing importance of air power.

LEFT: The M3 medium tank, produced from 1941, weighed around 30 tons, carried a 75mm sponson-mounted cannon, a turret-mounted 37mm, and three or four 30-cal machineguns. On open roads it could reach speeds of 26mph.

George Catlett Marshall (1880–1959)

On September 1, 1939, the day Germany invaded Poland, fifty-nine-year-old General George C. Marshall became chief of staff. Two days later Great Britain, France, Australia, and New Zealand declared war on the Third Reich. The Imperial Japanese Army had already been making territorial gains in China since 1931.

Marshall seemed a curious choice, having been a 1901 graduate of the Virginia Military Institute instead of West Point. He was not the ranking officer in the army, nor had he ever held a major combat command, but he had served as a superb staff officer with the operations section of General Pershing's GHQ in France. Pershing recognized the potential of Marshall and never forgot it, and Marshall never forgot Pershing's open tactics and fast-moving

offensives during World War I. During his term as assistant commandant at Fort Benning's Infantry School, Marshall imbued a generation of young officers with the same philosophy.

Ten months earlier, during a White House meeting, Marshall disagreed with Roosevelt over the lack of interest in modernizing the nation's military. He condemned the use of antiquated rifles, artillery, aircraft, and mechanized vehicles. The U.S. Army, with only 174,000 men, had fallen to nineteenth in the world, ahead of Bulgaria and next to Portugal, and had become, said Marshall, "ineffective." Of nine infantry divisions on paper, only three were organized as such, and those were at half strength. Marshall did not particularly care if his remarks offended the president. Roosevelt evidently approved of Marshall's earnest outspokenness and made him chief of staff.

With Roosevelt's support, Marshall became the principal spokesman at congressional hearings. While pressing for men, money, and arms, he directed the general staff to prepare manpower mobilization plans for an expanded field force. On September 27, 1940, Congress called up sixty thousand National Guardsmen. Eighteen days later lawmakers reinstated the draft by passing the Selective Service and Training Act. "For the first time in our history," Marshall told the nation, "we are beginning in a time of peace to prepare against the possibility of war."

During the next six years, Marshall transformed the general staff to a command post. He filled the department with a competency of officers unmatched by any commander in any previous war. He masterfully designed the grand strategy of the war and, to an exceptional degree, the staff planning required for industrial mobilization and logistical support.

When the impulsive president meddled in military affairs, Marshall exercised a unique talent for quashing Roosevelt's bad ideas and promoting his better ones, such as the decision to send destroyers to Great Britain, the lend-lease program, and the agreement that if the United States entered the war the "Europe First" policy (the defeat of Germany to take precedence over the defeat of Japan) would apply.

Marshall will always be remembered, not because he rebuilt the armed services from scratch and carried them to victory in World War II, but because as secretary of state (1947–1949) he designed the European Recovery Plan, or Marshall Plan, which integrated the economies of Europe and accelerated recovery.

LEFT: General George Catlett Marshall (1880–1959) served with the AEF in Europe during World War I and as chief of staff, U. S. Army (1939–1945), in World War II. Marshall retired during the war but was recalled in 1944 to serve as a five-star general of the army. After the war he became secretary of state during the administration of President Harry S. Truman.

ABOVE: During World War II, every branch of the service produced their own posters. For the first time, women were vigorously recruited to join the army

During the summer of 1941, the United States drifted slowly towards war. Marshall and his navy counterpart, Admiral Harold Stark, correctly anticipated a two-front war against Germany and Japan and drafted the plans necessary to mobilize the country. By September the newly designated Army of the United States ballooned to 1.2 million men, most of them serving enlistments of one year. Few of the men were trained. The rapidly expanding army did not have the infrastructure, logistics, or weaponry to support the growth. Volunteers and draftees began flooding camps to begin basic training. They received spotless new uniforms and boots, a modest amount of camping equipment, but trained with broomsticks because of the shortage of rifles.

A few months later, on December 7, 1941, the Japanese bombed the naval base at Pearl Harbor and decimated the Pacific Fleet. On December 8 the United States went to war against Japan. Two days later Germany and Italy declared war on the United States. The "Europe First" strategy was on the books, but the army needed weeks of training before it would be prepared to go anywhere in force. Congress also had to confront the problem of one-year enlistments. Once again, General Marshall's patience and skill in presenting his case to Congress resulted in arbitrarily extending enlistments by a narrow vote in the House of 203 to 202.

On February 9, 1942, Anglo-American planners met in Washington to discuss strategy. They recognized the importance of keeping Russia in the war by opening a second front. Great Britain would provide the springboard, but in 1942 the British chiefs of staff doubted such an expedition would succeed. Despite reaching no agreement on invading Europe, American troops continued to pour into Great Britain, including the first American strategic bombing squadrons. British Prime Minister Winston Churchill suggested striking the Axis through the "soft underbelly" of the Mediterranean. Roosevelt agreed, and plans for crossing the channel in 1942 were postponed and replaced by Operation Torch, the seizure of French Morocco, Algeria, and Tunis.

ABOVE: In December 1943, General Dwight D. Eisenhower became commander-in-chief of all allied forces in Western Europe.

The meeting also marked the formation of the Joint Chiefs of Staff (JCS). The JCS became the American component of the Anglo-American Combined Chiefs of Staff (CCS). The formation of the JCS materialized without any official directive. U.S. Navy Admiral William Leahy became the first chairman of the JCS with Admiral Ernest King representing the navy and General Marshall representing the army. Major General Henry H. "Hap" Arnold, the army air chief, also shared the table, signifying the emerging role of air power. The JCS is as essential today as in 1942, and now makes its home in the Pentagon.

The North African Campaign – Operation Torch

General Marshall assigned the task of commanding Operation Torch to fifty-two-year-old Lieutenant General Dwight D. "Ike" Eisenhower, who was already in England and studying ways to open a second front in Europe, not North Africa. Torch involved three major strategies: to establish a foothold for future combat against Italy and Germany; to prevent German Field Marshal Erwin Rommel from capturing North Africa and the Suez Canal while bringing relief to the British Eighth Army; and to prevent the former French navy and one hundred thousand French troops under Vichy France Admiral Jean François Darlan from supporting Rommel.

Meeting the November deadline meant immediate and massive improvisation. For planning purposes, Eisenhower moved headquarters to Gibraltar. Army troops received training in amphibious warfare. Shipyards converted passenger liners into infantry transports. Flyers practiced takeoffs from aircraft carriers. Although U.S. Marines had already conducted successful amphibious landings in the Solomon Islands, Torch would be the largest amphibious operation ever undertaken and included a joint Anglo-American force of 107,000 men. It also meant that American troops would be serving under British commanders, and British troops would be serving under American commanders.

BELOW RIGHT: On November 8, 1942, U.S. Rangers pass 81mm mortar rounds down into an assault craft. White armbands are worn to identify friendly forces during the attack.

BELOW: Passenger liners soon became gutted and converted into troopships, and once elegant staterooms were filled with cots stacked four high with a 16–18-inch crawl space between each layer.

In October 1942, prior to the scheduled landings, Eisenhower sent Major General Mark W. Clark and three officers on a secret and dangerous mission to secure information on Vichy forces in North Africa. Clark entered into talks with French officers in an effort to obtain their agreement to not impede Torch landings. The mission failed, and Clark's party barely escaped.

On November 8 the first elements of Major General George S. Patton's 34,300-man Western Task Force, which embarked in the States, landed along a 200-mile front in French Morocco. Patton encountered sporadic resistance, especially around the central city of Casablanca. By November 11 French resistance began to collapse. American soldiers took possession of the airfield at Port Lyautey, and P-40F Warhawk fighters transported by the escort carrier *Chenago* quickly achieved air supremacy.

At Oran, Algeria, Major General Lloyd Fredendall's Center Task Force of thirty-nine thousand American soldiers, which had been based in England, encountered the stiffest Vichy resistance. Second Battalion, 509th Parachute Infantry Regiment, flying from England was only partly successful in capturing airfields. As the landings progressed, troops established a beachhead, penetrated Oran, and on November 10 the French defenders capitulated.

The Eastern Task Force, commanded by Major General Charles Ryder and comprising ten thousand U.S. troops and twenty-three thousand British soldiers, also from England, landed at Algiers and took possession of the city on November 10 with barely a skirmish. The troops found Admiral Darlan at Algiers and took him into custody. Darlan broke with the Vichy and ordered an immediate ceasefire by all French troops and agreed to help the Allies drive the Germans out of Tunisia. Darlan's assistance lasted about six weeks. On December 24 a student acting on orders from the alleged "Resistance" assassinated

ABOVE: On December 5, 1942, elements from the 1st Rangers march past agave plants during exercises in Africa.

Darlan. Exactly where the order originated is not clear, but it was widely know than Free French leader Charles de Gaulle, who was in England, became infuriated when he learned that Eisenhower had retained Darlan as leader of the French forces in North Africa.

The Race for Tunisia

On November 17, with Allied forces occupying French North Africa, the *Wehrmacht* began transporting one thousand German troops a day into northern Tunisia. The Allies were not quite ready for a major overland engagement, but British Lieutenant General Kenneth A.N. Anderson, with elements that would become the First British Army, moved into the mountains southwest of Bizerte, butted against aggressive German troops, and halted. Eisenhower rushed General Fredendall's II Army Corps into the area on Anderson's right, but the year ended in stalemate with Anderson's First Army facing General

Jürgen von Arnim's Fifth Panzer Army in north-central Tunisia.

Field Marshal Rommel feared his vaunted *Afrika Corps* could be trapped at Mareth if Anderson and Fredendall struck his rear at the same time Lieutenant General Sir Bernard L. Montgomery's British Eighth Army assaulted from the south and struck his flank. On February 14, instead of waiting for developments, Rommel launched a two-pronged armor-led surprise attack closely supported by *Luftwaffe* fighters and dive-bombers. The mini-blitzkrieg scattered Fredendall's loosely deployed II Corps, rolled up the

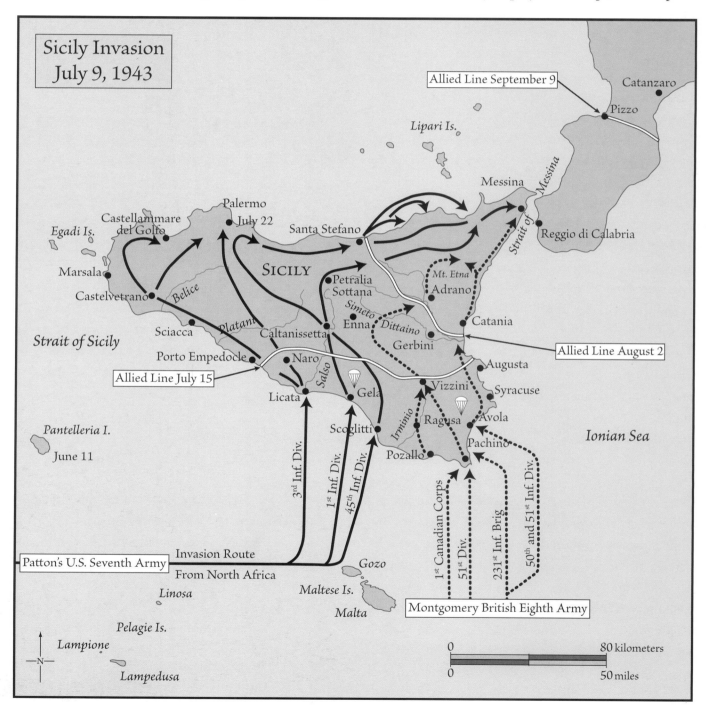

RIGHT: On July 9, 1943, General Patton's Seventh Army crossed the Mediterranean Sea from North Africa, landed on three beaches in southern Sicily, and swept through the island while British forces assaulted the southeastern coast of the island.

First Armored Division, and on February 18 surged through the Kasserine Pass. Fearing the loss of his vital supply base at Tebessa, Eisenhower rushed reinforcements as American and British troops attempted to regroup. On February 20, when Arnim failed to support Rommel's attack, the German assault began running out of fuel, and before losing momentum Rommel backtracked to Mareth as quickly as he had come.

For the first time, green American troops understood how it felt to be attacked by skillful German veterans enjoying superior weapons and air supremacy. Eisenhower investigated what went wrong and concluded that while the Americans had put up a remarkably tenacious fight, it had been poorly organized on the ground and poorly supported in the air. General Patton succeeded Fredendall as commander of the U.S. II Corps, and the U.S. Army Air Forces (AAF) changed tactics and adopted the British system of air support.

In April, Patton's revitalized II Corps aggressively changed from a secondary role at Kasserine Pass to one of major impact. Under Patton's leadership, the II Corps won the first significant American victory against German forces at El Guettar. Patton then plunged eastward, linked up with Montgomery's Eighth Army, and began driving Italian General Giovanni Messe from Mareth. On May 13 the Battle of Tunisia ended with the surrender of 240,000 Germans and Italians. Operations in North Africa cost the Axis 620,000 men. From November 1942 to May 1943, Americans suffered 18,500 casualties. Churchill and Roosevelt's decision to make North Africa the proving ground returned dividends. The Allies now had a springboard for operations in the Mediterranean, battle-hardened men with tactical training, and a successful template for mounting joint operations in the future.

LEFT: On July 22, 1943, General George Patton reviews troops from the 1st Infantry Division near Petralia Sottana, urging them to make a rapid lunge across northern Sicily in an effort to beat British General Bernard Montgomery to the city of Messina.

Sicily—Operation Husky

In January 1943 Roosevelt, Churchill, and the CCS held strategy talks at Casablanca. They mutually agreed to postpone the cross-channel attack until 1944 and to undertake another Mediterranean operation with Sicily the objective. In exchange for delaying cross-channel operations at the request of the British, Churchill agreed to Roosevelt's request for expanding operations in the Pacific. Roosevelt proclaimed, and Churchill agreed to accept, nothing but the enemy's "unconditional surrender," a policy of debatable practicality.

BELOW: On July 21, 1943, U.S. Rangers march through Palermo, Sicily, ahead of the main body of the 3rd Infantry Division.

GEORGE S. PATTON (1885-1945)

In 1943 George "Old Blood and Guts" Patton turned fifty-eight, but he never let age slow him down. Patton had been born into the army. He came from an old Virginia military family, entered the Virginia Military Institute at the earliest age possible, graduated from West Point in 1909, and joined the cavalry. Always energetic, remarkably capable, combative, and blunt, Patton never changed. He earned his captaincy serving with General Pershing's punitive expedition in pursuit of Pancho Villa (March 15, 1916–February 5, 1917), and when Pershing went to France, Patton went with him. He became the first American officer to receive tank training, set up the AEF Tank School, and led the First Tank Brigade in the Saint-Mihiel and Meuse-Argonne offensives.

World War I made Patton a tank man, and during the next two decades he spent his time advancing the virtues of mechanized armor and preparing for the next war. During the years of Hitler's expansion of the Third Reich, Patton successively commanded the Third Cavalry (December 1938–July 1940), the Second Armored Brigade (July–November 1940), and the I Armored Corps (January 15, 1942). He assisted in the final planning of Operation Torch and commanded the Western Task Force during the invasion of French Morocco. Following the reverses at Kasserine Pass, he replaced General Fredendall and took command of the II Army Corps.

Patton also had a penchant for making impolitic statements to the press, often against his counterpart in the British army, General Sir Bernard Montgomery. Having once been stripped from command for doing so, Patton promised Eisenhower he would behave, and on the eve of the Sicilian campaign Eisenhower put him in charge of the Seventh Army.

In Sicily Patton demonstrated his genius for tactics, but he immediately afterwards suffered public criticism and censure for an August 1943 face-slapping episode at a hospital where he found a so-called "coward" crouching among the wounded. Once again, an incident cost Patton his command. Eisenhower, however, turned Patton's misbehavior into an opportunity. He brought Patton to London, used his presence in England to decoy the Germans into believing the Allies would invade France at Calais instead of Normandy, and kept the general on the shelf for several months before placing him in charge of the newly created Third Army.

When Eisenhower finally turned Patton loose, the Third Army wheeled through France and spearheaded the push into central Germany. Patton's armored columns eventually pressed into Czechoslovakia, and had he had his way, he would have turned the Third Army against the Soviets. Once again Patton lost his command because of brash political outspokenness. On December 21, 1945, he died in Heidelberg of congestive heart failure, brought on by an automobile accident. His death may have come as a blessing. Patton, a true warrior with a fine military mind, could never be content with peace.

RIGHT: Lieutenant General George S. Patton, in addition to being a superb commander, also had a reputation for pitting himself against his British allies, which frequently got him into trouble with his superiors.

Eisenhower's staff had for months been working on Operation Husky, the invasion of Sicily. On June 9, following a monthlong bombardment of Axis air bases on Sardinia, Sicily, and Italy, Allied invasion convoys appeared off the southern coast of Sicily. Patton's newly activated Seventh Army, the first numbered U.S. field army to see action in World War II, assaulted beaches on the southwestern side of Sicily while Montgomery's Eighth British Army went ashore on the southeastern side. American troops fanned out to the west, their primary mission to seize airfields and protect the British flank.

Operation Husky also marked the debut of the 82nd Airborne, commanded by Brigadier General Matthew B. Ridgway. The general had never used a parachute when the 82nd Infantry Division suddenly became an airborne unit. Ridgeway eventually participated in many jumps and glider assaults, but at Sicily he came ashore in landing craft. His parachutists made two night drops, but suffered heavy casualties the second night when friendly antiaircraft (AA) on ships of the Allied fleet mistook the transports carrying the 504th Parachute Infantry Regiment for enemy aircraft.

On July 15–23, though German resistance stopped Montgomery south of Catania and blocked the British drive on the capital of Messina, Patton's army swept through western Sicily. General Sir Harold R.L.G. Alexander, Allied ground commander, ordered Patton to ease the pressure on Montgomery and press on to Palermo. Patton captured Palermo, turned east, and using a number of small amphibious end-runs, outflanked German positions on the northern coastal road and closed on Messina. On August 17 Montgomery's Eighth Army joined Patton's Seventh Army at Messina, just as the last Axis troops evacuated Sicily.

The campaign ended with a few flaws. Not only did the majority of German defenders escape across the Straits of Messina to the Italian peninsula, but

bickering between Patton and Montgomery resulted in two separate campaigns instead of one well-coordinated assault. There were also noticeable positives, in particular Patton's dash across the northern coastal road where, by using a series of small amphibious landings, he demonstrated a tactical insight far beyond the operational proficiency of other American commanders. The success of the five-week campaign can be partly attributed to substantial improvements in AAF air tactics, which Patton used to advantage as the Seventh Army rolled across the island.

In addition to great quantities of weapons, the Axis lost more than 164,000 troops, among them 32,000 Germans, as opposed to American losses of 7,319 and British losses of 9,353. As expected, German resistance had been professional and tenacious, as opposed to Italian resistance, which accounted for 80 percent of Axis losses.

Under Patton, the American army came of age in Sicily, earning the respect of the British Tommy and the British high command.

ABOVE: M4A3 Sherman tanks disgorge themselves from a landing ship tank (LST), which had the capacity of carrying 40 to 70 tanks weighing 25 to 40 tons each.

ABOVE: British and American reconnaissance troops (M5 light tank and M8 armored cars) confer on road to Rome.

BELOW: An M10 tank destroyer rumbles through the streets of Artena, Italy.

Italy—Operations Avalanche and Shingle

With Sicily in Allied control, Eisenhower had options, but after Patton's face-slapping incident, he temporarily sidelined his best general. Major General Omar N. Bradley, another rising star, had brilliantly commanded the II Corps of Seventh Army during the Sicilian campaign and seemed to be the right general to succeed Patton, but Eisenhower wanted Bradley, his old classmate from West Point, back in England to plan the cross-channel invasion of France. So Eisenhower turned operations in Italy over to forty-seven-year-old Lieutenant General Mark W. Clark, who had commanded the Fifth Army in Morocco.

Clark began planning the invasion of Salerno in January 1943. The political situation in Italy had become volatile. On July 24 the war-weary Italian nation toppled Benito Mussolini from power during the Sicilian campaign and replaced him with Field Marshal Pietro Badoglio, who announced he would continue hostilities but soon entered into secret peace talks with the Allies. On September 3, the same day that Italy signed an armistice, Montgomery's British Eighth Army landed on the toe of the Italian boot. Six days later a second British amphibious force landed at Taranto and began moving toward Foggia. On September 9 Clark's Fifth Army, composed of the British X Corps and the American VI Corps, sailed up the west coast of Italy and went ashore under heavy fire at Salerno. The three-prong Anglo-American

attack was intended to gain a foothold in Italy coincident with the Italian armistice, but Field Marshal Albert von Kesselring's army group was still there. The Germans quickly disarmed the Italians and took possession of their fortifications. After two months of intense fighting, the Allied armies had advanced no farther than the Gustav Line, a defensive position ten miles deep that ran from one side of Italy to the other with Monte Cassino in between. Hitler decided to hold as much of Italy as possible, and the Germans fought as fiercely and pugnaciously as ever, contesting every foot of ground in the winter mud of the snow-covered spine of the Italian peninsula.

Frustrated by fighting in terrain where the enemy had the advantage, Clark launched an amphibious landing behind German lines at Anzio (Operation Shingle). He intended to cut German communications by a swift movement into the interior, but Major General John P. Lucas, commanding the VI Corps, talked Clark into waiting to consolidate the beachhead before moving inland. Clark made the mistake of agreeing. Kesselring brought German reinforcements from the north and the east and nearly drove fifty thousand Anglo-American troops back into the Tyrrhenian Sea. The costly tactical mistake delayed operations in Italy until mid-May, when British General Alexander consolidated Anglo-American armies in Italy into the Fifteenth Army Group and broke through the Gustav Line. On June 4, two days before the Normandy invasion, Clark's Fifth Army marched into Rome.

Mark Clark wanted glory, but he did not find it in Italy. He had difficulty conducting, coordinating, and sustaining operations, and he suffered from confusion and uninspired leadership among his subordinates throughout the campaign, caused in part from the deployment of troops from twenty-two different nations, few of whom were familiar with Anglo-American operations. From September 3, 1943, when the Allies first landed in Italy, to May 2, 1945, when the Germans surrendered unconditionally among the foothills of the Italian Alps, the Allies suffered 312,000 casualties, the Germans 435,000. The CCS seemed content to let the Italian campaign drag, knowing that Hitler would continue to divert German troops from France, while in England an Allied Expeditionary Force composed of 3 million men congregated for the great crusade to liberate Western Europe.

ABOVE: Any American who lived through the years of World War II might still recognize this familiar poster.

FAR LEFT: On 29 August 1944, C Battery, 598th Field Artillery Battalion, fire 105mm howitzers across the Arno River.

LEFT: American docks were constantly busy providing equipment to the armies of the United States and its Allies, enough to equip 2,000 infantry divisions. Deckhands watch as cranes lift a jeep, an armored vehicle, and a 2 1/2-ton truck onto a freighter.

GENERAL DWIGHT DAVID "IKE" EISENHOWER (1890–1969)

Dwight David Eisenhower grew up in Abilene, Kansas, and in 1915 graduated from West Point, just in time to participate in World War I. Like George Patton, Ike became a tank instructor. He also served under General Douglas MacArthur in the Philippines (1933–1939) and learned to fly. After returning to the states, he worked for General George C. Marshall in the operations division of the U.S. Army staff in Washington. Although he had served under some of America's finest generals, Ike had never commanded troops in the field when Marshall put him in charge of the Anglo-American landings in North Africa, Sicily, and Italy.

As supreme commander of a mixed force of all arms and nationalities, Ike devised a system of unified command that General Alexander of the British Army, Admiral Sir Andrew Cunningham of the Royal Navy, and General Sir Arthur Tedder all liked, and they served willingly as his subordinate. Eisenhower's greatest chore would be working with the French, and Charles de Gaulle in particular.

"High command, particularly Allied command, in war," wrote Eisenhower, "carries with it a lot of things that were never included in our textbooks." Though a novice politician, Eisenhower developed a style that pleased Roosevelt, Churchill, and even Stalin, which eventually saved thousands of lives.

In January 1944, and to Eisenhower's surprise, Roosevelt and Churchill moved him to London to command Operation Overlord, the Allied invasion of France. He ran Supreme Headquarters Allied Expeditionary Forces (SHAEF) using the same unified system that worked so well during North African and Mediterranean operations. He told the air arm what he wanted but not how to do it. For Operation Neptune (the Normandy landings) he left the details to the naval and air technicians and to British Field Marshal Montgomery. The arrangement worked because Ike knew how to unify people of different skills to achieve a common purpose.

After the Normandy landings on June 6, 1944, Eisenhower waited until August before moving headquarters to France to take over the general direction of the army groups commanded by Generals Bradley and Montgomery. Despite many obstacles, he conducted a systematic and methodical advance along a broad front.

Eisenhower's strategic talents, original ideas, great strength of character, and amiable disposition made him a gifted leader. The people of the United States recognized Ike's leadership and in 1952 elected him president. He served two terms.

BELOW: General Eisenhower gives men of the 101st Airborne Division a pep talk on the eve of the Normandy Invasion.

Strategy and Policy—1943

Conferences between Roosevelt, Churchill, and the CCS guided the war. The January 14–23, 1943, Casablanca Conference delayed the cross-channel invasion until 1944. The May 15–25 "Trident" Conference in Washington stepped up the strategic bombing offensive against Germany and German-occupied Europe and set a tentative date of May 1, 1944, for crossing the channel. An August 14–24, 1943, "Quadrant" conference at Quebec resulted in an agreement to intensify the war against Japan and to draw the U.S.S.R into a closer relationship with the western Allies. Two months later, foreign ministers from the U.S., U.K., and USSR met in Moscow to lay the groundwork for the Cairo-Tehran "Sextant-Eureka" conferences scheduled in November and December. There they agreed that China should become the fourth member of the alliance, and they also agreed to form a postwar international organization, which subsequently became the United Nations (U.N.). The two Cairo conferences, which excluded the USSR, were important because Roosevelt and Churchill needed to keep China in the war. The November Tehran Conference included Josef Stalin, during which he was informed that the channel crossing would occur in late May or early June 1944, and he agreed to launch a major Soviet offensive at the same time.

Thunder from Sky—Operation Pointblank

During World War II, General Henry "Hap" Arnold became the architect of American air power. His concept of air tactics made the AAF the mightiest aerial striking power of the war. His simple slogan, "Keep 'em Flying," made the long-range Strategic Air Force the most pulverizing weapon in the Allies arsenal.

In 1943 the U.S. Eighth Air Force, commanded by General Carl Spaatz, operated from British airfields and began a round-the-clock aerial offensive.

While Air Marshal Sir Arthur Harris's RAF Bomber Command made night runs against the economy and morale of the German people, the Eighth Air Force concentrated on daylight precision bombing against aircraft industrial targets and *Luftwaffe* installations. Both commands used new technology, a "pathfinder" system that located targets by radar, and a "window"

BELOW: British, American, French, and Soviet generals and diplomats meet to strike agreements on war policy.

BOTTOM: In preparation for Operation Overlord, soldiers perform a daily physical fitness regimen.

ABOVE: An M9 60mm Bazooka breaks into two parts to facilitate transport.

24s began shuttle-bombing operations with Harris's British Bomber Command, striking submarine bases. During the year, bombing missions extended from the Baltic Sea to the oil fields of Ploesti, Rumania. While daylight attacks proved more effective than night attacks, Allied fighters did not have the range to protect the big bombers until December, when the first long-range P-51 fighter escorts of the Ninth Air Force, commanded by Lieutenant General Lewis H. Brereton, became available.

In early 1944 Eisenhower began looking ahead to crossing the channel. For inexplicable reasons, the strategic air striking force remained independent of Eisenhower's command. Nevertheless, Eisenhower made one critical decision that went contrary to the advice of his air chiefs when he diverted assets of the Eighth Air Force from bombing German industrial and oil centers and put them to work destroying the French transportation network behind the invasion beaches, thereby denying the *Wehrmacht* the infrastructure needed to transfer troops and equipment. Eisenhower wanted nothing to stand in the way of Operation Overlord.

system made from strips of metalized paper, which, when dropped from planes, jammed German electronic air defenses.

In June 1943 Spaatz's B-17 Flying Fortresses and B-

Military Organization

The first five months of 1944 witnessed the greatest buildup of military power in the history of the world. From SHAEF headquarters in England, Eisenhower appointed the commanders to lead the operation with the approval of their respective governments. He chose General Montgomery to lead the ground forces, British Admiral Bertram Ramsey to lead naval operations, and Air Marshal Harris to command air operations. He appointed General Bradley, who had been at the planning table since January, commander of the First Army. As soon as a lodgment was secured, Eisenhower planned to put Bradley in charge of the Twelfth Army Group with Lieutenant General Courtney Hodges taking over the First Army and George Patton the Third Army.

The basic military unit continued to be the infantry division, and as one might expect, the organization of American and British divisions were much alike. The typical strength of a division ranged from about sixteen thousand to eighteen thousand men and consisted of a general headquarters, a reconnaissance unit, three regiments of infantry, and three 800-man battalions per regiment. Each battalion contained three to four infantry companies and a heavy artillery unit armed with mortars, heavy machine guns, and motorized artillery. Included in the division were a number of field artillery batteries, antitank weapons, and antiaircraft guns. Each division had at least one engineering company, a signal company, and several service companies such as medical, transportation, maintenance, and military police.

The typical infantry division in 1944 came equipped with about 18,000 rifles, carbines, and pistols; 1,200 light machine guns; 40 heavy machine guns; 360 mortars; 72 field guns; 110 antitank guns; 145 AA guns; which altogether provided more than five times the firepower of a 1940 division. More than 3,300 vehicles transported the division.

An armored division could contain more than fourteen thousand men and almost four hundred

LEFT: In September 1944, elements of the 60th Infantry Regiment shield themselves behind an M4 medium tank during the advance into Belgium.

RIGHT: American Airborne divisions typically included two parachute infantry regiments and one glider infantry regiment. Here a C-47 tows a Waco glider bound for the far side of the Rhine as part of Operation Varsity, March 24, 1945.

tanks (232 medium and 158 light). It would also have a motorized infantry regiment, three battalions of field artillery, an AA battalion, a battalion of engineers, and the standard service companies. The Second and Third Armored divisions were organized as "heavy" divisions. Starting in September 1943 the other fourteen armored divisions were converted to "light" divisions. Tanks for the light divisions totaled only 263 (186 medium and 77 light) with authorized personnel strength of 10,937.

Airborne divisions made major contributions in World War II. They were similar to an infantry division, the difference being that they came from the air. Their purpose varied but was usually intended to mount surprise attacks, operate behind enemy lines, and cause immense disruption. Airborne troops, however, could not carry heavy weapons or move quickly behind enemy lines without motorized transportation, and they were completely dependent upon air support. At the beginning of the war the actual strength of an airborne division was usually less than nine thousand men and consisted of a headquarters; a reconnaissance unit; two parachute and one glider infantry regiments, each made up of three battalions; a field artillery battalion; an antiaircraft/antitank battalion; a battalion of engineers; and service companies.

An army corps normally had operational control of two to four divisions, but sometimes as many as six. Each corps contained, in addition to its divisions, about three thousand men, including a headquarters, reconnaissance unit, engineers, artillery, signal troops, and other services.

An army, such as Patton's Third Army, consisted of its own staff of personnel, and controlled two or more

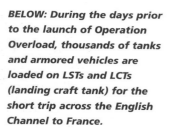

BELOW: During the days prior to the launch of Operation Overload, thousands of tanks and armored vehicles are loaded on LSTs and LCTs (landing craft tank) for the short trip across the English Channel to France.

corps. Two or more armies formed an army group, such as Bradley's Twelfth Army Group. The 4,581,000 men and women who fought in Western Europe did not all go into France at the same time, but nearly half of them did. They were tough young Americans, hardened by the Great Depression, and they would not back down to anyone.

Operation Overlord —The Normandy Invasion

On the eve of D-Day, General Eisenhower's brief instructions to his commanders could not have been more precise: "You will enter the continent of Europe and, in conjunction with the other United Nations, undertake operations aimed at the heart of Germany and the destruction of her armed forces." In five months Eisenhower had put nearly 3 million troops

ABOVE: On May 22, 1944, two weeks before D-Day, long lines form for chow. The buildup for the Normandy invasion (Operation Overlord) became massive. Most of the American soldiers congregated in bases in southern England, where they learned the true meaning of "hurry up and wait."

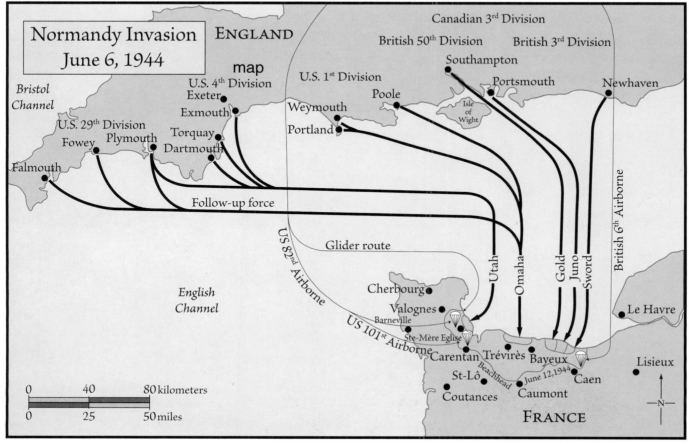

LEFT: The map of the Normandy invasion shows the routes taken by Allied forces as the massive amphibious and airborne operation departed from England for France.

THE 82ND AIRBORNE DIVISION

On August 25, 1917, the army formed the 82nd Infantry Division at Camp Gordon, Georgia. Because the division contained soldiers from all forty-eight states, it became known as the "All Americans" and wore the now familiar "AA" shoulder patch. Fighting as infantry in 1918, the 82nd participated in three major campaigns, among them Argonne Forest, where Sergeant Alvin York earned the Medal of Honor for outstanding heroism. The army demobilized the 82nd after World War I and for twenty years it remained active only in the memories of "All–American" veterans who served in the unit.

On March 25, 1942, the army reactivated the 82nd under the command of Major General Omar N. Bradley. Bradley was transferred to command the Twenty-eighth Division after only four months, turning the division over to Matthew Ridgway, who gave the All Americans parachute training and turned the unit into the army's first airborne division. Ridgway, who had never worn a parachute or jumped from an airplane, quickly overcame his inexperience.

Combat operations began on July 9, 1943, when the 82nd Airborne made its first parachute assault over Sicily. Two months later the 82nd's parachute regiments dropped near Salerno to help bolster the crumbling beachhead while the division's 325th Glider Infantry Regiment landed amphibiously. In November most of the division went to England to prepare for the invasion of France, but Ridgway detached the 504th Parachute Infantry Regiment for the Anzio Invasion. A German diarist nicknamed the paratroopers "Devils in Baggy Pants."

With two combat jumps and heavy combat in Sicily and Italy to their credit, the 82nd prepared for the invasion of Normandy. Having lost so many men in Italy, and with the 504th at Anzio (the regiment didn't leave for England until the end of March 1944), the division had two new regiments attached, the 507th and the 508th.

Late on June 5 General Ridgway joined three parachute infantry regiments and one reinforced glider regiment as men climbed aboard hundreds of planes and gliders for the largest airborne assault in history. When dropped from the sky they landed all over the Normandy countryside. Scattered among hedgerows, towns, and trees, they floundered about searching for comrades. After organizing into a patchwork of mixed units, they secured the exits from Utah Beach, cut communications, and created bedlam behind enemy lines.

Despite a chaotic beginning, the 82nd Airborne remained in combat for thirty-three days without relief or reinforcement. They reported every mission accomplished and claimed that no ground gained was ever lost. The cost came high with 5,245 paratroopers killed, wounded, or missing.

Reorganized in the United Kingdom, the 82nd became part of General Ridgway's XVIII Airborne Corps, comprised of the 17th, 82nd, and 101st Airborne Divisions. Together, they fought all over France and Germany. When the army deactivated the XVIII Corps in 1945, only the 82nd Airborne survived. The division made its home at Fort Bragg, North Carolina, and still does.

LEFT: On September 17, 1944, during Operation Market Garden, the 82nd Airborne Division is dropped by C-47s near Nijmegen, Holland.

together for a gigantic amphibious operation from southern England to the Normandy peninsula of France. He had also kept the Germans puzzled regarding his choice of landing beaches.

In May 1944 he informed the CCS that his force was ready and named June 5 D-Day. The Allied plan designated an assault on five beaches by elements from five army corps. General Bradley's First U.S. Army drew the assignment at Omaha and Utah beaches, and to his left General Sir Miles Dempsey's British Second Army (including a Canadian corps) drew the assignment of assaulting beaches code-named Gold, Juno, and Sword. Two airborne divisions, the 82nd and 101st, arranged to drop more than sixteen thousand troops behind the American beaches five hours before the assault to facilitate a linkup between the Utah and Omaha beachheads and pave the way for capturing Cherbourg.

Bad weather delayed the landings until the morning of June 6. At dawn 600 warships opened fire on the beaches, followed by a swarm of Allied air combat missions that during the first twenty-four hours flew more than one hundred thousand sorties. Some twenty-five hundred heavy bombers dropped ten thousand

tons of explosives while seven thousand fighters and fighter-bombers combed the area for targets.

Then came the assault. Some 4,000 ships transported 176,475 troops, 3,000 guns, 1,500 tanks, and 15,000 vehicles and disembarked everything at sea to landing craft assigned to the five beaches. By noon, Allied forces established a firm toehold on every beach but "Bloody Omaha," which stretched across six miles of shore with a 100-foot cliff overlooking the right flank.

Omaha Beach

On Omaha Beach, everything went wrong for the "Big Red One." Major General Leonard T. Gerow, commanding the V Corps, waded ashore and attempted to direct operations. German defenses were the heaviest, the terrain among the worst, and enemy artillery fire exceptionally accurate. As the day progressed thousands of soldiers—now soaked, cold, bloodied, and overloaded with equipment—began to believe they would be driven back into the sea.

ABOVE: A landing craft assault (LCA) is about 41 feet long and 10 feet wide and carries a crew of four, 880 pounds of material, and 35 men. Disembarking from this LCA on D-Day, soldiers from the 1st Infantry Division wade ashore to Omaha Beach.

LEFT: On D-Day, the U.S. 1st and 29th Infantry Divisions stream ashore on Omaha Beach and begin working their way up the bluffs of the Normandy peninsula.

RIGHT: In August 1944, during Seventh Army operations in Southern France, M10 tank derstroyers are lowered into an LST at St. Tropez.

FAR RIGHT: On August 18, 1944, an AA halftrack is emplaced by a beach exit road in the center of Beach Alpha Red, Cavalaire, Southern France.

BELOW: An American jeep heads toward Mont St. Michel, which was liberated shortly after the beginning of Operation Cobra.

BELOW RIGHT: U.S. troops disembark from a landing craft infantry (LCI), which carries 250 men fully equipped, into a LCA, which will transport 35 men to the beach.

Gerow looked about for Sherman tanks but could find none. The tanks had been fitted with flotation screens but offloaded too far from shore. They sank with their crews before reaching the beach. Nor could Gerow attract any air cover, although thousands of Allied planes were everywhere else. Heavy bombers from the Eighth Air Force were to have softened up the area, but pilots overflew the German bunkers and dropped their bombs three miles inland.

To complicate matters, the "Big Red One's" Sixteenth Regiment had been directed to the wrong area, a heavily defended sector of Omaha Beach. The soldiers spent hours huddled under a seawall watching as their comrades stumbled ashore into withering artillery and machinegun fire. Hundreds fell dead on the beach. Colonel George Taylor, commanding the Sixteenth Regiment, shouted, "Two kinds of people are staying on this beach! The dead and those who are going to die! Now let's get the hell out of here!" The regiment, weathering a hail of fire, struggled inland.

Colonel James E. Rudder's Second and Fifth Ranger battalions, delayed by a navigation error, came ashore on the western extremity of Omaha late. They were to have landed under the 100-foot cliff, scaled it in advance of the main landings, and destroyed the German coastal batteries. Instead, the rangers landed under furious enemy fire and were forced to remain on the stone-covered beach for most of the day. After Colonel Taylor started the plunge inland, Rudder advanced the rangers and finally outflanked the German position. Fifty years later Steven Spielberg immortalized Rudder's rangers and produced the film *Saving Private Ryan*.

When Gerow's V Corps took control of Omaha Beach, all concerns over the success of Operation Overlord ceased. By evening the Allies had 135,000 troops in France. Casualties exceeded ten thousand,

mostly among the First and Twenty-ninth Infantry Divisions at Omaha, where the strongest German defenses in Normandy were located. The situation could have been much worse had Hitler not been deceived into believing the initial attack would come at Pas de Calais, 200 miles away.

Breakout—Operation Cobra

A checkerboard of small fields boxed by thick and deep hedgerows on the Normandy peninsula reduced the Allied advance to a crawl as the defending Germans took every advantage of the terrain, but the beachheads continued to expand and interlock. Major General Joseph Lawton Collins, after landing at Utah Beach, swung up the peninsula and captured the port of Cherbourg, opening a supply base. By late July, Allied forces had grown to a million men with 150,000 vehicles and 500,000 tons of supplies ashore.

On July 25 General Spaatz's long-range bombers dropped forty-two hundred tons of explosives on the German line west of St.-Lô and opened a gap. Bradley's First Army broke through the gap and on July 31 reached Avranches. At this juncture Bradley turned the First Army over to General Hodges and incorporated General Patton's newly arrived Third Army into the new Twelfth Army Group. In early August, while Hodges fought off a determined German counterattack at Avranches, Patton's Third Army stormed through the gap and swung through Brittany to Le Mans. On August 25 the V Corps, spearheaded by French General Jacques Leclerc's Second Armored Division, liberated Paris. After Paris fell, both Bradley and Montgomery began the race to the Rhine.

Bradley's swift assault across central France isolated a German corps south of the Loire, along with dozens of enemy outposts. German soldiers wandered about for weeks searching for a way to surrender.

Race to the Rhine

On September 1, 1944, Eisenhower arrived in France, assumed command of all ground operations, and directed his army group commanders to advance along a broad front to the German border. The Rhine River bordered northeastern France, swung through western Germany, and flowed into the North Sea after passing through the Netherlands. The broad river formed a natural barrier to penetrating Germany's hinterland, and the enemy took special

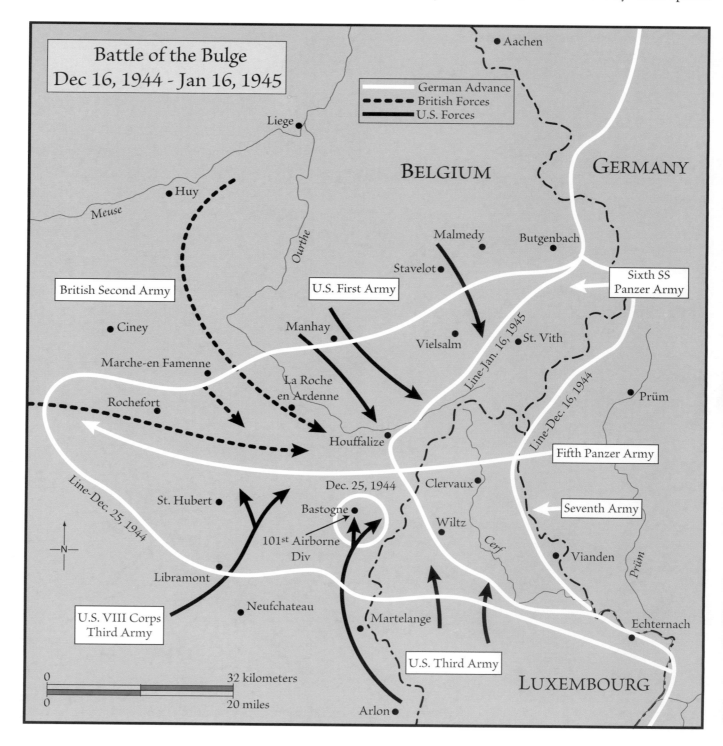

Battle of the Bulge
Dec 16, 1944 - Jan 16, 1945

German Advance
British Forces
U.S. Forces

Aachen

Liege

BELGIUM   GERMANY

Huy

Meuse

Malmedy   Butgenbach

Stavelot

Sixth SS
Panzer Army

British Second Army

U.S. First Army

Ciney

Manhay   Vielsalm   St. Vith

Line-Jan. 16, 1945

Marche-en Famenne

La Roche
en Ardenne   Prüm

Rochefort   Line-Dec. 16, 1944

Houffalize

Fifth Panzer Army

Dec. 25, 1944   Clervaux

Line-Dec. 25, 1944

St. Hubert   Bastogne   Seventh Army

Wiltz

101st Airborne
Div   Cerf

—N—   Vianden

Prüm

Libramont

Neufchateau   Echternach

U.S. VIII Corps
Third Army   Martelange

U.S. Third Army

0   32 kilometers

0   20 miles   LUXEMBOURG

Arlon

RIGHT: During the Ardennes campaign in December 1944, the German army swept into Belgium and created a huge bulge in the Allies' line, isolating an American force at Bastogne. The campaign became best known as the Battle of the Bulge.

pains to protect it by building and fortifying the Siegfried Line.

Two weeks prior to Eisenhower's arrival in France, Lieutenant General Alexander Patch landed the Seventh Army on the coast of southern France. Moving rapidly north, Major General Lucien K. Truscott's VI Corps, spearheading the attack, practically destroyed the German Nineteenth Army. On September 11 Patch made contact with Patton's Third Army west of Dijon. The southern invasion force then became the Sixth Army Group under the command of Lieutenant General Jacob M. Devers. Eisenhower now had another one hundred thousand veterans for the invasion of Germany.

The U.S. Army's drive to the Rhine soon became an epic of determination and resolve. At times the Allied armies moved so rapidly they ran out of fuel and supplies. General Montgomery's bold "Market Garden" Operation to drop three airborne divisions, among them the U.S. 82nd Airborne, behind enemy lines as stepping stones to crossing the Rhine in the Netherlands ended in a disappointing repulse in mid-September at Arnhem. The setback gave Hitler time to bring in reinforcements and prepare a counterattack.

Battle of the Bulge (Ardennes)

On October 28 Eisenhower ordered a November offensive aimed at destroying all German forces west of the Rhine and opening ways for crossing the river. Patton captured Metz, Devers' group liberated Strasbourg, and Bradley's First and Ninth Armies broke through at Aachen, but the Hürtgen Forest became a major obstacle. Winter closed rapidly, leaving the Allies on the German frontier, and there they paused to recuperate from the autumn battles and to gather strength for a final offensive.

On December 16 the Germans struck first, hurling two *panzer* divisions against General Hodges' First Army in an effort to plunge across the

ABOVE: On March 26, 1945, under cover of a smokescreen, elements of the 98th Division, U.S. Third Army, await orders to board assault boats for a Rhine River crossing at Oberwesel, Germany.

BELOW: On December 29, 1944, elements from the 101st Airborne Division move east out of Bastogne to meet the German attack.

LEFT: Remagen Bridge was captured intact by a task force of 9th Armored Division. It became a highway into Germany.

BELOW LEFT: The fighting intensified as the end neared as troops had to fight for every inch of ground, sometimes against youths and old men.

Meuse River and seize the Allies' logistical center at Antwerp. Hitler hoped to destroy Allied forces north of a line stretching from Bastogne to Antwerp, just as the Germans had done in 1940. His generals did not agree, but they followed orders. The Germans launched the assault after a period of rain, fog, and snow blanketed aerial observation and hampered combat operations. The ensuing Battle of the Bulge evolved into the largest battle fought by the U.S. Army during World War II. As soon as Eisenhower understood the extent and implications of the offensive, he threw every asset at his disposal into the fight. Germans flooded through the area, and every GI from St.-Vith to Bastogne dug deeper into their foxholes, counted their rounds, and like soldiers of yore, tried to make every shot count.

AUDIE L. MURPHY (1924–1971)

Born in Farmersville, Hunt County, Texas, to a dirt-poor family of sharecroppers, Audie Murphy wanted to be a U.S. Marine, but being underage, lean, and small, recruiters turned him down. He eventually joined the army to become a paratrooper, but no airborne unit would take him. So Private Murphy received basic infantry training and went to North Africa on the eve of the Sicily campaign as a common GI assigned to the Fifteenth Infantry Regiment of the Third Infantry Division.

Eighteen-year-old Murphy soon proved to be distinctively uncommon. Because of his youth and diminutive size, his comrades nicknamed him "Baby." Company commanders tried to keep him in the rear, but Murphy had a natural aptitude for infantry fighting. His combat career began when the day he watched a buddy die from an enemy bullet, and an enemy die from a bullet of his own. He fought in Sicily, Salerno, Anzio, Rome, through France, and finally into Germany. By the summer of 1944 his chest was already filled with decorations for valor, having earned the Distinguished Service Cross and the Medal of Honor during the Seventh Army's campaign across France. By V-E Day he had killed more than 240 Germans, single-handedly destroyed a German tank in one battle, held off six tanks in another, received a battlefield commission, and had become the most decorated soldier in World War II, winning every medal his country offered.

When the war ended Murphy asked himself, "When I was a child, I was told that men were branded by war. Has the brand been put on me? Have the years of blood and ruin stripped me of all decency?…I may be branded by war, but I will not be defeated by it…I will learn to live again."

Lionized by the American press as the quintessential American, Murphy decided to shed his brand and cash in on his popularity. He went to Hollywood and met David McClure, a fellow veteran and writer, who turned Murphy's journal and memories into a best seller, *To Hell and Back*, which became one of the most moving memoirs of the war. After starring in several low-budget westerns, Murphy played his own part in the film version of *To Hell and Back* and later starred in John Huston's classic, *The Red Badge of Courage*.

During his Hollywood career, Murphy's life slowly eroded. The dark side continued to plague him. He died in a plane crash at the age of forty-six.

BELOW: Second Lieutenant Audie L. Murphy (1924–1971) prepares to move out with his MI rifle somewhere near Holtzwirh, France, where on January 26, 1945, he earned the Medal of Honor for "indomitable courage and refusal to give an inch of ground."

Recovering from Market Garden in encampments near Rheims, France, the 82nd and 101st Airborne divisions were General Eisenhower's only strategic reserves. On the evening of December 17 Eisenhower decided to commit his reserves and the airborne divisions moved out by truck to Belgium the next day: the 82nd to Werbomont to help stop *Kampfgruppe Peiper* and the 101st to the key crossroads town of Bastogne. The All Americans linked up with the Seventh Armored Division at St.-Vith, detained the advance of the Sixth Panzer Army, causing delays fatal to Hitler's plan.

Acting division commander Brigadier General Anthony C. McAuliffe's truckborne 101st Airborne Division reached Bastogne on the 19th where McAuliffe gathered about eighteen thousand troops and resisted all efforts by the Fifth Panzer Army to overrun the perimeter. When the German's demanded the surrender of Bastogne, McAuliffe gruffly replied, "Nuts."

Hitler demanded that Bastogne be captured, and the battle raged from December 26 until January 2, 1945. Patton's Third Army, far to the south, executed a remarkable 90-degree turn to the north, struck the German flank, punched a hole in the Fifth Panzer Army, and opened the way to Bastogne. The skies cleared, the AAF began pulverizing German supply trains running reinforcements and supplies to St.-Vith, and German tanks and vehicles on the field began running out of fuel.

On January 3 the Allies counterattacked and, supported by air cover, pushed the Germans out of

ABOVE: On March 23, 1945, in England, the first of the new army C-46 transports board paratroopers from the 17th Airborne Division and the 1st Allied Airborne Division for operations across the Rhine.

RIGHT: As reinforcements from the U.S. 78th Infantry Division, Ninth Army, move towards Dinslaken, they pass German refugees going in the opposite direction.

the Ardennes and back to the Rhine. The Third Reich never recovered from the Battle of the Bulge. More than a million men participated in the desperate winter struggle. The German army lost 120,000 men, 600 tanks and assault weapons, 1,600 planes, and 6,000 vehicles. Allied losses, mostly American, were about 7,000 killed, 33,000 wounded, and 21,000 captured or missing. Eighty-six prisoners, captured by the First SS Panzer division at Malmédy, were lined up on December 17 and ruthlessly executed.

Unconditional Surrender

While Allied forces recovered from the Battle of the Bulge, Roosevelt, Churchill, and Stalin met on February 4, 1945, at Yalta, in the Crimea of the USSR, to agree on terms for settling the war. Roosevelt, severely incapacitated, had but two

RIGHT: On April 9, 1945, although the fighting in much of Germany has subsided, elements of the 35th Infantry Division, Ninth Army, remain cautious as they clear the buildings and streets in Herne, Germany.

months to live and during the conference probably made some of the worst decisions of his life. The Allied leaders arrived at a common understanding to enforce unconditional surrender on Germany, a four-power occupation of Germany after the war (to include France), and the disarmament of German armed forces. The pact included reparations, which was one of the conditions after World War I that led to World War II. Roosevelt also agreed to allow the Soviet Union to enter the war against Japan and receive their share of repossessed Japanese territories, which opened the door for the Soviet Union's involvement in China and Manchuria. With unconditional surrender a matter of uninfringeable

agreement, Germany continued to fight, although Hitler's military control of the Third Reich had already severely diminished.

On March 7, 1945, a two-battalion task force of the U.S. Ninth Armored Division found the Ludendorf Railroad Bridge at Remagen thinly guarded and crossed over the Rhine. Eisenhower immediately changed his plans for concentric attacks along the river and began pouring divisions across the bridge at Remagen. General Patton, who had been dragging bridging equipment and a navy detachment with landing craft in his army train, threw the Fifth Division across at Oppenheim. Patton's spearheads broke through light opposition and within forty-eight hours had plunged more than 100 miles east of the Rhine. On March 25 Hodges' First Army broke out of the Remagen bridgehead, followed by Devers' Sixth Army Group and Patch's Seventh Army. Allied forces fanned out and raced eastward to link up with Soviet troops on the Elbe. On May 7, 1945, Germany unconditionally surrendered to the members of the Grand Alliance. The war in Europe was over.

On April 12, 1945, when President Roosevelt died, the reins of the U.S. government passed to Vice President Harry S. Truman of Missouri, a man yet to be tested in the arena of high diplomacy and international politics. There were still decisions to be made. None of them would be easy.

BELOW: On May 9, 1945, Oberstgeneral Alfred Jodl and Admiral Hans von Friedburg sit before Allied commanders in Rheims and sign documents of unconditional surrender.

CHAPTER 5

WORLD WAR II IN THE PACIFIC 1941–1945

BELOW: In addition to its traditional coastal defense role, the Coast Artillery Corps was responsible for antiaircraft artillery.

WE NEED YOU!
COAST ARTILLERY CORPS U.S.A.

RIGHT: Lieutenant General Hideki Tojo (1884–1948), who belonged to the aggressive expansionist group in the Japanese government, in 1941 became a full general and prime minister. His rigidity and belligerence in foreign policy matters ultimately led to war with the United States.

Since 1931 Imperial Japan had pursued a policy of aggressive expansion in China on the pretense of protecting the emperor's interests. Chinese Communists, supported by the Soviet Union, were already skirmishing with Chinese Nationalist forces when the Imperial Japanese Army created the so-called Mukden Incident for the purpose of occupying Chinese Manchuria. By 1937 continued Japanese intrusions evolved into war with China, and when no other nation interceded to halt the expanding conflict, Imperial General Headquarters (IGH) began looking for more conquests.

In 1940, after France surrendered to Germany, Japan moved toward a broader war by sending troops into French Indochina. On September 26, 1940, President Roosevelt ordered an embargo on shipments to Japan of scrap iron and steel, which the latter called an "unfriendly act" because the United States had been Japan's major source of natural resources. One day later Japan signed a pact with Germany and Italy and became the third member of the Axis. Although each partner pledged to the others ten years of aid, the agreement did not require Japan to go to war with Great Britain or her allies. Japan committed its first miscalculation, believing in 1940 that Britain would collapse.

On July 26, 1941, after Japan's refusal to withdraw from Indochina, Roosevelt and Churchill froze Japanese assets. Three months later Lieutenant General Hideki Tojo, a zealous militarist, came into power and adopted a secret plan for simultaneous offenses against the U.S. Pacific Fleet at Pearl Harbor, the Philippines, and the oil-rich islands of British Malaya and the Netherlands East Indies. Tojo believed that if Japan destroyed the Pacific Fleet, in particular America's battleships and aircraft carriers, the United States would be unable to wage war in the Pacific for many months, if at all.

Pearl Harbor

Civilian and military authorities in the United States were keenly aware of Japan's preparations for war. They expected the blow to fall on Malaya, possibly the Philippines, but nobody worried much about Hawaii's string of tropical islands in the middle of the Pacific so far from the land of *Nippon*. U.S. intelligence had broken Japan's secret code and followed troop and ship movements, but cryptanalysts lost track of Vice Admiral Chuichi Nagumo's First Air Fleet when on November 25, 1941, a strike force of six aircraft carriers with 360 planes, escorted by two battleships, two heavy cruisers, and nine destroyers, sailed into the North Pacific.

Although Pearl Harbor may be best remembered as home to Admiral Husband E. Kimmel's U.S. Pacific Fleet, it was also Major General Walter C. Short's main army base, the largest in the Pacific with forty-three thousand troops spread among two infantry divisions, coast artillery, an air corps, and supporting services. Both officers had been alerted that a large Japanese battle squadron had sailed from the Kurile Islands on November 25 for an unknown destination and to be vigilant. Instead of sending out reconnaissance patrols, General Short parked aircraft on Hickam, Wheeler, Bellows, and Haleiwa fields together to discourage sabotage. Of course the general knew such clustering would make the planes vulnerable to air attack, but what were the chances of attack form the air? The Marine Corps and the navy also operated airfields, but Admiral Kimmel was no more vigilant than General Short.

Despite warnings—in one instance from their own alert island-based radar at Opana—neither Kimmel nor Short took defensive measures until too late. Before dawn on December 7, 1941, the first wave of 148 "Val" dive-bombers, "Kate" torpedo-planes, and "Zeke" fighters flew off Japanese carriers positioned 220 miles north of Oahu. A second wave of 170 planes followed. While the main strike was aimed at the U.S. fleet, Nagumo also wanted the island's airfields neutralized. A few minutes before 8:00 A.M., the first Vals flew over Hickam Field and woke everyone up. Army pilots at Hickam did not get a plane in the air until three hours later.

Of eight U.S. battleships in Pearl Harbor, three were sunk, one capsized, and the others were severely damaged. Three light cruisers, three destroyers, and several other ships also went to the bottom. Of 231 army planes, only eighty-seven could fly. Of 250 navy and marine planes only fifty-four could fly. The army suffered 226 killed and 396 wounded. The navy and marines lost more than 3,000 killed and 876 wounded. The Japanese would certainly have accomplished their mission had the three American aircraft carriers—*Enterprise*, *Lexington*, and

BELOW: Lieutenant General Walter Campbell Short (1880–1949) took command of the Hawaiian department, and because he was caught poorly prepared during the December 7, 1941, Japanese attack on Pearl Harbor, the army recalled and retired him in February 1942.

ABOVE: Posters of the U.S. Army projected patriotism, and many young volunteers became lured by the calling.

Saratoga—usually based at Pearl Harbor, not been at sea. The U.S. Pacific Fleet had been severely wounded, but not mortally.

The following day President Roosevelt, referring to December 7 as a "date that will live in infamy," asked Congress for a declaration of war against Japan. Admiral Ernest J. King, commander-in-chief, U.S. Fleet, wasted little time cashiering Admiral Kimmel and on December 31, 1941, replaced him with Admiral Chester W. Nimitz. Short continued to serve at Pearl Harbor, but only until February, when General Marshall shuffled him into retirement.

Japan's Invasion of the Philippines

With American naval power crippled, the Japanese seized Guam on December 10 and put the first troops ashore on the principal Philippine island of Luzon. Now free to roam as they pleased, the Japanese gobbled up Wake Island, Hong Kong, and Singapore, and then moved on Malaya, Burma, the Solomon Islands, and the Netherlands East Indies. To protect operations to the west and south, it became essential for the Japanese to occupy the Philippines, which meant ousting the Americans.

The largest segment of MacArthur's ground strength lay in Major General Jonathan M. Wainwright's I Corps north of Manila and Brigadier General George M. Parker's smaller II Corps south of the city. When on December 10–12 Japanese forces made amphibious landings at Aparri and Vigan in northern Luzon and at Legaspi to the south, MacArthur no longer had planes to mount a counterattack because all but seventeen of his B-17 bombers and thirty-four of his P-40 fighters had been destroyed on December 8. After a quick assessment of conditions, MacArthur decided to make a last-ditch defense in the mountainous jungles of the Bataan Peninsula, the northern arm of Manila Bay. MacArthur had long before decided how to hold the

GENERAL DOUGLAS MACARTHUR (1880–1964)

In 1941 sixty-one-year-old Douglas MacArthur was no longer a young man. The son of General Arthur MacArthur, he had been born into the army at Little Rock Barracks in Arkansas. He graduated first in the West Point class of 1903, and went to the Philippines to serve as his father's aide.

MacArthur's career skyrocketed in the army. He was nominated for the Medal of Honor in 1914 during the Veracruz expedition, and after World War I began, he helped to organize the Forty-second Rainbow Division and became the division's chief of staff. He fought in the Aisne-Marne campaign, led a brigade at St.-Mihiel, and again during the Meuse-Argonne campaigns. He was highly decorated for his bravery including two Distinguished

Service crosses. After the war MacArthur spent four years as superintendent at West Point.

In 1928 the army promoted MacArthur to major general and sent him back to the Philippines. MacArthur enjoyed life among the Filipinos. Returning to the United States he served as the army chief of staff from 1930 to 1935. After the island archipelago achieved independence in 1935, MacArthur retired from the army to become the Philippine government's field marshal. The arrangement lasted about a year. In 1937, as relations between Japan and American worsened, Roosevelt recalled MacArthur to active duty and appointed him to be commander of U.S. Army Forces in the Far East.

By December 1941 MacArthur's American and Filipino ground forces consisted of about 130,000 men, including 22,400 Regulars (more than half of them Philippine Scouts), 3,000 Philippine constabulary, and a Filipino army of 107,000 partly trained and armed volunteers.

MacArthur posted most of this force on Luzon.

The first indication that Japan might attack the Philippines came from Washington when Admiral Nagumo's strike force moved secretly into the Pacific. Reality struck shortly after noon on December 8 when eighty-four Japanese fighters and 108 twin-engine bombers walloped Clark and Iba airfields while Major General Lewis H. Brereton's pilots were eating lunch. Only one U.S. fighter squadron managed to get aloft.

The Japanese offensive marked the beginning of MacArthur's hectic World War II career. Later, in 1950, he would play a prominent role in the Korean War. Long after the old soldier's military career ended, he persistently cautioned Presidents John F. Kennedy and Lyndon B. Johnson to avoid becoming involved in Vietnam, but nobody listened

LEFT: In 1942, when ordered to leave the Philippines by President Roosevelt, General Douglas MacArthur (second from left) vowed he would return. In October 1944 he returned to command the amphibious landings on Leyte.

RIGHT: On December 8–20, 1941, Japanese naval and army forces invade the Philippines with overpowering forces against a Filipino-American army commanded by General Douglas MacArthur.

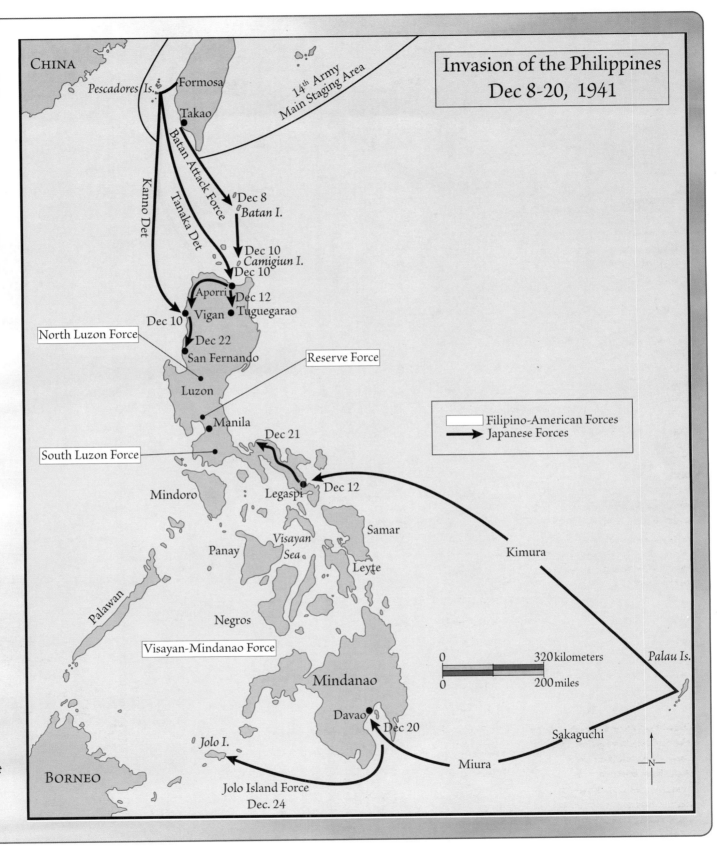

Invasion of the Philippines
Dec 8-20, 1941

CHINA

Pescadores Is.   Formosa

Takao

14th Army Main Staging Area

Batan Attack Force

Kanno Det

Tanaka Det

Dec 8
Batan I.

Dec 10
Camigiun I.
Dec 10

Aporri   Dec 12
Vigan   Tuguegarao
Dec 10

North Luzon Force

Dec 22
San Fernando

Reserve Force

Luzon

Manila   Dec 21

South Luzon Force

Legaspi   Dec 12

Mindoro

Panay   Visayan Sea

Samar

Leyte

Kimura

Palawan

Negros

Visayan-Mindanao Force

Filipino-American Forces
Japanese Forces

0   320 kilometers
0   200 miles

Palau Is.

Mindanao

Davao   Dec 20

Jolo I.   Sakaguchi

Miura

BORNEO

Jolo Island Force
Dec. 24

—N—

Philippines, but the defense had been predicated on the availability of the U.S. Pacific Fleet to bring in reinforcements and carrier air power. With the

Pacific Fleet incapacitated, MacArthur consolidated his troops on Bataan. Had he tried to defend Manila, his entire force would have been irrevocably lost.

By January 7, the army's relentless defense of the peninsula offered the only hope of rescue by sea. A tall range of impassable mountains divided the peninsula. Wainwright's I Corps held the left with Parker's II Corps on the right. The supply situation became deplorable, exacerbated by twenty thousand refugees with mouths to feed. The Americans went on half rations at once, and when the main Japanese attack on January 26 threatened to split the American position, MacArthur withdrew up the peninsula to where the artillery on Corregidor could provide additional support.

By March 11 the situation became untenable. Roosevelt ordered MacArthur to abandon the Philippines, leave immediately for Australia, and take command of Allied forces in the South Pacific. MacArthur unwillingly obeyed and turned the command over to Wainwright. Before departing, he told the people he left behind, "I shall return." On April 1, 1942, General MacArthur was awarded the Medal of Honor "For conspicuous leadership...gallantry and intrepidity above and beyond the call of duty in action against invading Japanese forces, and for the heroic conduct of defensive and offensive operations on the Bataan Peninsula."

On April 3 General Masaharu Homma's offensive broke through the American lines. Wainwright's corps disintegrated. Those who escaped moved to the island of Corregidor. The others—regulars and Philipine Scouts—became part of the 90-mile "Death March" to the prisoner compound at Camp O'Donnell, where 1,253 Americans died from mental and physical exhaustion, malnutrition, lack of medical care, and savage treatment. Wainwright escaped to Corregidor and courageously held out against overwhelming odds. On May 6, out of supplies and ammunition, he unconditionally surrendered the remnants of his small, exhausted force.

ABOVE: The gas-operated, magazine-fed, .30-caliber M1 carbine became the standard short-barreled rifle of the U.S. Army. During the war, more than six million were produced. The semi-automatic carbine could not quite match the muzzle velocity or the accuracy of the Garand M1 rifle.

RIGHT: In 1936, the gas-operated, eight-round clip-fed .30-caliber Garand M1 rifle became the standard rifle for the U.S. Army. The M1 weighed 9.5 pounds, was 43.6 inches long, and had a muzzle velocity of 2,750 feet per second. More than five million rifles were produced during the war.

RIGHT: On May 6, 1942, after the fall of Corregidor, the Japanese rounded up 11,500 American and Filipino prisoners and marched them across torturous roads to miserable prisoner of war camps.

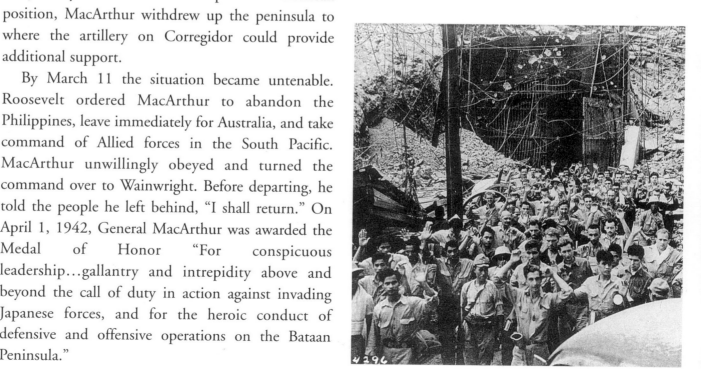

ALEXANDER R. NININGER, JR.

Born in Georgia, raised in Fort Lauderdale, Florida, Alexander R. "Sandy" Nininger seemed an unlikely candidate for West Point, preferring music, art, and drama to firearms. Nevertheless, he wanted to go to the Military Academy and obtained his appointment the hard way, by the tough competitive examination route.

In October 1941, having just completed the infantry officer's course at Fort Benning, Georgia, Second Lieutenant Nininger arrived home on leave. There he found urgent orders directing him to the Philippines. Arriving at Manila in one of the last transports to reach the islands, Nininger became a platoon leader in Company A, First Battalion, Fifty-seventh Infantry Regiment, Philippine Scouts, one of the best Filipino-American units in the army.

Nininger was still adjusting to his new role when Japanese infantry landed on Luzon. After Christmas, MacArthur declared Manila an open city and began shuttling forces onto Bataan. Colonel George S. Clarke, commanding the Fifty-seventh Infantry, ordered Nininger's battalion to cover the withdrawal of Brigadier General George M. Parker's II Corps. Nininger's company drew the assignment of manning the left flank with Company K, but swampy terrain prevented the two companies from connecting.

On January 9 General Homma began exerting heavy pressure against MacArthur's thin lines on Bataan. For two days Nininger platoon faced the main Japanese assault with Company I overrun and Company K about to be surrounded. The Scouts rallied, gained a little ground, but Company K remained engulfed.

Nininger told his company commander, First Lieutenant Fred Yeager, that he had studied the terrain and with ten good men he could pull out Company K. Yeager agreed, and Nininger picked ten of his sturdiest anti-sniper Filipinos. Armed with a rifle, a pistol, and a load of hand grenades, Nininger led his men down an irrigation ditch and emerged behind Japanese lines. He spotted an enemy sniper and shot him out of a tree. The fighting quickly intensified.

Nininger and his scouts infiltrated the Japanese position, picking off snipers as they advanced. When Major Royal Reynolds, the battalion commander, ordered the detachment out of the area, Nininger told his scouts to remain where they were and went forward alone. Out of rifle ammunition, Nininger disappeared into the thick *cogan* grass, a pistol in one hand and a hand grenade in the other. Company K rallied, advanced into the area, and spotted Nininger, who though wounded three times was still conducting a one-man war. As he staggered through the grass, three Japanese stepped out of the grass and drove their bayonets through his shattered body. Nininger whirled and blasted away with his pistol. When help arrived, they found him dead beside the enemy.

On January 12, 1942, "Sandy" Nininger became the first American soldier to receive the Medal of Honor in World War II. He also became the first in the West Point class of 1941 to be killed in battle.

ABOVE: Lieutenant Alexander R. Nininger served with the 57th Infantry, Philippine Scouts, and after withdrawing to Bataan in January 1942, he earned the Medal of Honor after fighting Japanese soldiers in hand-to-hand combat.

LEFT: On April 3–9, 1942, the Japanese broke through MacArthur's lines and forced the surrender of thousands of American and Filipino troops, most of whom were subjected to the 90-mile "Death March" to the prisoner compound at Camp O'Donnell.

LEFT: In August 1936, General MacArthur retired from the U.S. Army and became field marshal for the Philippine government. When in July 1941 President Roosevelt recalled MacArthur as a commander U.S. Forces in the Far East, he had already built a dedicated Filipino army of capable officers and men.

LEFT: A Filipino regiment stands at attention during inspection. Many Filipino companies became scouting units for American forces serving on the island.

The loss of the Philippines was a foregone conclusion, but the Japanese received their first lesson in the skill, gallantry, and determination of the American soldier. The campaign also occupied the Japanese war machine for five months, giving the U.S. Army and Navy time to gather strength. The Japanese never expected such resistance, especially from the Filipino forces trained by MacArthur. For the balance of the war, the Filipinos continued to be a constant source of trouble for Japan.

The Turning Tide

By May 1942 the staggering triumphs of the Japanese war machine planted the notion of invincibility in the minds of Imperial General Headquarters. The success of the army exceeded their wildest expectations, and now nothing could stop them. The vastness of the new empire tempted IGH to go farther, to New Guinea, Australia, and the remote American base at Midway. In Japanese hands Midway would force the American fleet to take refuge on the West Coast. In such overconfidence lay the seeds of defeat.

During May and early June, the U.S. Navy picked up the slack and in the battle of the Coral Sea turned back the Japanese invasion force headed for Port Moresby, New Guinea. Three weeks later, American cryptanalysts uncovered Japanese plans to capture Midway. Admiral Nimitz rushed his only three aircraft carriers to the area and in early June sank the enemy's four flattops and turned back the Japanese armada. The defeats stunned IGH and opened the way for the Allies to go on the offensive. The First Marine Division mounted an amphibious expedition and assaulted Guadalcanal and Tulagi in the Solomon Islands, and MacArthur put plans in place for repulsing the Japanese invasion of New Guinea's Papuan peninsula.

When in March 1942 MacArthur arrived in Australia, he found, to his dismay, few troops to command other than Australian militia units and a handful of flyers from the AAF. During the next three months Australia's Seventh Division arrived from North Africa, and two U.S. National Guard divisions, the Thirty-second and the Forty-first, arrived from the States. MacArthur also managed to assemble six fighter squadrons and two bomber squadrons. With no more than this, he prepared to attack Major General Tomitoro Horii's Eighteenth Army, which since July 21 had been moving slowly through New Guinea's Owen Stanley Mountains toward Port Moresby.

In September, when Horii's advanced elements came within thirty miles of Port Moresby, Allied resistance suddenly stiffened. Australian Major General Edmond F. Hering, commanding the Allied force, applied pressure, and through virtually impassable jungles and swamps, began moving Horii's forces back across the mountains. The offensive—short of artillery and rations and with men racked by disease—bogged down in a swampy area around the villages of Buna and Gona on the coast of the Solomon Sea. MacArthur realized he had serious logistics problems and dispatched Lieutenant General Robert L. Eichelberger (USA) into the area with supplies and reinforcements. On January 22 American infantry stormed the last enemy lodgment at Buna and recaptured Papua. Sixty percent of the 13,646 Americans surviving the campaign were incapacitated by disease, as opposed to 2,783 killed and wounded in battle.

RIGHT: On May 4, 1944, Major General William H. Gill (left) arrived in Australia with the 32nd Infantry Division to join General MacArthur's leapfrogging campaign across northern New Guinea.

On December 9 the First Marine Division, having done the heavy work on Guadalcanal, turned the rest of the island campaign over to General Alexander Patch's XIV Army Corps and the Second Marine Division. Patch's force struck swiftly, driving the defeated enemy across Guadalcanal to Cape

ABOVE: Over 1.25 million Thompson submachineguns were produced in the United Staes during the war. This is an M1A1 with a thirty-round box magazine attached.

Esperance, where Japanese destroyers managed to pull thirteen thousand disease-ridden survivors from the island.

Of all the places GIs fought during World War II, the heat, stench, insects, and jungles of Guadalcanal and Papua ranked among the worst, but the two campaigns knocked the arrogance out of the Japanese and put them for the first time on the defensive.

A New Strategy

In March 1942 the Combined Chiefs of Staff (CCS) sectored off areas of responsibility in the Far East. Great Britain took responsibility for operations in Southeast Asia, including India, Burma, and the Indian Ocean. MacArthur commanded the Southwest Pacific Area, which stretched from Australia through New Guinea, the Netherlands Indies, and the Philippines. Admiral Nimitz took the rest of area, including part of the Solomon Islands along with the entire Pacific. Nimitz divided his command into three operational areas: the North Pacific, the Central Pacific, and the South Pacific. Marines had taken the initiative during early operations in the Pacific, but they were now outnumbered by the army.

The favorable outcomes of early 1943, combined with the strengthening of all arms of the services, led the JCS to formulate the first concrete strategy for

winning the war against Japan. As the navy gathered strength at sea, the JCS decided to launch two converging offensives toward the Japanese home islands. Using army ground forces, land-based air power, and a fleet of old battleships and cruisers, MacArthur would leapfrog across the northern coast of New Guinea, drawing closer to the Philippines. MacArthur admitted that he had learned a lesson. When he observed the horrible condition of the disease-racked soldiers returning from the Papuan campaign, he pledged, "No more Bunas." Hereafter, his policy would be to bypass Japanese strongholds, leaving places like Rabaul behind to wither away. MacArthur never lost sight of his promise to return to the Philippines.

The second offensive formulated by the JCS involved the widely scattered Japanese-controlled islands of the Pacific. The AAF needed air bases for long-range bombers, and the JCS gave Admiral Nimitz the task of getting them by strategic island hopping. Nimitz, however, could not avoid every enemy stronghold because the Japanese had built mutually supporting air bases on dozens of widely scattered atolls. With army divisions flowing into the South Pacific, and the increased need for more troops, the island-hopping offensive could no longer be left exclusively to marines.

The success of the JCS strategy depended upon improved techniques for amphibious warfare and tactical air power. Putting troops ashore in the face of a dug-in and determined enemy had always required complicated and risky maneuvers. Early efforts in World War II demonstrated that the success of amphibious assaults depended upon air and sea supremacy together with overwhelming combat power. To minimize casualties during amphibious operations, special landing craft had to be produced to transport infantry, tanks, and artillery ashore while naval gunfire and direct air support softened up

THE WOMEN'S ARMY CORPS

On May 14, 1942, Congress established the Women's Army Auxiliary Corps. When on May 27 recruiting began, thirteen thousand women stormed the registration centers. The original mission of the corps was to train women for positions that released men for duty in combat divisions. The women performed so well that Congress, on September 1, 1943, gave the auxiliary military status as part of the U.S. Army and renamed it the Women's Army Corps (WAC).

The army assigned WACs to duties in administration, communications, medical care, supply, intelligence, and in total some 235 different army jobs. In many registration centers, recruiters ran out of application forms. "If the guys can take it," one volunteer said of her new life in olive drab, "so can I." Eleanor Roosevelt took special interest in the program, and with WAC director Ovetta Culp Hobby traveled about the country recruiting female college students, especially those with nurse's training, who joined the Army Nurse Corps, which had become a permanent part of the army's medical establishment in 1901.

Nowhere on the front lines were nurses needed more than in the South Pacific, where malaria, dysentery, and jungle infections racked up casualties faster than bullets and shrapnel. After weeks of fighting in the jungles of Guadalcanal, Papua, and Bougainville, men came out of the areas emaciated, racked with fever, and their bodies covered with sores. Medics could apply bandages and administer doses of sulfa and quinine in the field, but only the hospitals on Australia, attended by army doctors and nurses, could bring the soldier back to health.

The army also learned that women could fly and adapted to instruments faster than men. The Women's Auxiliary Ferrying Squadron (WAFS) came into existence, but female flyers were never given the opportunity to demonstrate their skills in war zones.

Eventually, more than 143,000 women served as WACs, the largest of the women's services in World War II. MacArthur and Eisenhower praised their work and in 1946 asked Congress to include WACs in the regular army, thus making it a permanent career field for women. Congress debated the issue for two years, finally agreeing in June 1948 to allow women to serve in the Organized Reserve Corps as well as the regular army. Colonel Hobby built the Women's Army Corps from scratch, earned the Distinguished Service Medal for her achievements, and later became a member of President Eisenhower's cabinet.

BELOW: In June 1944, African American nurses provide treatment in the surgical ward at the 268th Station Hospital, Milne Bay, New Guinea.

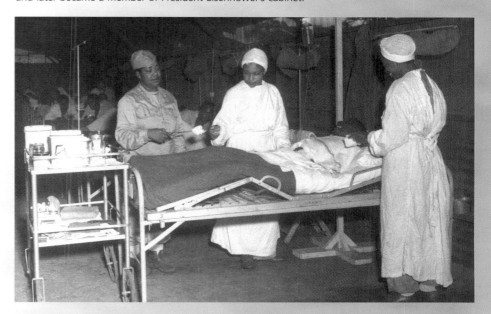

ABOVE: WACs endured the same cramped quarters as men on troopships.

ABOVE: A four-woman WAFS aircrew ferry a bomber to an airfield.

JOSEPH W. "VINEGAR JOE" STILWELL (1883–1946)

During the war in the Pacific, the rugged and strategic fighting in Burma received little attention. Without turning the Japanese out of Burma, the Allied front in China could not have been maintained, which would have freed more than a hundred thousand Japanese soldiers for service in the Pacific.

Saving Burma was mainly a British task, but General Joseph W. Stilwell, of Florida, had been serving as military attaché to China since 1935 and had taken a personal interest in the Sino-Japanese War. In January 1942 the JCS decided to get involved in Burma and sent Stilwell back to China to keep Chiang Kai-shek's disorganized nationalist army in the war. Appointed commanding general of U.S. Army forces in China-Burma-India (CBI), Stilwell flew to Chungking with a small staff, secured command of Chinese forces in Burma from Chiang, and from one Chinese division built eight more.

Often outspokenly impatient and irascible (hence his nickname "Vinegar Joe"), Stilwell never got along with Chiang. Always hampered by a lack of supplies and conflicting orders from Chiang, Stilwell was forced to withdraw his Chinese forces into India. "The Japs ran us out of Burma," Stilwell admitted, "We took a hell of a beating! I think we ought to find out what caused it, go back and retake it." Much like MacArthur, Stilwell intended to keep his word.

He trained three Chinese divisions in India to U.S. Army standards and began sending AAF transports over "the Hump" to airlift supplies to elements of his Chinese army operating out of Kunming. He coaxed Admiral Lord Louis Mountbatten, commander of CBI forces, into the Salween-Myitkyina-Mogaung offensive that liberated northern Burma. Stilwell relations with Chiang were always strained because of clashing agendas. Chiang wanted to fight Chinese communists, and Stilwell wanted to fight the Japanese. He eventually turned his CBI command over to General Albert C. Wedemeyer, who implemented the rest of "Vinegar Joe's" strategy and opened the Burma Road into China.

Stilwell had not seen the last of war. When General Simon Bolivar Buckner was killed on Okinawa, Stilwell took command of the Tenth Army from U.S. Marine Corps General Roy Geiger, who had taken command during the interim. Stilwell finished the campaign, and was present for the September 2, 1945, Japanese surrender ceremony in Tokyo Bay.

ABOVE: In 1945, Lieutenant General Joseph "Vinegar Joe" Stillwell (right) confers with Lieutenant General Simon Bolivar Buckner Jr., commander of the U.S. Tenth Army, shortly before the latter's death on Okinawa.

ABOVE: In the China-Burma-India Theater U.S. Army rations are loaded onto river barges in India and barged to Assam, where they will be reloaded onto planes and flown over the hump to China.

RESUPPLY BY AIR

The jungles of southeast Asia make resupply by vehicle difficult at the best of times and impossible at others. The Allies, however, used their aerial superiority to drop materiel from low-flying transports such as the Douglas C-47 (known under a variety of names such as Skytrain or Dakota) and the Curtiss C-46 Commando.

BELOW LEFT: The cargo hold of a C-47 is stuffed with ready-to-drop supplies.

BELOW RIGHT: A C-47 aircrew prepare to make a drop.

BOTTOM: A C-46 Commando from Major General Paul L. Williams Troop Carrier Forces drop supplies to ground forces.

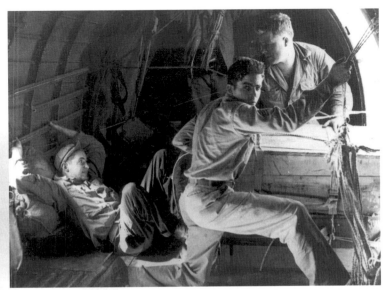

RIGHT: A radioman locates a safe spot to communicate with the command post, perhaps spotting or sending coordinates to direct artillery or close air support.

enemy emplacements behind the beaches. MacArthur measured his leaps up the 2,000-mile northern coast of New Guinea by the range of his fighter-bombers—200 miles. Nimitz used carrier air power to support and defend landing operations. As soon as captured airfields could be repaired, land-based aircraft took over the fighter-bomber chore and released carrier task forces for operations elsewhere.

The offensive envisioned by the JCS never got underway until September 1943, mainly because of operations in the Solomons. Neither MacArthur nor Nimitz intended to assault Japan's powerful naval air base at Rabaul, but extensive Allied operations could not be conducted as long as air and sea attacks from Rabaul remained unimpeded. While ground forces pushed north through the Solomons, Vice Admiral William F. "Bull" Halsey's carrier aircraft pounded Rabaul from the sea. On June 30 General Walter

RIGHT: A radioman locates a safe spot to communicate with the command post, perhaps spotting or sending coordinates to direct artillery or close air support.

BELOW: An M4 medium tank snakes through the jungle searching for Japanese dug-in fortifications and bunkers camouflaged among the thick foliage.

Krueger's Sixth Army, under the direction of MacArthur, secured new airfields on Woodlark and Trobriand Islands in the Solomon Sea. The struggle for air superiority in the Solomons continued throughout 1943. By autumn, the Japanese had lost three thousand planes and pilots in the Solomons, opening the way for MacArthur's New Guinea campaign.

MacArthur also secured the U.S. Seventh Fleet, commanded by Vice Admiral Thomas C. Kinkaid, for the purpose of controlling coastal operations along the New Guinea coast while Rear Admiral Daniel E. Barbey fashioned a series of amphibious operations. The Seventh Fleet remained in MacArthur's command for the balance of the war, earning the nickname "MacArthur's Navy."

The New Guinea Campaign

In September 1943 Japan still occupied most of New Guinea. MacArthur wanted full possession of the island as a springboard to the Philippines. By mid-month, Australian General Sir Thomas Blamey, using Australian and American infantry and U.S. paratroopers, defeated the Japanese at Lae and Salamaua, advanced to Finschhafen (on the tip of the Huon Peninsula), and paved the way for bringing in Lieutenant General George C. Kenney's Fifth Air Force. General Kreuger's Sixth Army took over the next task and, using elements from the First Cavalry Division, landed on New Britain and established air bases 100 miles from Rabaul.

MacArthur could now take the Eighteenth Army wherever he pleased on New Guinea. In rapid succession, MacArthur's divisions began to leapfrog across the 2,000-mile northern coast of New Guinea. On January 2 a regimental combat team from the Thirty-second division captured the Japanese garrison at Saidor. On February 29 the First U.S. Cavalry,

ABOVE: On June 23, 1944, Company H, 20th Infantry Regiment, 6th Army Division, sets up an 81mm mortar on Wakde Island, New Guinea.

Operations on New Guinea April-Sept 1944

July 30, 1944
July 2, 1944
May 27, 1944
May 17, 1944
Sansapor
Sarong
Noemfoor
Blak
Geelvink Bay
Sarmi
April 22, 1944
Admiralty Is.
Los Negros
Manus
Feb. 29, 1944
Atlantic Ocean
Hollandia
Aitape
Wewak
Madang
Jan. 2, 1944
Dec. 26, 1943
Rabaul
—N—
NEW GUINEA
Aroe Is.
Saidor
Finschhafen
Lae
New Britain
Sept. 22, 1943
Sept. 4, 1943
Arafura Sea
Salamaua
Buna
Port Moresby
0
800 kilometers
0
500 miles
Australia

LEFT: In September 1943, operations on northeastern New Guinea started out slowly, but in the early months of 1944 rapidly accelerated using leapfrog tactics.

accompanied by MacArthur in person, assaulted the Admiralty Islands. On April 22 the American Twenty-fourth and Forty-first Infantry Divisions, supported by the Seventh Fleet and Seventh Amphibious Force, landed at Aitape and Hollandia. By then MacArthur, through excellent staff planning and skillful coordination of land, sea, and air forces, had perfected the most ingenious formula for amphibious operations. At the cost of 100 dead and 1,000 Americans wounded during the Hollandia-Aitape operation, the Japanese lost more than 10,000 killed or missing. By July 30, 1944, Allied forces had completely destroyed Japanese power on New Guinea. Six weeks later MacArthur's forces leaped across the Halmahera Sea to the Moluccas and began landing planes on Morotai. From there MacArthur could almost see the southern tip of Mindanao in the Philippines, though it was still 350 miles away.

Island-hopping in the Pacific

By early 1943 Admiral Nimitz now had plenty of soldiers to augment the marines in the Pacific. He had also assigned Vice Admiral Raymond A. Spruance's Fifth Fleet, consisting of seven battleships, seven heavy and three light cruisers, eigth carriers, and thirty-four destroyers, to lead the island-hopping campaign. Like MacArthur, Nimitz's forces still had many lessons to learn about amphibious landings, although Rear Admiral Richmond Kelly Turner had masterminded most of the Pacific Fleet's amphibious operations in the Solomons.

Makin and Tarawa atolls in the Gilbert Islands (Operation Galvanic) lay 1,500 miles south of Hawaii and represented the first critical step in recapturing the Pacific. Although only 250 Japanese combat troops defended Makin, it took the 165th Infantry Regiment, 27th Infantry Division, four days

to smoke the enemy out of its defensive works. Marine Major General Holland M. "Howling Mad" Smith, commander of the newly established V Amphibious Corps, became so annoyed by the army's sloth-like performance at Makin that he refused to put the unit ashore on Tarawa. The principal enemy base at Betio, garrisoned by 4,836 naval troops, turned out to be a bloodier struggle than Holland Smith anticipated. After seventy-six hours of fighting, the Second Marine Division lost 990 killed and 2,391 wounded. The Japanese fought to the death, often relying on hand-to-hand combat. Only sevventeen defenders surrendered. Heavy casualties revealed the need for a more intensive pre-landing bombardment, heavier artillery, improvements in communications and air support, and the increased use of armored amphibious tractors (Landing Vehicles, Tracked) to protect troops coming ashore.

Tarawa casualties slowed down arrangements for Operation Flintlock, the invasion of the Marshall Islands, where Japanese forces occupied the atolls of Kwajalein, Eniwetok, and the twin islands of Roi and Namur. This time General Smith took the Seventh Infantry Division and put it ashore on the southeastern flank of Kwajalein's lagoon. The Japanese staged their usual suicidal resistance, and from January 29 to February 7, 1944, 7,870 enemy soldiers fought to the death. Using lessons learned at Tarawa, army and marine troops overran enemy defenses, losing only 372 killed and about 1,000 wounded.

On February 17 Admiral Turner put marines and the 106th Infantry Division on Eniwetok Atoll, and using close-in fighting and flame-throwers to smoke out the enemy, wiped out Japan's 1st Amphibious Brigade, a veteran combat unit 2,200 strong.

Operation Flintlock set up the invasion of the Marianas, where air bases could finally be built for the long-range strategic bombing of Japan.

ABOVE: In early July 1944, Hawaiian troops in camouflage suits at a command post near the Japanese-held airstrip on Noemfoor Island (Geelvink Bay, New Guinea), use an SCR300 radio to communicate with naval support.

BELOW: On February 1, 1944, tanks from the 7th Infantry Division landed on the southeastern flank of the lagoon at Kwajalein in the Marshall Islands and drove inland toward the airfield.

ABOVE: The Tarawa campaign saw U.S. Marines attack the island while, on November 20, 1943, the 165th Infantry Regiment of the 27th Army Division begin operations against Japanese held Makin Island.

The Mariana Islands (Operation Forager)

Assaulting the Marianas required a giant leap across more than 700 miles of open water, but doing so the summer of 1944 led to another important turning point in the war. Large Japanese forces occupied three principle islands, Saipan, Guam, and Tinian. All three locations contained strategically important airfields. Saipan lay 1,250 nautical miles south-southeast of Tokyo, and the new B-29 bombers boasted a range of 3,000 miles. Operations against the Marianas also penetrated Japan's crucial defensive perimeter, and when Nimitz's staff planned the operation, everyone expected the enemy to pour immense resources into defending the area, and Imperial General Headquarters made every attempts to do so.

On June 15, nine days after the invasion of Normandy, Admiral Spruance's force of more than 530 ships and auxiliaries arrived off Saipan with 127,000 troops. Ahead of the invasion fleet came Vice Admiral Marc Mitscher's carriers and battleships to pound shore installations and achieve air supremacy. While two marine divisions assaulted Saipan's beaches, Major General Ralph C. Smith's Twenty-seventh Infantry Division tagged along in reserve. On the morning of June 15, marines went ashore on eight beaches. Two nights later, as the result of heavy resistance, Smith took the Twenty-seventh Division ashore. Marine Lieutenant General Holland "Howling Mad" Smith became immediately annoyed by the performance of the Twenty-seventh Division and provoked a long, bitter interservice controversy by summarily relieving army General Smith. The action spawned a still undecided army-marine controversy, which had more to do with different doctrines than personalities. On June 18, despite the quarreling among generals, Americans captured Saipan's largest airfield. Then on July 7, perhaps seeking retribution for their general's removal, the Twenty-seventh Division faced and annihilated a suicide attack by three thousand fanatical Japanese intoxicated on sake and committed to death.

On July 13, in addition to losing Saipan, Japan lost 27,000 men against American casualties of 3,126 killed and 13,160 wounded. Admiral Mitscher's carrier planes, in what navy flyers called the "Great Marianas Turkey Shoot," destroyed 346 Japanese aircraft and sank an enemy carrier.

In November the AAF's Twentieth Air Force began flying strategic bombing missions against Japan, which indirectly led to one of the bloodiest and costliest battles in the Pacific on a five-mile-long volcanic island named Iwo Jima.

Return to the Philippines

In July 1944, as marines and the Seventy-seventh Army Division assaulted Guam and Tinian, Roosevelt met with MacArthur and Nimitz at Pearl Harbor to discuss strategy. Nimitz favored a move on Formosa or China. MacArthur insisted the Philippines be freed first. Roosevelt accepted MacArthur's proposal but authorized Nimitz to formulate plans for assaults on Iwo Jima and Okinawa.

On October 7 Admiral Halsey's Third Fleet carrier planes began pulverizing Japan's air forces and airfields on the Philippines and Formosa. The success of the attacks allowed MacArthur to move the scheduled Leyte invasion from December 20 to October 20. At the time General Tomoyuki Yamashita had about 350,000 Japanese troops spread about the Philippines. MacArthur's amphibious force consisted of some seven hundred vessels carrying two hundred thousand men from General Krueger's Sixth Army. "MacArthur's Navy," Admiral Kinkaid's Seventh Fleet, accompanied the invasion force. Among Kinkaid's considerable fleet were 6 battleships (restored survivors of Pearl Harbor), and a squadron of sixteen escort carriers. Admiral Mitscher's carrier groups, now part of

BELOW: During operations in the Marshall Islands, Major General Ralph C. Smith (left) and Captain Merlin O'Neill (right) of the U.S. Coast Guard meet with Admiral Chester W. Nimitz (center) at sea.

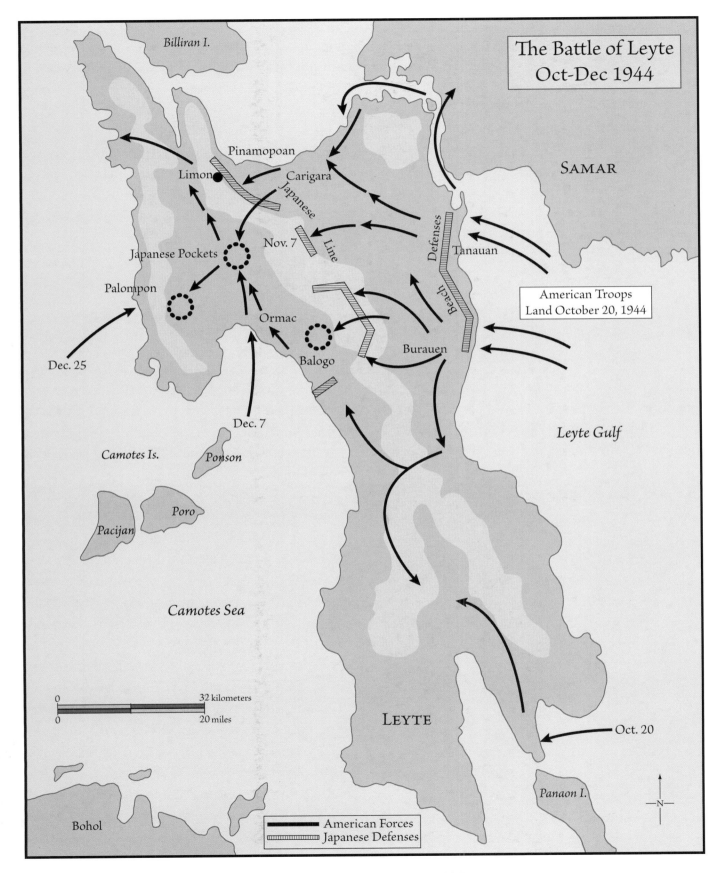

Billiran I.

Pinamopoan

Limon

Carigara

Japanese

SAMAR

Japanese Pockets

Nov. 7

Line

Defenses

Tanauan

Palompon

Beach

Dec. 25

Ormac

American Troops
Land October 20, 1944

Balogo

Burauen

Dec. 7

Leyte Gulf

Camotes Is.

Ponson

Poro

Pacijan

Camotes Sea

LEYTE

32 kilometers

20 miles

Oct. 20

Bohol

Panaon I.

—N—

American Forces
Japanese Defenses

The Battle of Leyte
Oct-Dec 1944

LEFT: On October 20, 1944, operations for the liberation of the Philippines began with American troop landings on the island of Leyte and continued to the end of the year.

ABOVE: On October 20, 1944, troops of the 77th Infantry Division come ashore against weak resistance at Leyte.

Following behind the establishment of the beachhead came the charismatic old general. He waded ashore, climbed on the platform of a truck with a microphone in his hand, and during a pelting monsoon, said, "This is the Voice of Freedom, General MacArthur speaking. People of the Philippines, I have returned." By midnight, General Krueger had 132,000 men and 200,000 tons of supplies ashore.

While General Yamashita attempted to pour reinforcements into Leyte, the Japanese navy launched a tardy all-out three-pronged attack to cripple the American invasion. Admiral Kinkaid smashed the southern Japanese force in the Surigao Strait while Halsey's carrier planes damaged and repulsed the Japanese center force in the Sibuyan Sea. Lured away from Leyte Gulf by a Japanese feint, Halsey steamed north and destroyed the Japanese northern carrier force off Cape Engaño. The naval battle ended the Japanese fleet as an organized fighting force and guaranteed MacArthur's success in the Philippines.

Halsey's Third Fleet, added another one thousand aircraft to the assault.

On October 20 leading elements from Major General Franklin C. Silbert's X Corps and Lieutenant General John R. Hodge's XXIV Corps came ashore on Leyte against light resistance from the enemy.

MacArthur's forces began working their way up the Philippines. On December 15 an army brigade captured Mindoro, marooning 135,000 Japanese soldiers behind the American advance. On January 9 General Krueger landed 64,000 troops at Lingayen, north of Manila. Major General Oscar W. Griswold put the XIV Corps in motion on the right while Major General Innis P. Swift's I Corps moved on the left. Griswold's corps began pushing through Japanese resistance to rescue some 50,000 prisoners held at the 617-acre compound at Camp O'Donnell while a separate division pressed ahead to capture Clark Field.

On January 30, 1945, General Eichelberger's Eighth Army made amphibious landings north and south of Manila. In late February the Thirty-seventh Infantry Division linked with the First Cavalry Division and the Eleventh Airborne Division for

ABOVE: With the Leyte beachhead secured, photographers record General MacArthur's promised return to the Philippines.

several days of house-to-house fighting in the Philippine capital. On March 4 resistance ended. Parts of Manila lay in rubble, its streets strewn with burned vehicles and 16,665 dead Japanese soldiers.

The Final Stepping Stones

The pear-shaped, eight-square-mile island of Iwo Jima might have been by-passed had it not been strategically located in the middle of the air route used by B-29s flying between Saipan and Tokyo. Capturing Iwo Jima became a task shouldered exclusively by three marine divisions because the army was organizing the Okinawa assault. On March 16, 1945, after killing 21,000 Japanese during four weeks of fighting, marines secured Iwo Jima. The next day sixteen AAF B-29s returning from Japan made emergency landings on the island. By war's end, 2,251 damaged B-29s took refuge on Iwo, sparing the lives of 24,761 flyers.

On March 14, as operations began winding down on Iwo Jima, Admiral Mitscher's carrier planes began preliminary air operations against enemy airfields on Kyushu and the Ryukyu group, the latter being the southernmost islands of the Japanese homeland, although more than 300 nautical miles from Kyushu. Okinawa, the largest in the group, became the focal

ABOVE: Men of the 77th Infantry Division move single file into the interior with machineguns and tripods slung over their shoulders.

target of "Operation Iceberg." Organized under Nimitz's command (MacArthur was still fighting on the Philippines), Admiral Spruance's Fifth Fleet planned to land 183,000 troops from thirteen hundred naval vessels on the beaches at Hagushi. Lieutenant General Simon Bolivar Buckner commanded the Tenth Army, which included the XXIV Corps under Major General John R. Hodge, and the III Marine Amphibious Corps under Major General Roy S. Geiger. Vice Admiral Richmond Kelly Turner directed Okinawa's amphibious operations, which would be the largest and most complicated undertaking in the Pacific. Operation Iceberg relied entirely on Admiral Mitscher's carrier planes to control the air.

On April 1, 1945, General Buckner's Tenth Army began landing in eight waves along an eight-mile front at Hagushi. The Thirty-second Japanese Army (130,000 men), under the command of Lieutenant General Mitsuru Ushijima, offered little resistance

LEFT: On March 26, 1945, men of the 1st Battalion, 306th Infantry Regiment, 77th Division, fight their way across Kerama Island, located 25 miles west of Okinawa.

ABOVE: *Lieutenant General Simon Bolivar Buckner, Jr. (left), Vice Admiral Richmond Kelley Turner (center), and Marine Corps Brigadier General Oliver P. Smith (right) confer on Turner's flagship to plan the invasion of Okinawa.*

BELOW: *President Harry S. Truman arrives in Japan to congratulate General Douglas MacArthur on the conclusion of the war with Japan.*

against the landing because his troops were waiting in elaborately designed underground and interlocked defensive systems inland. The Japanese also deployed some three thousand kamikaze suicide planes to strike the American invasion fleet on the theory that sinking or driving the ships away would improve General Ushijima's chances of isolating and defeating the Americans on the island. Kamikazes took a heavy toll on American ships and naval personnel, but Mitscher's carrier planes took a heavier toll on Japanese aircraft. By most accounts, the Japanese lost eight thousand planes during the Okinawa campaign.

Okinawa ranked as one of the most violent campaigns of the war and presaged the quality of determined resistance Americans would confront when invading Japan's mainland.

On June 18 a Japanese artillery shell killed General Buckner, and on June 22, the final day of the battle, General Ushijima committed hara-kiri (ceremonial suicide). The eighty-three-day battle eradicated the Twenty-second Japanese army, but cost 12,374 American lives and 36,656 wounded, an unexpectedly high percentage of which included navy casualties caused by kamikazes.

The Setting Sun

The JCS expected the Japanese to defend the home islands with even more ferocity than Okinawa, using as many as 4 million undefeated and fanatic troops to fight to the death. Estimates of Allied casualties ran as high as 1.5 million men, but plans went ahead for the invasion of Kyushu in November, followed by the invasion of Honshu during the spring of 1946.

On July 16, 1945, while the JCS agonized over casualty estimates, the army exploded the first experimental atomic bomb at Alamogordo, New Mexico. High-level debates followed in Washington over the use of atomic weapons. Putting aside the question of morality, Secretary of State Henry L.

Stimson recommended that the bombs be deployed, and in late July, President Truman agreed. On August 6 the AAF dropped the first atomic bomb on Hiroshima and killed 78,150 civilians outright and injured 70,000 more. Three days later a second bomb fell on Nagasaki, killing 40,000 more civilians and injuring 25,000. On August 10 the recently reformed Japanese government accepted Allied demands for unconditional surrender, and four days later (V-J Day) signed an armistice. On August 15 General MacArthur flew to Tokyo as Supreme Commander to accept, on September 2 with other Allied officers, the official surrender of Japan.

The Butcher's Bill

During World War II the United States mobilized 14.9 million men and women. Most of them (10.4 million) served in the army. Of the 292,100 servicemen who died, and the 571,822 who were wounded, most of them belonged to the army. Japan mobilized a force of 7.4 million men, and lost more than 1.5 million killed because of suicidal tactics as opposed to only 500,000 wounded. American bombing campaigns took the lives of 300,000 Japanese civilians.

Fifty million people died in World War II, but another war to end all wars slipped through the fingers of politicians. Communism, the next world threat, remained alive and well.

RIGHT: On September 2, 1945, General Macarthur and other Allied representatives watch as Japanese Foreign Minister Mamoru Shigemetsu steps forward to sign the official surrender agreement on board the USS Missouri in Tokyo Bay.

LEFT: On August 29, 1945, jubilant Allied prisoners of war cheer their liberators as they are released from the Aomori compound near Yokohama, Japan.

CHAPTER 6

COLD WAR: THE KOREAN CONFLICT 1945–1952

The United States exited World War II as a great international power, but with global commitments that included the protection of Allied interests in liberated areas as well as the economic recovery of defeated enemies. Congress vacillated under increasing public pressure to "bring the boys home," and soldiers overseas clamored for accelerated separation. After all, the United States enjoyed a monopoly on atomic weapons—the power of mass self-destruction. Because advocates of air power argued that the bomb made armies and navies obsolete, cutting other service branches sounded sensible to Congress.

In early 1946 former British Prime Minister Winston Churchill came to America and warned, "An Iron Curtain has descended across the [European] continent, allowing police governments to rule Eastern Europe." Indeed, the Soviet Union did a turnabout, changing from ally to adversary. President Truman, perhaps reacting to Churchill's advice, asked for a postwar army of 1.5 million, a navy of six hundred thousand, and an air force of four hundred thousand. Neither Congress nor the American people wanted to support such a force. Old, obsolete thinking still prevailed in Congress. In two years the army scaled back from 10 million soldiers to fewer than a half-million—sixth in size to the armies of the world.

In 1947 the feeble American army began preparing for Soviet armored intervention into Western Europe, and the AAF began training for nuclear war. Congress decided to strip the AAF out of the army and formed the U.S. Air Force (USAF), a new independent service branch that should have been created in the 1930s but occurred only after air generals convinced legislators that other branches of service would not longer be needed in the nuclear age. Such naiveté on the part of Congress cannot be explained when short-range rockets, jet engines, and German V-2 long-range missiles capable of delivering nuclear warheads already existed. Congress also created the Department of Defense (DOD), gave formal status to the Joint Chiefs of Staff (JCS), and created the Central Intelligence Agency (CIA). Even President Truman, seeking election in 1948, changed

BELOW: In April 1946, former British Prime Minister Winston Churchill (left) came to the United States and met with President Harry S. Truman (right). At Fulton, Missouri, Churchill made his famous speech, and warned, "From Stettin in the Baltic to Trieste in the Adriatic, and iron curtain has descended across the [European] continent."

colors and ran on a platform advocating a reduction in military spending.

Congressional military strategy, or rather the absence of having a strategy at all, received a jolt in 1949 when Soviet Russia detonated a nuclear explosion, canceled the U.S. monopoly on atomic weapons, and threatened mutual annihilation should the world's two powers engage in war. Friction from this confrontation developed into what militarists called the "Cold War." The seminal mushroom cloud had barely settled over the USSR when efforts to expand communism in the Far East took center stage.

Prelude to the Korean War

During the Potsdam Conference of July 17–August 2, 1945, Josef Stalin made it perfectly clear that he wanted half of the Korean peninsula. When Churchill refused to discuss the subject, Stalin turned to Truman, who also avoided the topic. On August 8, dissatisfied with the outcome of the conference, the USSR declared war on Japan for no reason other than to promote Soviet geopolitical interests in the Far East. Seven days later Japan surrendered. Stalin immediately demanded answers on his Korean claims, and on that day Truman authorized and Stalin acquiesced to the arbitrary establishment of the thirty-eighth degree of latitude, thereby dividing Korea into two political spheres. The USSR would receive the Japanese surrender in North Korea, and the U.S. would receive the Japanese surrender in South Korea. After the surrender Stalin declared the thirty-eighth parallel a political boundary and lowered the Iron Curtain.

In 1947 the U.S. referred the Soviet Union's action to the U.N. The multinational organization failed to obtain agreement from the USSR to establish an independent Korea and hold free national elections. Instead the USSR set up a puppet government at Pyongyang, organized the North Korean Army (NKA), and began staging raids, sabotage, and guerrilla infiltrations into South Korea. U.S. Army troops, which had been performing constabulary duties, evacuated South Korea in June 1949, leaving behind a small military advisory group to organize the Republic of Korea (ROK) Army.

By early 1950 the well-trained and Russian-equipped NKA consisted of ten divisions (130,000 men) with another 100,000 men in reserve, a brigade of Soviet T-34 medium tanks, and an air force of 180 Yakovlev-9 (Yak) propeller-driven fighters.

The ROK army—trained more as a police force than a combat force—consisted of 100,000 men in eight divisions but without any appreciable artillery, tanks, or fighter planes.

Outbreak of War

In an early morning driving rain on June 25, 1950, NKA Marshal Choe Yong Gun crossed the thirty-eighth parallel into South Korea with ninety thousand men and hundreds of Soviet-made tanks. Four ROK divisions scattered along the border melted away. Nobody in the United States anticipated the attack. The CIA had never made an effort to understand the ruthless and unpredictable nature of North Korean leader Kim-Il-song, nor were they aware that the Red Chinese, after conferring with Stalin, encouraged the invasion. On June 28 NKA troops captured the South Korean capital of Seoul before most of the world knew what was happening.

On June 27 President Truman ordered seventy-year-old General Douglas MacArthur, commanding U.S. forces in the Far East, to

BELOW: In 1945, General Douglas MacArthur (right) gets his first look at the harsh winter landscape of North Korea.

ABOVE: *There were still recruiting posters during the Korean War, but very few compared with World War II.*

aid South Korea with whatever resources he could muster. MacArthur furnished a small amount of air support, blockaded the North Korean coast with the depleted U.S. Seventh Fleet, and on June 28 personally arrived south of Seoul to reconnoiter the front on the day the Korean capital fell. He landed at Suwon airfield in the middle of a strafing attack by Yak fighters. MacArthur advised Truman that the ROK army would never be able to curb the sudden invasion. MacArthur's report resulted in heated discussions in Washington about how much authority to give the general and how much military response to employ. MacArthur ignored the decision to confine air operations to South Korean airspace and made a unilateral decision to cross the thirty-eighth parallel and strike NKA airbases in North Korea. B-26 and B-29 pilots began flying missions over Korea but because of inadequate communications did not know where to drop their bombs.

Having been boycotted by the USSR in its efforts to legalize the thirty-eighth parallel, the U.N. put MacArthur in charge of troops from sixteen participating nations and crowned him Commander in Chief, United Nations Command. On June 29–30 Truman ratified MacArthur's decision to use air power throughout the Korean peninsula and authorized the use of ground troops.

Although the USAF, the navy, and the marines would contribute mightily to the Korean War, the army bore the brunt of repulsing the invasion. Because Congress, with Truman's blessing, had recently cut back the regular army, MacArthur's ground forces in Japan consisted of four understrength divisions divided into two skeleton army corps having a few old antitank weapons but no medium tanks, heavy artillery, or armored vehicles. Despite severe unpreparedness, MacArthur hastily fed three divisions into South Korea to retain a toehold at Pusan.

On July 4 C-54 Skymaster transports airlifted Lieutenant Colonel Charles B. Smith's 440-man infantry battalion to Osan. An NKA division supported by tanks struck Task Force Smith in the morning. Smith's 2.36-inch bazooka rockets bounced off armor-plated Soviet tanks. A two-gun 75 mm recoilless rifle platoon also failed to stop the tanks. ROK troops fled, leaving Smith's battalion surrounded. After seven hours of desperate fighting, Smith could no longer hold a defensive position. With the battalion's ammunition running low, the survivors cut their way free.

Thirty miles south of Osan, Major General William F. Dean's Twenty-fourth Division slowed the NKA advance by trading terrain for time, enabling the Twenty-fifth Division and the First Cavalry to

RIGHT: *On July 5, 1950, ten days after the North Korean army plunged across the 38th Parallel, the* Pacific Stars and Stripes *publish the first issue showing action photographs.*

reach South Korea with reinforcements. Surrounded on three sides, Dean's Twenty-fourth Division fought a delaying action for five days at Taejon. On July 22 the First Cavalry Division relieved Dean with help from the Twenty-fifth Division on the right flank. With more American troops coming on the field, the ROK divisions reorganized, slowed the NKA advance, and established the Pusan perimeter.

The Pusan Perimeter

The survival of South Korea depended upon holding the Pusan perimeter—a line bounded on the east and south by the sea and on the west by the Naktong River. The perimeter formed two legs of a right angle, one ninety miles long and the other about sixty miles long. The task of defending this sprawling zone fell mainly on American troops using old World War II weapons and fixed-wing propeller-driven aircraft. A few Bell H-13 helicopters made an appearance for the first time on a battlefield to perform medical

evacuations, but the new Sikorsky H-5s had not yet arrived. Communications were deplorable. Major General Edward M. Almond, MacArthur's chief of staff, commuted around the battlefield in an old Navy spotter plane. Lieutenant General Walton H. Walker, commanding the Eighth Army, rode about in a jeep making observations from the ground and issuing orders on the spot.

LEFT: On August 24, 1950, a 46-ton M26 Pershing tank detours around a broken bridge in the Tabu-dong area during the defense of the Pusan perimeter.

LEFT: The first casualty evacuations by helicopter began in Korea and were flown to Mobile Army Surgical Hospitals (MASH) for immediate treatment. Survival rates in the Korea War dropped to 25 deaths per 1,000 wounded, compared with 45 per thousand during World War II.

RIGHT: The 140-mile Pusan Perimeter developed in the tight southeastern corner of South Korea, without which the United States would have been unable to feed reinforcements and equipment to the crumbling ROK army. The area also became the launching pad for General Walton H. Walker's counterattack during the Inchon assault.

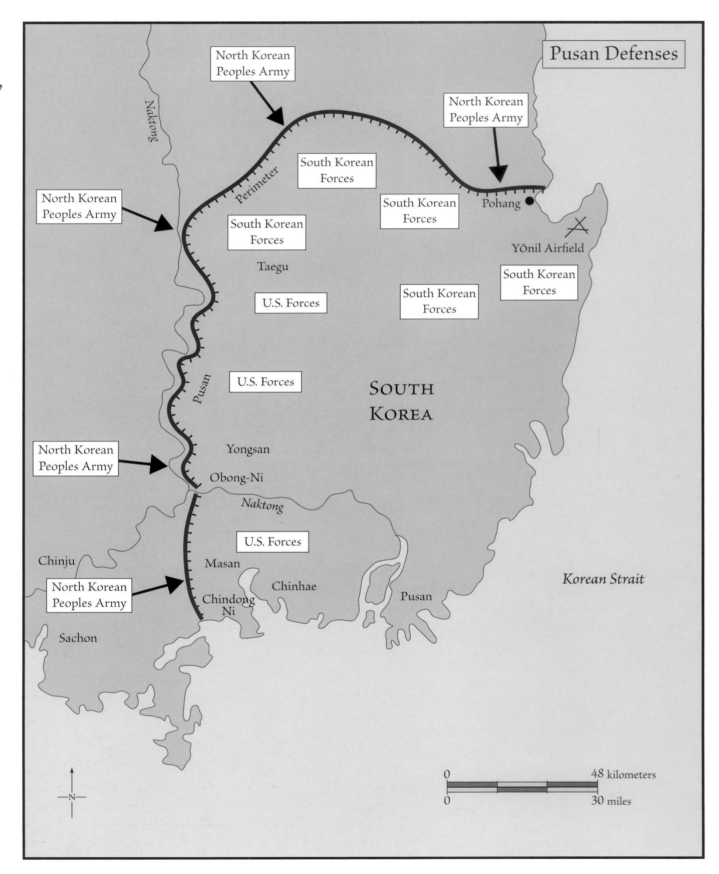

Pusan Defenses

North Korean Peoples Army

North Korean Peoples Army

North Korean Peoples Army

Naktong

Perimeter

South Korean Forces

South Korean Forces

South Korean Forces

Pohang

North Korean Peoples Army

South Korean Forces

Yōnil Airfield

South Korean Forces

Taegu

U.S. Forces

South Korean Forces

Pusan

U.S. Forces

SOUTH KOREA

North Korean Peoples Army

Yongsan

Obong-Ni

Naktong

U.S. Forces

Korean Strait

Chinju

Masan

North Korean Peoples Army

Chindong Ni

Chinhae

Pusan

Sachon

0   48 kilometers

0   30 miles

N

WALTON H. "JOHNNIE" WALKER (1889–1950)

On July 13, 1950, sixty-one-year-old Lieutenant General Walton H. "Johnnie" Walker of Belton, Texas, took command of the U.S. Eighth Army at Pusan. The nickname "Johnnie Walker" originated from his capacity to consume large quantities of his favorite brand of scotch. Walker found most of his army near Taegu, defending a thirty-five-mile front along the Naktong River. Four days later Walker absorbed command of thousands of disorganized and demoralized ROK army soldiers, though ROK troops never became official members of the Eighth Army.

Walker graduated from West Point in 1912 and received a Silver Star for gallantry in World War I. During World War II he commanded the XX Corps in General Patton's Third Army. The XX Corps won distinction in Europe as the "Ghost Corps" for the speed of its advance. In May 1945 the unit reached Linz, Austria, the deepest penetration east of Patton's army. After the war Walker went to Japan to command the Eighth Army, a "hollow force," hardly an army at all. Walker's four divisions were trimmed to two-thirds their authorized strength and equipment, and only 10 percent of the men had combat experience. The sad shape of the army annoyed Walker and probably accounted for his troublesome relationship with MacArthur.

With his back to the sea and in a tight corner, Walker exploited his one advantage: the ability to maneuver forces along interior lines. On July 29 he issued his famous "Stand or Die" directive, bluntly declaring, "There will be no Dunkirk, there will be no Bataan." Having been mentored by Patton, Walker's choice of words came as no surprise to anyone.

From August 5 to September 15, 1950, Walker conducted one of the most skillful mobile defensive operations in American history, made possible by intelligence operatives who broke the NKA code. He parried every NKA penetration by he timely shifting of his forces to close gaps.

Walker's primary objective was to keep the NKA engaged along the Pusan perimeter while MacArthur organized the X Corps for the invasion of Inchon. That the strategy worked is a standing tribute to both commanders, though they often disagreed on tactics. Walker's annoyance with MacArthur persisted during the campaign that later took the Eighth Army to the Manchurian border, where large-scale Chinese interventions led to the disastrous defeat of U.N. forces. Walker, who Patton called "a fighter in every sense of the word," claimed the repulse could have been prevented had MacArthur not divided the command. X Corps operated independently from Eighth Army under the command of Major General Edward M. Almond, making it impossible for him to synchronize operations in Korea.

On December 23, 1950, a Korean civilian truck struck Walker's jeep, killed the general, and eliminated one of MacArthur's sharpest critics.

ABOVE: Lieutenant General Walton H. "Johnnie" Walker (1889–1950) commanded the U.S. Eighth Army in Korea and got his picture on the cover of Time magazine for his stubborn defense of the Pusan perimeter.

RIGHT: In September 1950, soldiers serve a machinegun emplacement overlooking the Naktong River along the Pusan perimeter.

For six weeks Walker's Eighth Army and five shaken ROK divisions kept fourteen NKA infantry divisions and several tank regiments occupied along the 120-mile Pusan perimeter. Equipment shortages in Walker's command became so desperate that armored vehicles on display in the United States were pulled from exhibitions, reconditioned, and rushed to Korea. Meanwhile, the Seventh Fleet protected both sea flanks while the Far East Air Force, together with carrier-based aircraft, hammered NKA communications and provided close air support. By mid-September Walker had the Pusan perimeter reinforced, reorganized, and well supplied on the eve of the Inchon offensive.

Inchon—Operation Chromite

On August 12, 1950, while the Eighth Army still clawed to maintain its toehold on the Korean peninsula, MacArthur decided to assault Inchon. He did not wait for approval from the JCS but put his staff immediately to work to accomplish in one month what would normally have taken several. He formed the X Corps from the Seventh Infantry Division (the last of his occupation troops in Japan), brought five thousand ROK soldiers to Japan for training, and added the First Marine Division, part of which had been fighting at Pusan. He put General Almond, his chief of staff and a close friend, in charge of the X Corps, though outside of his own coterie few had anything good to say about the general.

The port of Inchon, located a few miles west of Seoul, lay in a harbor of bottomless mud flats

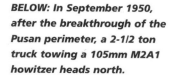

BELOW: In September 1950, after the breakthrough of the Pusan perimeter, a 2-1/2 ton truck towing a 105mm M2A1 howitzer heads north.

coursed by strong currents and surrounded by granite seawalls designed to hold back twenty-foot tides. The NKA considered the area unsuitable for

amphibious operations, posted only 2,200 troops at Inchon, but maintained a force of 21,500 in the nearby Seoul-Kimpo area. Two hundred and thirty ships, mostly American, participated in the operation. Assaulting Inchon required that the task force go up Flying Fish Channel precisely at high tide, thereby enabling troops to scale seawalls from ladders in their landing craft. After overrunning the small NKA force in the city, the next target became the Kimpo airport and Seoul, thereby liberating the South Korean capital and restoring President Syngman Rhee to power.

On the morning of September 15, landing craft churned through heavy seas off the island of Wolmi-do, the first point of assault, while rocket ships (LSMRs) and F4U-4 Corsair fighters pulverized shore installations with 5-inch high-velocity rockets.

LEFT: On September 15, 1950, during an inspection of landing areas in Inchon's harbor, MacArthur (center) sits aboard a navy launch, flanked by Vice Admiral Arthur D. Struble on his right and Brigadier General Courtney Whitney on his left.

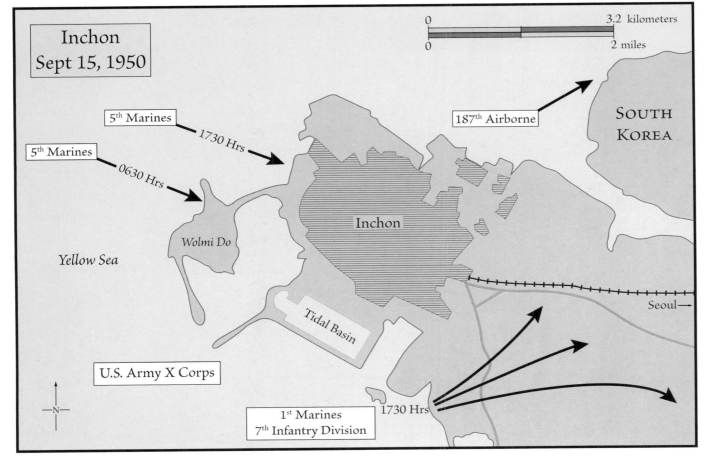

LEFT: Inchon had the reputation of being one of the most dangerous harbors in the world. Early assaults were made by specially trained marines and immediately followed up by the army's 7th Infantry Division and other elements from the X Corps.

At 6:33 A.M. the first wave waded ashore and, supported by air support, captured Wolmi-do in thirty minutes. MacArthur now had a beachhead.

At high tide, 5:30 P.M., LSTs (Landing Craft, Tanks) bumped against Inchon's seawall. Ladders went up, and elements from Major General Oliver P. Smith's First Marine Division dropped into the city. The invasion went without a hitch. By early morning Smith had more than fifteen thousand troops and fifteen hundred vehicles ashore, with the Seventh Infantry Division close behind. On September 17, while marines captured Kimpo airfield, the Seventh Infantry swung east and south and began cutting the railroads and highways supplying NKA forces on the Pusan perimeter. The assault astonished and confused the NKA. In tandem with MacArthur's landing, Walker's Eighth Army broke out of Pusan's perimeter and began driving the NKA north into the waiting Seventh Division. About thirty thousand NKA troops managed to escaped across the thirty-eighth parallel, but another 135,000 were either killed or taken prisoner in MacArthur's superbly executed trap.

BELOW: On September 20, 1950, following General Walker's breakthrough at the Pusan perimeter, reconnaissance troops from the 19th Infantry Regiment, 24th Infantry Division, move to the front after crossing the Naktong River.

BELOW RIGHT: On October 1, 1950, General MacArthur received permission from the United Nations and President Truman to cross the 38th Parallel and advance to the Yalu River on the Manchurian border.

A New and Mighty Enemy

The question became what to do next. President Truman wanted to limit the war to South Korea, fearing that a penetration into North Korea could bring Red China or Soviet Russia into the war. North Korea, however, still had an army that could threaten the South Korean government. The U.N. favored unifying Korea, which had been the original plan, so on September 27, 1950, Truman informed MacArthur that he could go into North Korea with the understanding that only ROK troops were to be used near Chinese or Soviet borders.

On October 1, ROK troops crossed the thirty-eighth parallel, followed by Walker's Eighth Army on the left and Almond's X Corps far over on the right. The U.N. call for restoration of peace, security, and unification throughout the peninsula received no response from North Korean leader Kim-Il-song, so the advance continued.

On October 15 MacArthur flew to Wake Island to post Truman on the course of the war and to assure him that Chinese threats of intervention were merely saber-rattling propaganda. The CIA expressed the same opinion. Both were wrong. Two months earlier Chinese Premier Chou En-lai distinctly warned that China would send troops into Korea if the Allies advanced north of the thirty-eighth parallel. Deeper

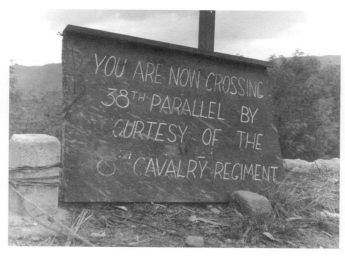

For twenty-four hours the Eighth Army encountered only light resistance as it pressed toward the Yalu, but on November 25 180,000 hidden Chinese troops struck the right flank, flooded through the ROK II Corps, hit the U.S. Second Division of the IX Corps, and threatened to envelop Walker's entire army.

Two days later 120,000 Chinese troops, advancing along both sides of the Chosin Reservoir, isolated the First Marine Division west of the reservoir. East of the reservoir they drove back the Third and Seventh Army Divisions of the X Corps.

MacArthur suddenly found both wings of his army in jeopardy and ordered a pullback. After some early disorder, the Eighth Army managed to disengage and withdrew to the thirty-eighth parallel. At the Chosin Reservoir, General Oliver Smith's First Marine Division fought its way out of envelopment, kept the way open for the withdrawal of the X Corps, and in a running battle in s

LEFT: On September 25, 1950, a knocked out bridge holds up the 2nd Infantry Division on the Hwang-gang River.

penetrations of American and ROK units were already reporting numerous Chinese units fighting alongside NKA units. MacArthur had his own agenda and did not care. If Red China entered the war, he would smash them with air power. In World War II he had never heard of bombing restrictions.

By October 20 U.N. forces had penetrated deep into North Korea, capturing Pyongyang. ROK elements advanced within fifty miles from China's Manchurian border. As the Allies began closing on the Yalu River, resistance became more unyielding. By early November thousands of Chinese troops filtering into North Korea were fighting beside NKA troops, but still not in sufficient numbers to check the Allied advance.

Meanwhile, on November 24, MacArthur ordered Walker's Eighth Army (nine divisions) to make a reconnaissance in force on the western side of the peninsula while General Almond's X Corps (five divisions) advanced up the eastern side. As two hundred thousand Allied combat troops began moving in bitter weather toward the Yalu River, some three hundred thousand Chinese troops (thirty divisions), accompanied by Soviet advisors and armed with Soviet weapons, crossed at night into North Korea.

BELOW: On December 13, 1950, during the evacuation of the X Army Corps from Hungnam, a soldier on watch from the 2nd Infantry Division tries to keep warm near his jeep.

ub-zero weather, fell back to Hungnam on the Sea of Japan and established a defensive perimeter. On December 5, supported by air cover, the navy began embarking 105,000 U.S. and ROK troops, 98,000 civilian refugees, and 350,000 tons of cargo and equipment from Hungnam to Pusan.

After what began as a brilliant campaign, MacArthur found himself with Walker's Eighth Army holding the line back below the thirty-eighth parallel and Almond's X Corps recovering at Pusan. MacArthur finally agreed with General Walker that the X Corps should be part of the Eighth Army, but he kept it in reserve at Pusan. On December 23, Walker died of injuries suffered in a vehicle accident and was replaced by fifty-five-year-old Lieutenant General Matthew B. Ridgway, the brilliant paratrooper commander of World War II.

What MacArthur should or should not have done when he sent forces across the thirty-eighth parallel on October 1 will remain a subject of debate as long as the Korean War is studied. When the U.N. and the JCS prohibited aerial reconnaissance north of the Yalu, it blindfolded MacArthur. When his request to bomb Yalu bridges was denied, the decision enabled China's army to cross unhindered. When his request to bomb North Korea's key entry port of Rachin near Vladivostok was also denied, he had no way of impeding the flow of Soviet weaponry. Nor could he bomb Chinese airfields, where Soviet jets flown by Russian pilots enjoyed the luxury of making sorties into Korea without fear of molestation while reposing in Manchuria. A serious misunderstanding existed between MacArthur and the JCS over Chinese intervention. MacArthur believed that if the Chinese intervened, he would be given authorization to extend air operations into Manchuria, but the U.N. and the JCS never intended to allow this.

RIGHT: On February 10, 1951, an M39 Armored Utility Vehicle of the 2nd Reconnaissance Company, 2nd Infantry Division near Chipyong-ri, heads into the field.

The 38th Parallel—Again

After MacArthur pulled back to the thirty-eighth parallel, Ridgway now had to hold it. Having fought in Europe rather than the Pacific, Ridgway arrived in Korea with a keener understanding of the influence of politics on armies. He had barely become settled when on January 1 four hundred thousand Chinese troops, augmented by one hundred thousand NKA troops, assaulted the Eighth Army's two hundred thousand troops and pushed them out of Seoul. Ridgway brought reserves from Pusan, stabilized his position about fifty miles south of the politically imposed parallel, and told his staff, "There will be no more discussion of retreat. We're going back." Ridgway organized Operation Ripper and on March 14 reoccupied Seoul. By March 31 Ridgway had portions of the army contesting for turf along the strategic parallel. For the next twelve months each side mounted offensives and parried with counteroffensives without moving more than ten to twenty miles one way or the other. Although Ridgway made gains using excellent tactics, he dutifully and diligently understood that the president and the JCS had decided to accept a stalemated war rather than become engaged in a major confrontation with China or Russia.

Old Soldiers Never Die

MacArthur agonized over watching men die while politicians erected barriers. Being an old-fashioned "unconditional surrender" man, he did not believe in limited wars. Nor did he conceal his dissatisfaction over the restrictions placed upon his battle plans. What Truman called a "police action," MacArthur called war, bloody and dirty as always. "In war, there is no substitution to victory," MacArthur declared, unaware that the expression of his feelings to Representative Joseph W. Martin, Jr., of Massachusetts, would promptly be made public. He did not believe the USSR would come to the aid of China, and he believed there would be no better time to confront the Soviets, unify Korea, defeat Red

ABOVE: On 13 April 1951, the world is shocked to learn that President Truman has recalled venerable General MacArthur for insubordination and replaced him with Lieutenant General Matthew B. Ridgeway.

ABOVE AND BEYOND THE CALL OF DUTY

In the bloody Korean War, which claimed more than 2 million lives, seventy-seven Americans earned the Medal of Honor, most of them posthumously.

Sergeant George D. Libby of Casco, Maine, a member of the Third Engineer Combat Battalion, lost his life on July 20, 1950, and became the first Medal of Honor recipient in the Korean War. Libby's battalion was among the first to reach Pusan when MacArthur ordered the Twenty-fourth Infantry Division to Korea. At Taejon, after the NKA began enveloping the division, Libby pushed a number of wounded men onto an M5 artillery tractor and posted himself to ride shotgun. On the way out of the trap, the tractor encountered an enemy roadblock. North Koreans poured a hail of fire at the truck, and Libby, interposed between the driver and the enemy, fired a stream of bullets back. Libby held on, blasting away at the enemy as bullets ripped through his body. The tractor crashed the roadblock, bringing the wounded safely to an aid station, but Libby lost his life in a courageous effort to save his buddies. In the decades following the war, thousands of Americans and Koreans have crossed the Libby Bridge over the Han River, named for the daring engineer who lost his life saving others.

Major General William F. Dean of Berkeley, California, took personal responsibility for the rear guard of his Twenty-fourth Division at Taejon. Knowing other divisions were on the way, Dean wanted to buy time by delaying the advance of the NKA. One of the last persons to see Dean remembered him holding a new 3.5-inch rocket launcher, and saying, "I just got me a tank!" A junior officer recalled seeing Dean stalking another T-34 tank accompanied by a small group of soldiers. After the general disappeared into the smoke of war, President Truman awarded him the Medal of Honor for his one-man stand against the enemy. Unknown for months to come, and completely cutoff from his division, Dean disappeared into the interior and eluded capture for 33 days. Freed by his captors during operation Big Switch (prisoner exchange), Dean eventually emerged from the murk of war to learn that he had been awarded the Medal of Honor.

Of the seventy-seven Medal of Honor recipients in the Korea War, sixty were enlisted men. The list ranged from buck private to major general. Melvin L. Brown, one of nineteen privates awarded the medal, came from Mahaffey, Pennsylvania. Sent to Korea, he became a member of the Eighth Engineer Combat Battalion with the First Cavalry Division. On September 4, 1950, Brown squatted atop a fifty-foot wall along the Pusan perimeter and fought off a horde of North Koreans with his .30-caliber M1 rifle and a belt of hand grenades slung around his chest. After running out of ammunition, he killed twelve more enemy soldiers with a shovel before dying of wounds. His story was little different from all the others, except in the details. Heroes came from all ranks, and sometimes it took a war to learn whom they were.

ABOVE: In 1951, Lieutenant General James Alward Van Fleet (1892–1992) also appeared on the cover of Time magazine after taking over the Eighth Army in Korea from General Ridgway.

China, and quash the spread of communism. He also wanted to use Chinese Nationalist troops in Korea and on the Chinese mainland. MacArthur voiced many opinions that tramped on presidential prerogatives. On April 11, 1951, after MacArthur's views became public, Truman recalled the supreme commander, replacing him with General Ridgway, with fifty-seven-year-old Lieutenant General James A. Van Fleet taking Ridgway's place as commander of combat forces in Korea. MacArthur understood the reasons behind his dismissal, but millions of Americans did not. Like the general, much of the public never quite agreed with the president's policy of no-win warfare.

With the front line now stabilized in the vicinity of the old border, General Van Fleet became increasingly frustrated with "fighting while negotiating," complaining that it affected morale and was not the way to defeat communist aggression. Truman vetoed Van Fleet's many efforts to take the offensive. When Van Fleet left Korea in 1953, he retired from the army, grumbling that the United States could have easily won the Korean War had Truman possessed the will.

When MacArthur made his famous parting address to Congress, reminding them that "Old soldiers never die," he could also have been speaking for Van Fleet.

An Unsettling Settlement

Van Fleet pushed the Eighth Army across the thirty-eighth parallel and established the "Kansas-Wyoming line" on excellent defensive terrain. In June 1951 fighting stopped and peace talks began. Intermittent clashes erupted as negotiators jockeyed for advantage and armies jockeyed for larger slices of the battlefield.

In May 1952 General Mark W. Clark replaced Ridgway in Tokyo as supreme commander. By then North Korea had built an army of eight hundred

thousand men, six hundred thousand of them Chinese. Clark never achieved the fame he coveted when commanding Allied forces during the 1943–1945 Italian campaign, and Korea looked like another opportunity. When Dwight D. Eisenhower won the 1952 presidential election, he did so on a promise to end the Korean War. Clark erroneously believed that Ike disapproved of Truman's policy and would resume offensive actions. Instead of using military force, Eisenhower applied threats, warning North Korea and its allies that the United States would "move decisively without inhibition in our use of weapons" and would not confine the fighting to Korea. The threat worked. On July 27, 1953, the fighting ended with an armistice that established a demilitarized zone separating the two Koreas along the old thirty-eighth parallel boundary. The First Cavalry Division and the Seventh Infantry Division remained in Korea for decades as insurance against a resumption of hostilities.

Two million Americans became involved in the Korean War, with 33,629 killed and 103,284

RIGHT: On May 6, 1951, during the see-saw fighting around the 38th Parallel, an 8-inch M115 howitzer of Battery C, 17th Field Artillery Battalion, 7th Infantry Division, shells Communist Chinese positions at Hwachon.

wounded. Of 10,218 Americans captured, only 3,746 were returned. The others died of starvation, wounds, or were murdered. The communist armies lost 1.6 million battle casualties, most of them Chinese, and at least four hundred thousand non-battle casualties.

The Korean War also brought racial integration, first as a combat necessity and then because President Truman ordered it. A new work environment enabling service personnel to advance up the chain of command by demonstrating superior ability and performance soon attracted ambitious young men and women regardless of race.

Drawing the line on the thirty-eighth parallel demonstrated that the United States intended to play a major role in world affairs and would continue to resist communist expansion in the free world. The Korean conflict also marked a basic change from the traditional American concept of total victory via unconditional surrender, giving way to a policy of negotiation and military constraint to achieve a political outcome. A decade later at Vietnam, another administration seemed to forget the pitfalls of Korean warfare and politics.

The war also proved the fallacy of the JCS strategy emanating from the late 1940s that diminished the need for an army or navy by declaring that all future wars would be decided by air power delivering nuclear weapons. Korea proved otherwise. Ground forces were here to stay.

ABOVE: On December 5, 1952, President-elect Dwight D. Eisenhower (left center) visits the 2nd Infantry Division headquarters, accompanied by Major General James C. Fry (right) and General Mark W. Clark.

LEFT: On July 29, 1953, tanks of the 7th Infantry Regiment, 3rd Infantry Division, prepare to move to new positions following the July 27 signing of the armistice at Panmunjon.

COLD WAR: VIETNAM 1952–1975

BELOW: On September 24, 1963, Secretary of Defense Robert McNamara (center) and U.S. Army Chief of Staff General Maxwell Taylor (left) confer with President John F. Kennedy prior to their visit to South Vietnam.

Despite the frustrations of the Korean War, the conflict revived a sense of purpose for the army. The war was not glorious, but it did hold the line against communist expansion—about all American and free-world politicians thought reasonable without risking Armageddon.

Aware of the unpopularity of the Korean War—mainly because of how it was conducted—President Eisenhower adopted a new American military policy, replacing limited war with massive retaliation. The policy, though largely rhetorical, called for the army to retain much of its ground strength from the Korean War while America built its nuclear arsenal. Congress, however, cut back the army and infuriated such notable generals as Matthew Ridgway and Maxwell D. Taylor. Both men retired in disgust. Until the 1960 elections, despite modestly successful efforts by Eisenhower to build a strategic reserve, the principal army forces overseas continued to be the Seventh Army in Germany and the Eighth Army in Korea.

During the 1960 election campaign, presidential hopeful Senator John F. Kennedy of Massachusetts charged that the nation was imperiled by a policy that neglected conventional forms of military power and relied too heavily on nuclear weapons—the same views that had been expressed by Ridgway and Taylor. The charge resonated with the public. Kennedy took office in January 1963 and appointed Robert S. McNamara, formerly head of the Ford Motor Company, secretary of defense, and General Taylor became Kennedy's military advisor. McNamara stripped the defense department of "dead wood" and brought in new blood, soon to be dubbed "defense intellectuals" by advocates and "whiz kids" by detractors. McNamara's goals were clear: to revitalize the armed services, and in particular, the army. Kennedy announced that the new army would have the capacity to respond to communist military challenges wherever they occurred with, if need be, nuclear power. The army had been essential in Korea, and Kennedy promised that it would continue to be strong. Communist disturbances in Vietnam ranked high among his concerns, despite warnings from Eisenhower and Kennedy's own diplomatic corps to avoid involvement.

When McNamara took control of the department of defense, the army had dwindled from its peak strength of 2.8 million troops during the Korean War to eleven understrength combat divisions. By November 1963, the month of President Kennedy's assassination, McNamara had rebuilt the army to sixteen combat-ready divisions. The new army could airlift an entire division from one continent to another. With Special Forces leading the way, the army became confident of its capability to fight and win not only limited wars, such as Korea, but unconventional wars as well. McNamara's ebullient confidence in America's military might spilled over to President Lyndon B. Johnson after the power-politician from Texas assumed control of the government following Kennedy's assassination. McNamara's policies, often questionable and sometimes misunderstood, caused considerable disarray among the military services, and those problems funneled into Johnson's administration.

Politics, War, and the Army

The conflict in Vietnam actually began the day World War II ended. On September 2, 1945, the same day Japan signed the surrender agreement, Ho Chi Minh's Vietnamese Liberation Army, under the command of General Vo Nguyen Giap, seized huge stores of abandoned Japanese weapons. Ho issued a "Declaration of Independence" modeled after the American document, but U.S. operatives in Vietnam said the new government was a screen controlled by a "100% Communist party."

The situation worsened when France, after reforming its government in 1945, decided to recapture Vietnam and retain it as a colony. The crisis escalated in 1953 when thousands of French paratroopers dropped into Dienbienphu and found themselves surrounded by North Vietnamese armed with Soviet weapons. Ho's communists kicked the

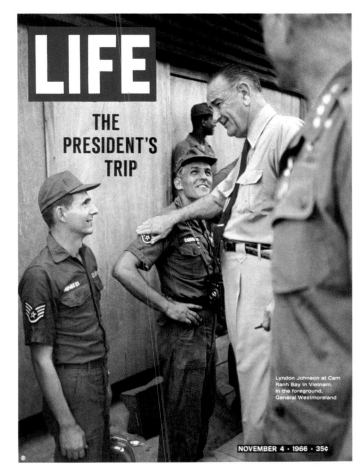

LIFE
THE PRESIDENT'S TRIP

Lyndon Johnson at Cam Ranh Bay in Vietnam. In the foreground, General Westmoreland

NOVEMBER 4 · 1966 · 35¢

LEFT: On November 4, 1966, Life's cover captures a moment during President Lyndon B. Johnson's visit to South Vietnam when he stops to chat with a pair of enlisted airmen.

French out of Vietnam but in the 1954 Geneva settlement obtained only half of what they wanted. Another demilitarized zone (DMZ), drawn at the seventeenth parallel (Ben Hai River), divided the Democratic Republic of Vietnam (North Vietnam) from the Republic of Vietnam (South Vietnam), and left the choice to Vietnamese families as to where they wanted to live. More than eight hundred thousand North Vietnamese relocated to South Vietnam, among them communist infiltrators. Only one hundred thousand South Vietnamese moved north because Ho's Vietminh agents encouraged communists to remain in the south and support the Viet Cong (VC) guerrilla movement.

In 1954, although strongly against military involvement in Vietnam, President Eisenhower sent a few army advisors to aid the resettlement effort.

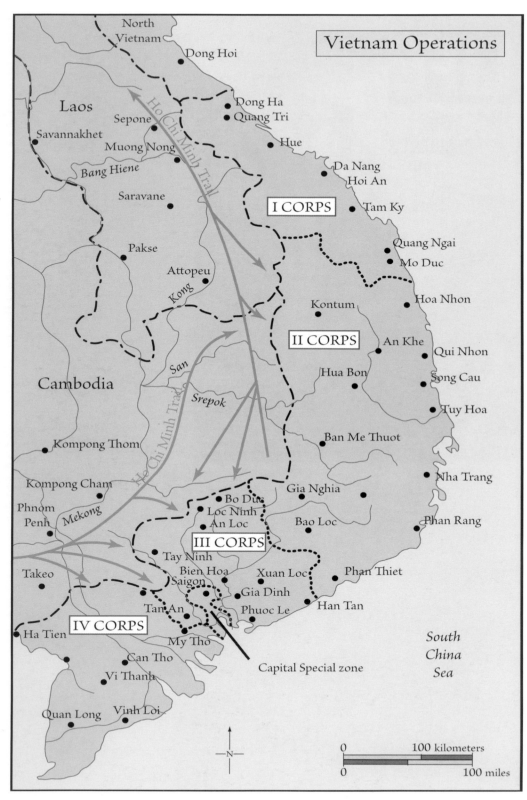

ABOVE: *Four army corps were each responsible for a different sector of South Vietnam. The problem of controlling the war partially emanated from the Ho Chi Minh trail, which consisted of a network of roads stretching from North Vietnam through eastern Laos to South Vietnam.*

Because of increased insurgency, he later increased America's involvement to four hundred specialists, ostensibly to aid in building President Ngo Dinh Diem's two hundred thousand-man Army of the Republic of (South) Vietnam (ARVN). Eisenhower wanted to help South Vietnam maintain its independence in the face of communist intervention from the north.

Elections to reunify the country were scheduled for 1956, but President Diem refused to participate. He insisted that free elections could not be held in North Vietnam. Ho had stacked the deck to favor his own election, and when parried by Diem's refusal, he ordered the VC to commence insurgency action. Assassinations, sabotage, and small hit-and-run military attacks soon spread terrorism and crippled local authority throughout South Vietnam.

As the South Vietnamese government slowly weakened, Eisenhower sent more military advisors. Despite instructions to function only in the rear, army personnel operating in the countryside found themselves drawn into skirmishes. On July 8, 1959, guerrillas killed Major Dale Buis and Master Sergeant Chester Ovnard, the first Americans to die in Vietnam. General Lyman H. Lemnitzer, the army's twenty-first chief of staff (1959–1960), told Eisenhower the U.S. could win in Vietnam and win the Cold War. The president had no intention of engaging American forces in an armed conflict and certainly did not want to test Lemnitzer's opinions in places like Vietnam. Lemnitzer, however, became chairman of the JCS on the eve of President Kennedy's election.

Kennedy held strong military views. He found more in common with Limnitzer's advice than with Eisenhower's and also believed that localized conflicts could be better contained by conventional means than massive nuclear retaliation. Kennedy called the strategy "flexible response," meaning that he intended to build a nuclear arsenal greater than the Soviets while simultaneously having multi-purpose conventional forces available at all times. He evidently listened to Limnitzer's advice on Vietnam because in 1962 he committed eleven thousand Americans, mostly from the army, to the Vietnam experiment. Serving in the Military Assistance Command, Vietnam (MACV), under General Paul D. Harkins, were Green Berets from Special Forces.

Special Forces in Vietnam

During the Korean War, Brigadier General Robert A. McClure suggested the formation of specialized units capable of conducting unconventional warfare missions behind enemy lines. On June 1952, the army's first U.S. Special Forces (USSF) volunteers reported at Fort Bragg, North Carolina.

Initial training included infiltration and land navigation techniques, using parachute drops or small boats to get behind enemy lines. Specialized training followed in weaponry, intelligence gathering, communications, sabotage, and languages. Army volunteers completing the diversified course became members of Special Forces (SF), a unique organization separated from the usual army chain of command.

In 1957 the First Special Forces Group entered Vietnam and trained fifty-eight Vietnamese soldiers in SF techniques. After finishing the course, the newly organized Vietnamese Special Forces (Luc Luong ?ac Biêt) trained Vietnamese Rangers. In 1961 mixed U.S.-Vietnamese SF teams began operating under the control of the CIA, mainly because President Kennedy wanted to expand the military's capability to conduct unconventional warfare. In 1962 the CIA sent the first SF missions into North Vietnam.

Special Forces became the chief instrument of counterinsurgency in Vietnam. While part of the goal

was to destroy guerrilla operations, the main objective was to win the allegiance of the people by enabling them to defend themselves. In 1962 Secretary McNamara decided that Special Forces should be used for paramilitary operations instead of pacification and restored the unit to army control. When the transfer occurred, SF had secured 879 villages and trained 52,636 villagers, 10,904 reaction force soldiers, 515 medics, 3,800 scouts, and 946 trail watchers. Because of the unreliability and incompetence of Vietnamese officers, pacified areas

ABOVE: Special Forces units were constantly active in the outlying hamlets where Viet Cong hid among the villagers. Here Special Forces Captain Vernon Gillespie questions two captured Viet Cong while scouting guerrilla activities in 1964.

LEFT: Captain Vernon Gillespie trudges through a village alongside a black-clad Viet Cong captured during a 1964 sweep.

CAPTAIN ROGER H. C. DONLON

In June 1964 thirty-year-old Captain Roger H. C. Donlon of the Seventh Special Forces Group arrived in Vietnam as an advisor. The army assigned him to Special Forces Detachment A-726 at Camp Nam Dong, situated in the Vietnamese mountains near the Laotian border. The unit consisted of his own twelve-man A-team, plus a 311-man South Vietnam force and sixty ethnic Nung (Montagnard) guards of Chinese origin.

Before dawn on July 6, 1964, and months before Americans became abundant in Vietnam, a reinforced battalion of VC struck the camp with mortars, grenades, and automatic weapons. Donlon gathered a detail and ran through a hail of small-arms fire to gather needed ammunition from a burning storage building. He then dodged exploding grenades in an effort to reach and defend the camp's main gate, where VC had stormed the entrance in an effort to overrun the camp. Donlon raised his AR-15 rifle—forerunner of the M16—and at point-blank range killed a swarm of VC assaulting the gate.

After suffering a severe stomach wound, Donlon dropped into a 60 mm mortar pit and laid down a covering fire, enabling others to fall back. He transferred the mortar in the pit to a better defensive position, but later, while dragging a wounded soldier to safety, suffered shrapnel wounds in his left shoulder.

Seeing an abandoned 57 mm recoilless rifle laying beside a nearby pit, Donlon retrieved it, gathered ammunition, and started back to the makeshift perimeter. An enemy hand grenade burst nearby and shrapnel ripped into his leg. Donlon ignored his injuries. He darted from one defensive position to another, urging even the wounded to fight back. He remained in the most heavily contested area, where a mortar shell exploded nearby and hurled shrapnel into his face and chest. At daylight, an army CV-2 Caribou arrived overhead and dropped supplies. After five hours of fighting the VC gave up and vanished into the jungle, leaving behind sixty-two dead. Nam Dong became the first clear victory in a yet undefined war.

On December 5, 1964, in a ceremony at the White House, President Johnson awarded Major Donlon the Vietnam War's first Medal of Honor. Donlon returned to Vietnam for another tour of duty, and after a twenty-seven-year career in the army, retired as a colonel.

LEFT: In a White House ceremony in the East Room on December 5, 1964, President Lyndon B. Johnson presents Captain Roger H. Donlon the first Medal of Honor awarded in the Vietnam War "for conspicuous gallantry above and beyond the call of duty in our present efforts in the Republic of Vietnam."

became more loyal to SF operatives than officials from Saigon.

Border camps with surveillance responsibilities along the Cambodian and Laotian borders became tempting targets for wandering VC and the People's Army of (North) Vietnam (PAVN). In July 1964 a reinforced VC battalion attacked the camp at Nam Dong where Captain Roger H.C. Donlon, commander of the camp, earned the first Medal of Honor awarded since the Korean War.

Because of extremely hazardous duty behind enemy lines, SF personnel served six to twelve months. In September 1968 Special Forces attained its greatest strength, having 3,542 personnel assigned in Vietnam. Secretary McNamara, and at times President Johnson, became personally involved in USSF missions into Laos, Cambodia, and North Vietnam. In August 1969 General Creighton Abrams began phasing out SF operations in Vietnam, and on February 22, 1973, ceased them altogether.

Special Forces, which started as an experiment in 1952, proved its value during the Vietnam War, and is today an essential body for gathering intelligence and targeting.

Incident in the Gulf of Tonkin

On August 2, 1964, the destroyer USS *Maddox* reported being attacked by at least three North Vietnamese Soviet-made torpedo boats in international waters. Two days later *Maddox* reported a second attack, though search aircraft located no torpedo boats.

If President Johnson wanted an excuse to involve the United States more deeply in South Vietnam's troubles, the incident paved the way. Congress passed the Gulf of Tonkin Resolution, giving the president authorization for expanded U.S. involvement. By the end of the year, troop strength in Vietnam rose to 2,400.

The "Ouch Level" Strategy

On February 7, 1965, VC attacked U.S. installations near the Pleiku Air base. President Johnson called it a deliberately hostile act and ordered retaliatory bombings against selected targets in North Vietnam. One target, Dong Hoi, lay along the coast a short distance above the DMZ. The VC responded by intensifying terrorism and sabotage activities against U.S. bases and personnel.

In 1965 President Johnson had two matters on his mind that would directly affect his legacy, the Vietnam War and the Great Society. Both drove Johnson's decision-making. Little did he realize that if the war failed, so would his Great Society.

Johnson did not expect to lose the Vietnam War because he, with Secretary of Defense McNamara and the "whiz kids," had devised the "ouch level" strategy. On that grandiloquent scheme, the president on March 2 authorized Operation "Rolling Thunder," a sustained bombing campaign organized around the strategic theory that a graduated and progressive bombing of North Vietnam would eventually force Ho Chi Minh to say "ouch," thereby leading to the termination of Hanoi's support of the VC and the preservation of South Vietnam's government. The success of the strategy, however, depended upon the degree of Johnson's willingness to bomb North Vietnam.

The president punctuated his determination by declaring: "We will not be defeated. We will not grow tired. We will not withdraw, either openly or under the cloak of meaningless agreement...and we will remain ready...for unconditional discussion." Over time, "meaningless" best described America's longest war.

McNamara attempted to speed up the "ouch level" by deploying more forces on the ground. On March 8, 1965, the Ninth Marine Expeditionary Brigade (first combat unit in Vietnam) landed at Danang in

the northern province of Quang Nam. No major engagement occurred for three months, although more ground forces arrived every week and more bombs fell on the enemy.

On June 28 the 173rd Airborne Brigade joined with the 503rd Infantry Brigade and two ARNV battalions for the first major offensive against the VC. The battle took place twenty miles northeast of Saigon in the province of Bien Hoa. Fifty thousand troops collaborated in the attack, revealing the rapid escalation of American involvement.

Major General Harry W.O. Kinnard's First Cavalry Division came ashore during the summer and established headquarters at Anh Khe, midway between Saigon and the DMZ. A flat highland base, troops called Anh Khe "the Golf Course." Kinnard had trained the division to go to war in helicopters, much like early cavalry units had gone to war on

ABOVE: Four days before the opening Battle of Ia Drang (October 19, 1965), recently arrived Company A, 1st Battalion, 5th Cavalry Regiment of the 1st Cavalry (Airmobile) Division, move quickly through a rice paddy during a sweep for Viet Cong.

RIGHT: Another company of 1st Cavalry Division fans out along a mountain stream looking for tracks left by a Viet Cong unit in the area.

horses. During October and November, Kinnard flew the division into western Pleiku Province to prevent PAVN regular troops from cutting South Vietnam in two. In the Battle of Ia Drang Valley, the First Cavalry repulsed the North Vietnamese and demonstrated the effectiveness of air mobility. Kinnard lost 305 killed; the PAVN, 3,561. General William C. Westmoreland, commander of the U.S. Military Assistance Command, Vietnam, applauded the kill ratio of twelve enemy to one friendly, confirming his approach to war as one of "attrition." The Ia Drang campaign became Westmoreland's "dress rehearsal" for fighting the war in Vietnam.

Generals understood the reasons for success in the Ia Drang Valley: The First Cavalry was a crack division composed of regulars. Johnson and McNamara deluded themselves into believing that any American division could perform equally as well. Kinnard had trained his men for two years, they knew each other, and they knew how to fight. Soon draftees began flowing into Vietnam. They were men who did not know each other, resented being there, and had never fired a weapon in combat. They resisted discipline, resorted to drinking and drugs, and in rare instances hated their officers enough to murder them in combat. Aided by news correspondents and publicists reproaching the war, the quality of American soldiers sent to Vietnam continued to decline as numbers increased.

Among Johnson's military peculiarities was his refusal to call up the Army Reserve or the National Guard. Both organizations could have provided men and women of experience along with their equipment. For most of the war Johnson deprived the army of this rich resource of veterans, relying instead on inductees unfitted and unprepared for combat conditions in Vietnam.

The Expanding War

Had President Johnson understood the theory of equilibrium, he would have known that an equal or greater force would oppose whatever force he applied. Hence, the "ouch" factor worked both ways.

Operations in 1966 got off to a good start. In January the 173rd Airborne Brigade destroyed one VC battalion and headquarters of another in

HELICOPTERS AT WAR

More helicopters were used for more purposes during the Vietnam War than ever before. Although earlier 1950 designs found service in the Korean War, they could not compare with the highly specialized models introduced during the Vietnam conflict, where military operations could not be conducted without them.

In 1961, four years before Americans became directly involved in fighting, two companies of Piasecki CH-21 Shawnee helicopters arrived by carrier and twelve days later lifted 1,000 ARNV paratroopers in the first helicopter assault in Vietnam. After larger helicopters became available, the army used the Shawnees to evacuate casualties, supply outlying camps, and provide rapid transportation for the disposition of troops. By the end of 1964, the United States had more than 250 helicopters in Vietnam.

Boeing medium-life CH-47 Chinooks and Bell UH-1H "Hueys" became the army's all-purpose workhorses, making it possible for airmobile units to avoid ambushes along roads and trails infested by the enemy. At An Khe, General Kinnard used 434 helicopters. He divided them into a battalion of attack helicopters, a battalion of assault support helicopters, an aerial rocket artillery battalion, and an air cavalry squadron. The army used armor-plated Chinooks for transporting men, medical evacuation, artillery emplacement, aircraft retrieval, and supply. The Bell Huey, perhaps the most versatile of all helicopters, carried troops and provided gunship escort, using 2.75 inch folding-fin aerial rockets and 7.62 mm forward-firing machineguns. Hueys also performed command and control, medical evacuation, reconnaissance, radio relay, base security, and about any other task a unit commander required. Some Hueys, called "slicks," were used exclusively to transport troops and carried no external armament, only two M60 machineguns mounted in the ship's doors.

Bell AH-1 Cobras with 7.62 mm miniguns, 40 mm grenade launcher, 20 mm cannon, antitank missiles, and various rockets arrived later and replaced the slower, under-firepowered gunships such as the UH-1B "Hog" and the ACH-47A. A favorite of the First Air Cavalry Division, gunships made plenty of noise.

ABOVE: *On October 13, 1968, members of Company A, 2nd Battalion, 5th Cavalry, prepare to jump from a hovering UH-1D of Company B, 227th Assault Helicopter Battalion, during operations near Quang Tri.*

LEFT: *On May 27, 1967, a UH-1D of Company B, 229th Assault Helicopter Battalion, lifts off after delivering supplies to Company A, 1st Battalion, 7th Cavalry, during Operation Pershing.*

BELOW: *On May 28, 1967, UH-1D Hueys of Company B, 1st Battalion, 9th Cavalry, flare as they pick up members from the Aerorifle Platoon during Operation Pershing.*

Helicopter sorties (one flight by one aircraft)

Total number of sorties	36,125,000
Attack sorties	3,932,000
Assault troop sorties	7,547,000
Cargo sorties	3,548,000
Reconnaissance, search and rescue	21,098,000

The United States lost ten helicopters over North Vietnam and 2,066 in South Vietnam. The army lost 564 pilots killed in action and about double that number of aircrew were KIA. No branch of the service lost a higher per capita ratio of men than army helicopter flyers, but the emergency medical evacuation helicopter, manned by fearless crews, airlifted nine hundred thousand patients "from battlefields, rice paddies, destroyed villages, and jungles at all hours of the night or day, under all weather conditions, in the face of intense enemy fire."

ABOVE: On February 27, 1966, troopers of the 2nd Battalion, 502nd Infantry Regiment (Airborne), First Brigade, 101st Airborne, congregate at the pick-up zone for a combat air assault by UH-1D helicopters during Operation Harrison.

BELOW: On November 19, 1966, men of Company C, 1st Battalion, 327th Infantry Regiment (Airborne), First Brigade, 101st Airborne, carefully follow a stream in search of Viet Cong during Operation Geronimo.

Operation Marauder. In February the 101st Airborne, together with the Second ROK Marine Brigade and the Fourth ARVN Regiment, conducted a sweeping search-and-destroy operation against the VC in Phu Yen Province. The early success of these missions led to more, at times involving twenty thousand troops.

With the VC under persistent attack in South Vietnam, Ho Chi Minh sent PAVN reinforcements, using infiltration routes through Laos and Cambodia, thereby involving both countries in the war. In June and July, Johnson authorized strategic air strikes against oil installations around Hanoi and the port of Haiphong but excluded airfields, power plants, ships, and targets within cities for fear of killing a Chinese or Russian operative and possibly enlarging the war. By autumn the United States had assumed the principal role in fighting the war. In a ten-week operation ("Attleboro"), which began on September 14, 1966, twenty-two thousand U.S. troops engaged VC and PAVN troops along the Cambodian border northwest of Saigon and broke up a planned communist offensive. By December 31, 1966, American military strength had risen to 389,000 troops, about one hundred thousand more than McNamara had anticipated at the beginning of the year. More men were getting killed, and more were on the way.

Search-and-destroy operations continued through 1967. Marines mainly operated along the DMZ and in the northern provinces of South Vietnam while army units covered the rest of the country. VC/PAVN efforts to expand operations in South Vietnam met with no success, but they relentlessly kept coming. General Westmoreland poured more green troops into the conflict, and American casualties mounted. His troop demands reached unanticipated levels. During December the 101st Airborne Division, 10,024 men and more than fifty-three hundred tons

of equipment, undertook the greatest airlift in history, flying directly from Fort Campbell, Kentucky, to South Vietnam in 369 C-141 Starfighters and twenty-two C-133 Cargomasters.

The Tet Offensive

On July 6, 1967, top North Vietnam politburo officials met in Hanoi to discuss ways to turn the conflict their way. The war had not been going well for the communists because they could not compete with American firepower and mobility. During the discussions General Giap suggested a massive masterstroke, much like the one that overcame the French at Dienbienphu.

Giap borrowed his plan from Chinese communist doctrine, asserting that from a general offensive would come a general uprising, during which the people of South Vietnam would turn against the Saigon government and unite in the communist

ABOVE: A "Black Scarf" member of the 1st Battalion, 2nd Infantry Regiment, carries an ax and machete and head toward the jungle where the 1st Infantry Division is conducting operations north of Phnoc Vinh.

cause. Giap also predicted that American resolve to continue the war would then be shattered by political and military defections. The plan fitted nicely into Ho's strategy.

Giap set the general offensive for January 30, 1968, the beginning of the holiday celebrating the Lunar New Year. To conceal the plan, North Vietnam staged a number of pointless but deceptive offensives along the DMZ, such as the siege of Khe Sanh, to distract attention away from Saigon and Hue. The Khe Sanh envelopment succeeded in obsessing the president. He had a scale model of the firebase made, kept it in the White House situation room, and requested daily status reports.

Although in November troops of the 101st Airborne captured documents outlining Giap's general offensive, CIA intelligence dismissed the information as propaganda. Lieutenant General Frederick C. Weyand, commanding the II Field Force and the ARVN III Corps near Saigon, tied increased communist radio traffic together with the sudden decrease of skirmishing in his operating area and prepared for trouble. He warned General Westmoreland and reinforced his fourteen combat battalions with thirteen more. Weyand's adjustments came just in time.

On January 30, more than 60,000 VC and PAVN troops broke the Tet holiday truce and launched uncoordinated attacks on allied bases and South Vietnamese towns. Some assaults began twenty-four hours earlier than others, giving army commanders time to recall ARVN troops to their units. U.S. forces went on alert, and Giap lost the element of surprise at Saigon and Hue. The offensive struck six major cities, thirty-six of forty-four provincial capitals, and sixty-four of 245 district capitals. Except for Saigon, Hue, and Khe Sanh, the fighting quickly ended. On February 25 marines recaptured Hue. On March 7, though VC reached the grounds of the American

WILLIAM C. WESTMORELAND (1914–2005)

Born in Spartansburg County, South Carolina, on March 26, 1914, William Childs Westmoreland attended The Citadel for a year before entering West Point in 1932. Commissioned into the artillery, he fought in the major campaigns of World War II, distinguishing himself at the Kasserine Pass and as colonel in the Ninth Infantry Division in France and Germany.

In January 1964 Westmoreland arrived in South Vietnam, replacing General Paul D. Harkins as commander of the U.S. Military Assistance Command, Vietnam. He immediately observed that the South Vietnamese lacked a "sense of urgency." He expected his role in Vietnam to be one of action, not contemplation. In August 1964 Johnson promoted Westmoreland to full general. It was now Westmoreland's war, but with restrictions.

Westmoreland continued the strategy of search-and-destroy, which at first seemed to be the correct tactic for waging a politically limited war based upon the president's "ouch" theory. While the strategy cleansed some areas of VC activity, General Giap filled the voids with elements from the PAVN.

The flaw in Johnson-McNamara's "ouch" strategy, which involved political, economic, military, and other strategic restraints, conflicted with Westmoreland's efforts to win the war. While the general's MACV staff worked on applying more firepower and technology (such as the carcinogenic defoliant Agent Orange), the other strategy of pacification, which initially showed progress, took a back seat. While Westmoreland engaged the communists in a war of attrition, Ho Chi Minh patiently laid plans in North Vietnam to frustrate and damage the American will to sustain the war by flooding South Vietnam with more PAVN troops. What astonished Westmoreland, and disappointed Johnson, was the resilience of the enemy to escalate the war despite enormous losses.

Westmoreland's problems were not all his fault, but it was his misfortune to be responsible for implementing a defective strategy designed by civilians who never understood the nature of the enemy.

In July 1968, following the victorious repulse of the communist Tet offensive, President Johnson recalled Westmoreland and appointed him army chief of staff. General Creighton Abrams, Westmoreland's former deputy, carried out a new presidential decree: to honorably hand off the war to the South Vietnamese.

In July 1972 Westmoreland retired from the army after thirty-six years of service.

ABOVE: General William Childs Westmoreland (1914-2005), in charge of Military Assistance Command, Vietnam (MACV), sought a strategic solution to the growing Viet Cong/North Vietnamese Army capability and wanted to raise the ante at a time when the civilian organization under President Johnson wanted to open negotiations to end the conflict.

ABOVE: Although Vietnam is often thought of as an infantryman's war, tanks played an important part also. Here a Marine Corps M48A3 Patton tank from 3rd Platoon, Company A, 1st Tank Battalion, supports the 1st Battalion, 5th Marine Regiment during street fighting in Hue on February 12, 1968.

RIGHT: A 48.5-ton Patton M48A3 tank rumbles down the road at more than thirty miles per hour. The big tank carries a 90mm main gun, two .30-calibre machine guns, one .50-caliber machine gun, and a crew of five. Every crew "personalizes" their tank's searchlight covers.

General Westmoreland was unwilling to wait for Johnson to bungle a won war. His first objective was to ferret out and dispose of the few VC and PAVN units still operating in South Vietnam. His plans hit an obstacle when a White House staff member discovered that Westmoreland and JCS chairman General Earle Weaver were preparing a request for another 206,000 troops and leaked the story to the press. A *New York Times* account mentioned nothing about the army's impressive victory and misled the public into believing that more troops were needed to recover from a serious military setback during the Tet offensive.

North Korean officials and propagandists studied the news media's impact on American public opinion and turned it to their advantage. Speaking of the Tet offensive, military historian Brigadier General S. L.A. Marshall, who made several tours to Vietnam to study the progress of the war, credited the news media for turning "a potential major victory…into a disastrous defeat through mistaken estimates, loss of nerve, and a tidal wave of defeatism."

The Post-Tet Offensive

Faced with irresolute political maneuvering in Washington, General Westmoreland wasted no time in launching an all-out effort to bring the fighting in South Vietnam to a final conclusion. On April 8,

Embassy in Saigon, fighting sputtered out. On March 20 PAVN units assaulting Khe Sanh melted away after suffering ten weeks of superior firepower.

Despite reports to the contrary in the press, the Tet offensive resulted in a military disaster for the communists. More than fifty-eight thousand VC/PAVN troops died in the assaults. Although Giap achieved surprise, he could not exploit it. The general uprising never took place, and South Vietnam did not rally to the communist cause. The VC were virtually wiped out, and after Tet the continuance of the war fell mainly upon North Vietnam.

Giap's third assumption—that the American government would lose its will to fight—showed positive signs of happening. During the Tet offensive, Johnson could not decide what to do. On February 24 he ordered the bombing of Hanoi. Six weeks later he halted the bombing and announced that the United States would seek a negotiated settlement. Men like Westmoreland and Weyand were astonished. After giving the communists a crushing tactical defeat, it appeared that Johnson was about to reward the communists with an undeserved strategic victory.

1968, more than one hundred thousand men from forty-two U.S. and thirty-seven ARVN battalions went on the offensive against communist forces in eleven provinces around Saigon as part of Operation Complete Victory. Eleven days later the First Cavalry Division, 101st Airborne Division, First ARVN Division, and elements from other units launched another offensive, Operation Delaware, against communist bases in the northern provinces.

The impact of the offensives resonated in Hanoi, and on May 5 the communists launched a counter-offensive targeting 122 military installations, airfields, and major cities, including Saigon. The attacks all failed, and Westmoreland envisioned victory in South Vietnam.

In late 1967 Secretary of Defense McNamara, once a proponent for escalating the war, changed his mind and turned dovish. McNamara, however, had also begun to confuse the president as well as the army, pressing for a more aggressive war with additional troops on one hand and a gradual bailout on the other. Later, he admitted that he "misunderstood the nature of the conflict."

BELOW: Many variants of the M113 Armored Personnel Carriers (APCs) served in Vietnam, such as the armored ambulance designated the M577A1 Field Aid Station, or "Angel Track," operating with the 11th Armored Cavalry Regiment, the largest U.S. Army armored formation to serve in Vietnam.

THE MY LAI MASSACRE

Following on the heels of the Tet offensive came the infamous My Lai (Song My) massacre. On March 16, 1968, more than two hundred unarmed Vietnamese civilians were slaughtered by U.S. soldiers of Company C, First Battalion, Twentieth Infantry Regiment, Eleventh Infantry Brigade, Twenty-third (American) Division. The division had been thrown together with a mixture of ad hoc brigades during the U.S. military buildup and suffered, by many accounts, from weak leadership that originated with division commander Major General Samuel H. Koster. Elements from Colonel Oran K. Henderson's Eleventh Brigade, dubbed by soldiers in other units as the "Butcher Brigade," had earned the reputation of being merely "bands of thugs."

Captain Ernest Medina of Charlie Company commanded one of those bands with his sidekick, platoon commander First Lieutenant William L. Calley, Jr. The unit specialized in airmobile search-and-destroy missions. On March 16, Medina planned to arrive at My Lai after the local women had departed for market. They expected to find elements of the Forty-eighth VC Local Force Battalion in the area. Instead, they found only women, children, and old men cooking breakfast.

For inexplicable reasons, Calley's platoon lost control and opened fire on the villagers. Those who escaped the initial firing were systematically rounded up, led to a ditch, and executed. The platoon continued to search through the village, setting fire to huts and killing everyone in sight. Warrant Officer Hugh Thompson, who had flown part of Medina's company to My Lai, observed what was happening on the ground and landed his helicopter between Calley's platoon and fleeing villagers, thus ending the massacre.

A year later an army board under Lieutenant General William Peers investigated the incident. The board was unable to find any specific reason for Company C's action. General Peers cited the frustrations of soldiers seeing buddies killed by snipers, mines, and booby traps as contributory, but he focused his sharpest criticism on thirty persons, mostly officers and the division commander, who knew about the atrocities but suppressed the incident. A small museum at My Lai claims that 504 civilians were killed that day. Despite the attention given to the incident by the media and Hollywood, such misconduct was extremely rare.

Charges against fourteen men were eventually dismissed or acquitted by court-martial except those against Lieutenant Calley, who became the unit's scapegoat and was sentenced to life imprisonment. In 1974 President Richard M. Nixon released Calley on parole.

ABOVE: On 23 January 1966, Lieutenant Daniel Hill of Company B, 2nd Battalion, 327th Infantry Regiment, First Brigade, 101st Airborne Division, sets fire to a village hut during Operation Van Buren. Such acts alienated U.S. forces from the rural population.

BELOW: Patrolling the swamps and jungles became a matter of watchful endurance for the infantry because the enemy always lay well-hidden and was always ready to take advantage of any lack of vigilance on the soldier's part.

BELOW: Early in the Vietnam conflict, the standard army M16 5.56mm assault rifle caused repeated problems due to stoppages. Toward the latter 1960s, the army introduced the M16A1, an improved model that overcame earlier problems and proved an excellent weapon for jungle operations.

So in January 1968, on the eve of the Tet offensive, Johnson brought in a trusted friend, Clark M. Clifford, as the new secretary of defense. In 1960 Clifford had not opposed involvement in Vietnam, and as recently as November 1967 he had urged Johnson to stand firm in Vietnam. When in the same month McNamara issued a memorandum advocating a negotiated peace, Clifford opposed it. Then came the Tet offensive. After General Westmoreland requested 206,000 more troops and the press misrepresented the request to the public, Clifford met with the staff of so-called "Wise Men," and against the advice of well-informed administration hawks, told Johnson that the United States could not attain its objectives in Vietnam and should begin peace negotiations. Johnson recalled Westmoreland, whose operations in April had begun to cleanse South Vietnam of communists, and replaced him with General Abrams.

On May 10, 1968, Johnson announced the first Paris peace talks between the United States and North Vietnam. He also announced that he would not seek another term as president. The peace talks abruptly ended during the summer when communists launched a third offensive. Johnson resumed B-52 bombing operations north of the DMZ and along Cambodian infiltration routes. When North Vietnam expressed interest in resuming peace negations, Johnson ordered a cessation of air, naval, and ground bombardments. As the president soon learned, these breaks merely provided time for the PAVN to stockpile supplies for future operations.

General Abrams clearly understood North Vietnam's strategy and his predecessor's mistakes. He discontinued Westmoreland's search-and-destroy tactics and reliance on body count as a measure of the enemy's attrition. He concentrated on population security, pacification, unifying combat operations, and upgrading South Vietnamese forces with better weapons and better training. He also discovered that the enemy could not wage an offensive without first stockpiling ammunition and supplies in a forward base because they lacked the transportation for sustaining logistics. Instead of large search-and-destroy missions, Abrams sent small-unit patrols into the interior to preempt offensives by destroying the enemy's forward logistics dumps, which were usually hidden by guerrillas operating in scattered hamlets and villages.

Abrams' operations against North Vietnamese infiltration routes eventually resulted in the Battle of "Hamburger Hill" in Quang Tri Province near the DMZ. On May 11, 1969, in one of the rare occasions of the war, entrenched PAVN regulars attempted to stand against the Third Battalion, 187th Infantry, on a lump of ground called Hill 937. After several unsuccessful assaults over a three-day period, the 3/187th called for reinforcements. The 101st Airborne sent in two brigades, along with a battalion from the Third ARVN. On May 18 a two-battalion assault took the summit but were driven off by torrential rain. Finally on May 20, after ten previous tries, a four-battalion assault drove the PAVN off the mountain and into Laos, leaving piles of corpses behind minced like hamburger. Once the PAVN withdrew from the hill, U.S. forces abandoned it as well. A few days later PAVN forces moved back to the hill unimpeded. Although only fifty-six Americans and five South Vietnamese were killed in the action, as opposed to 630 of the enemy, the media used the seemingly useless battle to symbolize the frustration of men dying to win tactical battles without ever achieving strategic victory.

Congress viewed photographs of 241 Americans killed in action during the battle for Hamburger Hill. Although most of the men had been killed somewhere else, the media lumped the deaths into the publicity ginned up over Hamburger Hill. In 1987 the public digested an embellished version of the battle when Paramount Pictures released *Hamburger Hill* as a major motion picture.

On April 30, 1969, U.S. forces in Vietnam peaked at 543,482 men and women. Antiwar correspondents clamored again when on June 8 twenty-five-year-old First Lieutenant Sharon A. Lane, a member of the Army Nurse Reserve Corps, became the only American woman killed by enemy fire in Vietnam. Bad publicity, pacifists, and Hamburger Hill led to the limitation of military operations in South Vietnam, the beginning of troop withdrawals, and the Vietnamization of the war.

The Beginning of the End

On January 20, 1969, Richard M. Nixon became the thirty-seventh president of the United States. His association with Vietnam traced back to October 1953, when as vice president in the Eisenhower administration he visited French Indo-China, observed the spread of communism, and in April 1954 urged dropping three tactical atomic bombs on Viet Minh positions at Dienbienphu. Eisenhower refused. Nixon then urged the president to send more technicians and supplies. Again Eisenhower refused. In 1968 Nixon emerged again, this time as an unlikely Republican candidate for president. Having

nothing to gain by confronting the Vietnam issue head-on, he concentrated his efforts on denouncing Johnson's domestic record, which lay in shambles. Prodded by the news media on Vietnam, Nixon said he had a "secret plan" to end the war, though later he admitted having nothing.

After inauguration Nixon declared that ending the Vietnam War would be his first priority. He believed that by continuing an aggressive war, as Johnson had done, Ho Chi Minh would ultimately achieve the objective of a unified Vietnam under communist rule. With peace talks under way, he suspended the bombing of North Vietnam and on May 14, 1969, announced a planned withdrawal from South Vietnam. The announcement led to the so-called "Nixon Doctrine," which turned problems in Asia over to Asian nations, "except for the threat of a major power involving nuclear weapons." Most observers interpreted the statement to mean that Nixon intended to abandon South Vietnam as soon as U.S. troops withdrew.

Instead of allowing peaceful negotiations, North Vietnam launched a summer offensive. Nixon responded by authorizing a resumption of bombing in North Vietnam and along the Ho Chi Minh Trail in Laos. By the end of 1969, Nixon was back to fighting a Johnson-style limited war, though he reduced U.S. forces in Vietnam by fifty thousand men and turned the responsibility for the defense of Saigon over South Vietnamese forces. Nixon denied any intention to abandon Vietnam, but the process had begun.

In 1970 President Johnson's war became President Nixon's war. Instead of negotiating a settlement, which North Vietnam seemed unready to discuss in light of America's reduction in forces, Nixon once again intensified the bombing of North Vietnam and expanded the war into Laos and Cambodia. However, another 150,000 American troops came home as further Vietnamization progressed.

ABOVE: 105mm howitzer firing from a fire support base.

ABOVE: Machinegun team clears a blockage during a firefight.

BELOW: A truck-mounted, M55 Quad .50 turret. The quads were mounted on M35- and M54-series trucks, but because of the absence of an air threat, they were used effectively in ground fighting. This is a reenactment photograph.

U.S. Military Strength and Combat Deaths in Vietnam		
Year ending	Military Strength	Combat Deaths
1965	154,000	1,636
1966	389,000	4,771
1967	480,000	9,699
1968	536,040	14,437
1969	484,326	6,727
1970	335,794	7,171
1971	158,119	942
1972	24,200	531

Maximum Deployed Strength: Army	
Deployed	440,691
Killed/died of wounds	30,644
Wounded	76,811
POWs/MIAs	2,904
Total combat casualties	130,359
Non-battle deaths	7,173

BELOW: President Richard M. Nixon (left) and Secretary of State Henry A. Kissinger became the architects of the Vietnam pullout, which Nixon announced on January 20, 1973, during inauguration day ceremonies.

On January 15, 1973, in response to Secretary of State Henry A. Kissinger's October 26, 1972, statement that "peace is at hand," President Nixon announced a halt to all offensive military action, including air strikes, shelling, and ground operations. The cease-fire agreement, signed eight days later, provided for the release of all U.S. prisoners of war, the withdrawal of remaining U.S. troops, and the establishment of an international force to supervise the truce.

The Abrams Legacy

No army general spent more time in Vietnam than General Creighton "Abe" Abrams, who arrived in 1967 and on July 3, 1968, superseded General Westmoreland as Commander, Military Assistance Command, Vietnam. His strategy and tactics, built around a theory of continuous night and day small "clear-and-hold" operations instead of occasional massive "search-and-destroy" missions, led to concentration on enemy bases of power and control of the population. He believed that the outcome of a war could never be decided until "both sides [were] fighting the same war," which was not quite the case in Vietnam, where different and inconsistent political agendas influenced strategy and outcome. Abrams contended with the same military and political limitations as did Westmoreland, but he found the key to fighting future wars. One diplomat, who observed the true genius in Abrams, remarked that the general "deserved a better war."

In June 1972 Abrams left Vietnam to become army chief of staff. He never wanted to see another Vietnam war where allies in collusion with corrupt members of the armed forces robbed commissaries, munitions dumps, and post exchanges, or a war where drug traffic boomed, red-light ghettos thrived, and venereal rates climbed to seven hundred cases per thousand. Abrams witnessed it all, and when he became chief of staff he concentrated on reform, readiness in all departments of the army, and in particular, the welfare and security of the American soldier.

Abrams passed away in 1974, but he left a legacy born of the Vietnam War. General John W. Vessey, chairman of the JCS (1982–1985), said it best: "When Americans watched the stunning success of our armed forces in Desert Storm, they were watching the Abrams vision in action. The modern equipment, the effective air support, the use of reserve components and, most of all, the advanced training which taught our people how to stay alive on the battlefield were all seeds planted by Abe."

Had Abrams lived another year, it might have been interesting to hear his comments when on April 30, 1975, Saigon fell to advancing North Vietnamese troops. During Operation Frequent Wind—the helicopter evacuation of the few remaining Americans in Saigon—the last two U.S. troops died supporting a cause they probably never understood.

PRISONERS OF WAR

In February and March 1973, 565 U.S. military and twenty-six civilians were released from North Vietnam prisons. At the time forty thousand communist prisoners were held in South Vietnam. About seventy U.S. prisoners died in POW camps: two were murdered, three died from brutality, and three perished from substandard medical care. At this time twenty-five hundred men were listed as missing in action (MIA).

Shot down on March 26, 1964, while flying a light reconnaissance plane, army Special Forces Caption Floyd James Thompson emerged as the longest held surviving POW of the war.

American prisoners were held in eleven North Vietnam prisons, four in Hanoi, six outside the city, and one near the Chinese border. POWs banded together, pledging to maintain a record that would reflect well upon themselves, the U.S. military, and the nation. Prison-camp authorities applied every means to extract intelligence, including torture, isolation, and psychological abuse. Prisoners were locked in stocks, malnourished, and bounced from one camp to another. In 1969, after Ho Chi Minh died and Nixon began withdrawals of American troops, torture ended and camps conditions improved. Only one American defected, Marine Private Robert R. Garwood. He returned to the United States in 1979 to face court-martial.

On March 29, 1973, when President Nixon announced "all our American POWs are on their way home," questions were raised about why there were so few. Conversely, the ratio of twenty-five hundred MIAs to seventy POWs made no sense to most Americans. The plot thickened when Private Garwood returned to the states and admitted seeing up to seventy Americans still being held against their will. In 1987 retired General John Vessey arrived in Vietnam to investigate the MIA matter but found the Vietnamese reluctant to provide information they previously denied having. POW/MIA affairs still remain clouded with more than two thousand Americans still listed as missing in action.

ABOVE: President Johnson never bombed downtown Hanoi, leaving the Hilton Hotel untouched by war.

BELOW: Secretary of Defense Melvin R. Laird visits the 82nd Airborne Division at Fort Bragg, North Carolina, to decorate soldiers and airmen who participated in the November 20–21, 1970, raid on the Son Tay prisoner of war compound (see below right).

CHAPTER 8
ENEMIES OLD AND NEW 1975–2005

BELOW: The United Nations, organized in San Francisco on June 26, 1945, seemed a brilliant war-ending idea at the time. Five years later the Korean War erupted, and others soon followed. The United States remains the backbone of the UN military force. Here a few Americans in the forward lines during the Korean War watch as shells explode on Communist positions.

On October 24, 1945, the United Nations Charter, ratified by twenty-nine nations, came into being and replaced the League of Nations, which on April 18, 1946, voted itself out of existence. The founding nations then established a twelve-member Security Council, in which China, France, Great Britain, the USSR, and the U.S. became permanent members. Major responsibilities of the UN included international peacekeeping and disarmament using tools of negotiation, diplomatic leverage, and the collective military assets of its members. The effectiveness of the UN on arms reduction varied over time and included nuclear test-ban treaties; agreements on the limitation of strategic weapons, such as nuclear arms, anti-ballistic missiles, biological, and chemical weapons; and treaties such as the Strategic Arms Limitations Talks (SALT). Four decades of UN-inspired negotiations did not stop the Cold War, the Korean War, the Vietnam War, or a hundred other mini-wars where governments or people believed they had a political, geographic, religious, or ethnic reason to rebel or make war.

The UN never had a reliable force of peacekeepers and relied mainly upon the five permanent members of the Security Council for manpower and weapons.

Those same five members often caused the problems, but not always, and some members consistently failed to provide military or peacekeeping resources for political reasons. Over time, China, France, the United Kingdom (U.K.), the USSR, and the United States managed to avoid fighting each other by creating an arsenal of nuclear technology capable of destroying civilization. During that same period of time, the UN became a massive bureaucracy with diminishing effectiveness and creeping corruption as more nations became members. As UN peacekeeping efforts became less efficient, the United States and the United Kingdom became increasingly involved in containing aggression and repelling international terrorism. The tools available for national defense and peacekeeping depended heavily on the decisions of national leaders.

Jimmy Carter and National Defense

Into the equation of international peacekeeping stepped former Georgia governor—as well as Annapolis graduate and onetime naval nuclear engineer—Jimmy Carter, who on January 20, 1977, became the thirty-ninth president of the United States. Carter believed deeply in a world at peace and the covenants of the United Nations. Having distanced himself from the Vietnam War and the shenanigans of the Nixon administration, Carter entered the White House as a fresh breath of air. He attempted to improve international relations and curb the proliferation of nuclear weapons. On June 18,

1979, he signed the SALT II agreement, but made the mistake of trying to set the example by reducing outlays for national defense. He cut the B-1 bomber program because he believed cruise missiles would be cheaper. He restricted the navy's shipbuilding plans and retarded the application of new technology. He axed the neutron bomb, and then allowed production of some parts. He prolonged procurement of tactical aircraft, MX missiles, and reduced spending for the standing army, its weapons, and its maintenance. The public applauded the cutbacks. Soaring domestic inflation, coupled with the impression that the military had lost the Vietnam War, set national defense initiatives back about five years.

In office six weeks, Carter experienced his first run-in with the army on March 9, 1977, when he announced that all U.S. ground troops (numbering thirty-two thousand) and tactical missiles were to be withdrawn from South Korea. The order touched off a controversy with Major General John K. Singlaub, who criticized the plan because of increased Soviet activity. Carter removed Singlaub from Korea and commenced the withdrawal. In December 1979, when the Soviet Union invaded Afghanistan, Carter cancelled the order.

Carter's optimistic hopes of a more peaceful future were shattered by disturbances in the Middle East and by his own miscalculations. By withdrawing support for the Shah of Iran, he opened the door for the return of Ayatollah Ruhollah Khomeini, the exiled and embittered senior Iranian Shiite cleric living in Paris. On January 16, 1979, the shah departed from Iran, and Khomeini returned to set up an Islamic republic. Rebellion and civil strife followed in the provinces, with uprisings expanding into Azerbaijan and Kurdistan. On November 3, 1979, Iranian militants broke into the U.S. Embassy compound at Tehran and took ninety hostages, among them sixty-six Americans. On December 2 another mob stormed the U.S.

LEFT: The M113 armored personnel carrier evolved through the 1960s from a gas-powered to a diesel-powered engine. In the 1970s, the M113A2 emerged with improved suspension and cooling. Again upgraded in the 1980s, modified M113s continued to play a key role during the Cold War.

Embassy at Tripoli, Libya, but took no hostages. UN negotiators failed to get the prisoners released from Iran. Carter's efforts failed also. Nobody recognized the hostage seizures in 1979 as acts of growing Islamic terrorism. Twenty-six years later, when Mahmoud Ahmadinejad became president of Iran, some of the

LEFT: The M60 main battle tank pictured here evolved from the M26 Pershing medium tank that first saw combat in Europe toward the end of World War II. The M26 evolved into the M46 Patton, followed by the M47, M48, and during the latter years of the Cold war, the M60, which were still seeing service during Desert Storm. By 1997, more than 15,000 had been built.

former embassy employees recognized him as being the leader of the hostage-takers.

On March 1, 1980, after awakening to the realities of a dangerous world and while campaigning for reelection, Carter agreed to the formation of a Rapid Deployment Force composed of one hundred thousand men (later two hundred thousand) from crack units of the army and the Marine Corps. Their mission was to respond and deploy quickly with naval and air support to crisis situations around the world. Reminded daily by headlines and magazine photos of the hostage crisis in Iran, Carter thought he had the perfect place to try his rapid deployment experiment and authorized Operation Blue Light, better known as "Desert One."

Desert One

On April 24, 1980, army Colonel Charles Beckwith organized a dangerous mission to rescue fifty-three hostages still held in Tehran. The complicated operation required six USAF C-130 transports flying from Egypt to rendezvous with eight commando-carrying navy RH-53D helicopters flying from the USS *Nimitz* and meet at a spot in the desert 200 miles from Tehran. President Carter had not taken very good care of his military assets. Two helicopters were forced to turn back because of mechanical trouble, and a third helicopter conked out after landing at Desert One.

Colonel Beckwith needed a minimum of six helicopters to perform the rescue, and having only five, he cancelled the operation. When withdrawing from the site, one of the remaining helicopters collided with a fuel-laden C-130 on the ground and killed five airmen and three marines. An official investigation justifiably criticized the mission's planning and command arrangements. Some called it Jimmy Carter's bad luck. The hostage crisis had already hurt America's international standing, and

under the Carter administration the U.S. government appeared weak and irresolute. The debacle at Desert One merely reinforced international opinion

Ronald Reagan Takes Control

On January 20, 1981, former governor of California and Hollywood actor Ronald Reagan became the fortieth president of the United States. He pledged to undo everything Jimmy Carter did wrong, and that was enough to ensure his election. Although Carter took steps to improve the military during the last year of his administration, his good intentions were not enough to convince the public that he had the ability to solve the nation's problems. Reagan promised to rearm America

and challenge the "Evil Empire," his favorite expression when referring to the Soviet Union.

Reagan faced an enormous task burdened by years of neglect. He understood the importance of creating an organization of competent military advisers and built a team around Secretary of Defense Caspar Weinberger, Secretary of the Army John O. Marsh (an infantry veteran), Chairman of the JCS General John W. Vessey, Jr., (an infantry division commander during the Vietnam War), and Army Chief of Staff General Edward C. Meyer (an advocate for reviving Special Forces).

Reagan began his first term by placing emphasis on weapons procurement. He reversed Carter's decision to defer production of the neutron bomb and on August 10, 1981, authorized full production on enhanced radiation weapons. He wanted nuclear devices that could be fitted to Lance missiles or deployed as eight-inch artillery shells. On October 2 he also reversed Carter's cancellation of the B-1 bomber and ordered them into production to replace the aging B-52 force. Carter had authorized the development of a "Stealth" bomber in the latter months of his administration but allowed the sensitive information to be leaked to the press for political gain prior to the national election. Reagan put the program on track for completion in the 1980s. He announced a new basing mode for MX intercontinental ballistic missiles (ICBMs) in hardened silos, accelerated the building of the Trident submarine, and stepped up the program for developing and producing better Pershing and Tomahawk cruise missile systems.

In an address on March 23, 1983, Reagan stunned Congress by announcing that the United States would pursue the feasibility of perfecting an antiballistic missile (ABM) defense system from outer space. Critics derided the "Star Wars Speech" as delusional, but supporters applauded the concept as

an important step in overcoming the mutually assured destruction mentality that dominated strategic thinking for the past two decades. Formed around an anti-ICBM space-based laser or energy beam defense system, the project, named the "Strategic Defense Initiative" (SDI), received stiff opposition from Congress. It also created immense alarm in the Soviet Union because it trampled on existing ABM agreements, which was precisely what Reagan intended.

Reagan also placed emphasis on increasing pay and benefits to a diminished standing army penalized by years of spiraling inflation. Too many exceptional but disaffected professionals in all ranks had either retired early or resigned to take more lucrative jobs in the civilian sector. The 1980 attempt to free hostages from Tehran demonstrated the weakness of the army to plan and successfully execute multi-service operations. In 1983, when Soviet and Cuban operatives attempted build a communist base on the tiny Caribbean island of Grenada, General John A. Wickham, Jr., the thirty-first army chief of staff, used the opportunity for intervention to study the level of the army's efficiency.

Rebuilding Professionalism

The importance of Urgent Fury lay in its impetus to refocus military attention on command and communication problems. Reagan established pools of "thinkers" and "reformers" to study ways of improving military preparedness and defense measures. The so-called "Military Reform Movement" met at West Point and concluded that army doctrine based upon the concept of "attrition warfare" had to be radically modified to "maneuver warfare." Army chief of staff General Wickham responded to the recommendations and began revising army doctrine to include emphasis on maneuver, defense in depth, offensive warfare concepts, and long-range strikes by deep interdiction

ABOVE: President Ronald Reagan at General John W. Vessey, Jr's retirement ceremony at Andrews Air Force Base in September 1985.

OPERATION URGENT FURY—GRENADA

On March 13, 1979, Maurice Bishop seized power of the former British colony of Grenada and established a socialist dictatorship. He sought ties with Cuba and the Soviet Union and soon had Russian construction workers and advisers at work on a new airport suitable for landing military planes. In October 1983 Bishop became dissatisfied with Cuban insolence and considered switching allegiance to the United States. Deputy Prime Minister Bernard Coard assumed power in a coup d'état and on October 19 stood by as assassins murdered Bishop.

On an appeal from Caribbean nations for help, President Reagan ordered U.S. forces to invade Grenada, uproot Cuban troops converting the island into a military base, evacuate six hundred U.S. students attending St. George's University Medical School, and stabilize the island.

Vice Admiral Joseph Metcalf III drew the assignment and hurriedly assembled a force of six thousand troops, including marines, army rangers, and elements from the 82nd Airborne Division. Metcalf launched Urgent Fury from the USS *Guam*, one of several ships carrying helicopter assault troops. At 5:00 A.M. on October 25, marines landed at Pearls Airport on the northern side of the island, stormed gun positions manned by Cubans, and secured the airfield. At the same hour, army rangers jumped from C-130 Hercules transports from an altitude of 500 feet into stiffer resistance at the Point Salinas airfield. A third force of three thousand men came ashore later in amphibious craft.

The final outcome of the operation was never in doubt (there were only one thousand Grenadian troops and about six hundred Cubans), but U.S. command coordination demonstrated how badly inter-service communications had deteriorated since Vietnam. The military had not decided on a policy of "jointness" when communicating between different service branches, and all the problems surfaced on Grenada. Several preventable friendly fire accidents occurred. Nor was there a single service commander on the ground to make tactical decisions. One soldier embellished the problems by reporting that his team had to use a pay phone to call the United States in order to patch in a navy fire controller. Although incredible communication and logistics foul-ups marred the entire operation, army and marine forces secured the island in sixty hours.

U.S. forces lost 18 killed and 83 wounded in Grenada, compared with enemy losses of 36 killed, 66 wounded, and 655 captured. Most Grenadian troops simply faded into the civilian population. In addition to Russians and Cubans, U.S. forces found North Koreans, East Germans, Bulgarians, and Libyans among the prisoners.

ABOVE LEFT: On October 25, 1983 U.S. Army rangers gather themselves together and move out on patrol from Salinas airport, Grenada.

ABOVE RIGHT: On October 28, 1983, on returning from Grenada, 1st Lieutenant Raymond A. Thomas, Sergeant Michael H. Cameron, and Private Allan S. Bishop (left to right) of the 2nd Battalion, 75th Rangers, receive the Combat Infantryman's Badge from army chief of staff General John A. Wickham, Jr.

BELOW LEFT: On October 25, 1983, troopers from the 82nd Airborne open fire on Cuban soldiers.

BELOW RIGHT: Rangers watch over Cuban prisoners, who surrendered in droves.

with weapons of increasing range. Because every new program required a name, the army called it "AirLand Battle" doctrine. Congress supported the program because it contained their ideas.

Reagan accepted General Wickham's recommendations and in the mid-1980s re-structured four regular army divisions into light divisions. These units became the Sixth, Seventh, and Twenty-fifth Light Infantry and the Tenth Mountain (Light Infantry) divisions. They were small divisions, having only 10,500 personnel. Lightly armed and equipped, they were extremely mobile compared with a conventional infantry division, and required fewer sorties to deploy than the two standing airborne divisions (82nd and 101st).

Midway through Reagan's second term, Congress passed sweeping defense legislation (Goldwater-Nichols Defense Reorganization Act) that supported much of the president's thinking. The chairman of the JCS became the senior military advisor to both the president and the secretary of defense, and the newly created position of vice chairman of the JCS became the second ranking officer in the military hierarchy. In addition to the chairman and vice chairman, the JCS included the chief of staff of the army, the chief of naval operations, the chief of staff of the air force, and the commandant of the Marine Corps. Each member had a supporting staff. The chairman was responsible to the secretary of defense for strategic direction and planning, contingency planning, programming, budgeting for military equipment, the development of joint doctrine, and the education and training for the employment of joint forces provided by each of the services. The chairman was also responsible for providing communication links between the secretary of defense, the president, and the unified commands. This legislation reverted the JCS from being a collegial body of officers, which occurred during the Johnson-Nixon-Carter administrations, to a true joint-service general staff with a single chief of staff. The wisdom of this change became manifest after the Iraqi invasion of Kuwait in 1990 and remains in effect and functional today.

Having served the maximum two terms as president, President Reagan departed from the White House in January 1989 and turned the reins of government over to George H. W. Bush. During his term as president, Reagan had rebuilt the military and negotiated the first major nuclear arms reduction agreement with the Soviet Union since the 1972 SALT Treaty. Having forced the USSR into an arms race, Reagan's policies eventually bankrupted the Soviet government and brought an end to the forty-year Cold War.

When Bush entered the White House in 1989, his problems were much different than those confronted by Reagan. He had a much different background than Reagan, having been a navy pilot during World War II, ambassador to the United Nations, a director of the CIA, a member of the House of Representatives, and for eight years Ronald Reagan's vice president. He understood the military and became an important factor in its resurrection. He also understood international politics and aided Soviet Premier Mikhail Gorbachev in officially ending the Cold War. Little did Bush realize that his first military problem would occur in Central America.

The New Army

Much had changed since the 1960s and the 1970s. President Reagan had built a standing army of 781,000 volunteers serving careers in armor, cavalry, air cavalry, mechanized infantry, light infantry, airborne, ranger, Special Forces, aviation, and artillery. Backing up the regulars were 261,000 reservists trained in combat, combat-support, and

BELOW: As missile technology advanced, so did antiaircraft/antimissile technology. During Desert Storm, the U.S. Army Air Defense Artillery deployed 29 Patriot missile batteries in the Middle East to shoot down Russian-made Iraqi Scud missiles. Official army figures claim 49 hits in 51 launches.

OPERATION JUST CAUSE—PANAMA

The Vietnam War accelerated international trafficking in drugs, which gave President George H. W. Bush a more insidious war to fight. One-time CIA informant Manuel A. Noriega, former chief of intelligence for the Panamanian Defense Force, took control of the military after the death General Omar Torrijos. In February 1988 federal grand juries in Miami and Tampa, Florida, indicted Noriega for running drugs. When Panamanian President Eric A. Delvalle attempted to arrest the general, Noriega ousted him. After voting on May 10, 1989, went against Noriega's candidate, the general nullified the election. President Bush became concerned and increased U.S. forces in the Canal Zone.

On December 16, 1989, Panamanian soldiers armed with AK-47s opened fire on four unarmed American officers driving to a restaurant. One officer died; another was wounded. On December 17 President Bush authorized Operation Just Cause, and Secretary of Defense Richard B. Cheney put twelve thousand men serving in the Canal Zone on heightened alert.

Bush handed the mission to army General Maxwell Thurman, who immediately mobilized a force of 22,500 marine and army troops. At 1:00 A.M. on December 20, armored vehicles from the Fifth Mechanized Infantry Division and attack helicopters moved out from bases in the Canal Zone. At the same time, C-130 and C-141 transports flew in the Second Brigade of the 82nd Airborne Division from Fort Bragg, North Carolina, and the Seventh Light Infantry Division from Fort Ord, California. The objective: to apprehend General Noriega and neutralize the six thousand-man Panamanian Defense Force.

Thurman divided the environs of Panama City into four tactical zones. A small force of marines took one sector; the army covered the rest, which included Panama City and the entire Canal Zone.

U.S forces swiftly overcame resistance in the capital and the countryside but were confronted with widespread looting in shopping areas. Snipers became active as U.S. forces began door-to-door searches for Noriega. On December 22 President Bush offered a $1 million reward for information leading to the capture of Noriega and dispatched another twenty-five army troops to aid in the search. On December 24 the Vatican Embassy in Panama City admitted sheltering Noriega but refused to hand him over. On January 3, 1990, the haggard Panamanian dictator surrendered to U.S. troops and was immediately flown to Florida for arraignment. By then twenty-three U.S. troops had been killed and 220 wounded, some from friendly fire.

In the aftermath the U.S., France, and the U.K vetoed an attempt by the UN Security Council to condemn the invasion. Panamanian drug smuggling, however, never stopped.

On December 20, 1989, elements from the 82nd Airborne parachuted onto Panama's airfield during Operation Just Cause and soon came under fire at the terminal.

TOP: The M110A2 eight-inch howitzer was the most accurate filed artillery weapon in the army inventory and could fire a 200-pound projectile almost 17 kilometers.

ABOVE: The M107 175mm self-propelled gun sits in the same chassis as the M110 above and fires a 174-pound projectile almost 33 kilometers, twice the distance of a M110 projectile.

general-support. They supplemented the regulars in all battalions but air cavalry, airborne infantry, motorized infantry, and ranger units. Another 285,000 men and women served in the Individual Ready Reserve and were subject to call according to their military occupational specialties.

The National Guard, numbering more than 452,000 men and women, were better trained and better equipped than ever before. Guardsmen were expected to be deployable thirty to sixty days after call-up. They totaled 43 percent of the army's combat units and 20 percent of its support units. Like reservists, they carried the latest weaponry and equipment and were developing the skills necessary to become helicopter pilots.

As the army grew in size and strength, it regained public support. Educational standards improved and revitalized the Reserved Officer Training Corps

(ROTC), which had originated with the National Defense Act of 1916. Although the reserved officer served as the backbone of army combat leadership in World War II and the Korean War, changing public attitudes in the 1960s and 1970s had devastated the program. The Reagan administration put ROTC back on track, and between 1986 and 1990, thirty-two thousand men and women received commissions in the U.S. Army, National Guard, or Army Reserve.

Until 1987 Special Forces had been spread about different commands. On April 9 Secretary of the Army Marsh approved the establishment of a Special Forces. Marsh integrated into Special Forces soldiers who were technically and tactically proficient, expert at performing insertion missions, and capable of foreign internal operations. Special warfare schools formed rangers and other SF groups into a single integrated fighting concept consistent with the new AirLand Battle doctrine, thereby ensuring unanimity of action and purpose in any future emergency.

AirLand Battle Doctrine

The AirLand Battle concept had been knocked about since 1976 as a fundamental warfighting doctrine. Although the concept resurfaced in 1982, it remained unsettled until 1986 when army leaders realized that the service needed a more flexible doctrine with stronger interservice integration. The doctrine resulted from a changing approach to the battlefield, which could no longer be viewed from a ground-based perspective but must be seen as one employing airpower in conjunction with ground operations.

AirLand Battle centered on strong and fluid interservice coordination in three phases: "deep" (forward of friendly troops), "close" (the main battle area), and "rear" (behind the combat force). "Deep" meant attacking enemy forces with combined air assets and long-range artillery, thereby wearing down the enemy before it could engage in "close" combat.

"Deep" also meant the deployment of Special Forces behind enemy lines for disrupting communications, intelligence gathering, targeting, and special mission assignments. Army tacticians believed a smaller force could always defeat a much larger force by following AirLand Battle doctrine.

The New Weapons

Reagan put money into firepower and mobility. Heading the list of new armored vehicles were M1A1 Abrams main battle tanks, named for the general who preached mobility. Thirty-five battalions of

the behemoths had been formed during Reagan's administration with more scheduled for the early 1990s. The M1A1 incorporated a fifteen hundred horsepower diesel turbine engine, chobham armor, a ballistic computer, and a laser rangefinder with thermal imagery. The tank carried two machine guns and a highly accurate 120 mm cannon that could

BELOW: The Bradley Infantry Fighting Vehicle replaced the M113 APC and, in addition to a 25mm cannon, provided the added capability of launching Stinger missiles. The Bradley has a crew of three and can transport a six-man fully equipped infantry squad.

BELOW: On August 1, 2004, a Bradley M2A3 and a Humvee of the 39th Brigade Combat Team goes on patrol near Al Taji in Iraq. The Bradley wears active and passive armor panels on hull front and sides and has a complex viewing system on the turret.

ABOVE: *The Army Tactical Missile System (ATACMS) consists of ground-launched missile systems featuring surface-to-surface guided missiles that can hurl an antipersonnel/antimateriel (APAM) warhead deep into enemy territory.*

BELOW: *A Patriot missile roars from its launcher. Although primarily employed as an antiaircraft weapon, the Patriot has been used against Iraqi Scud surface-to-surface missiles."*

destroy an enemy target two miles away.

Supplementing M1A1 tanks were M2 and M3 Bradley fighting vehicles designed to carry men and weapons into battle with speed and safety. The Bradleys replaced the earlier M113 armored personnel carriers and came equipped with a machinegun, a 25mm cannon, and twin launchers for tube launched, optically tracked, wire-guided (TOW) missiles. The M2s and M3s were double armor-plated, fully amphibious, and capable of cross-country speeds of forty-one miles per hour.

The army also developed better artillery and rocketry. Armor-plated 155 mm M109 and the 203 mm M110 self-propelled howitzers supplemented the non-armored and towed 155 mm M114 howitzers, the 155 mm M198 howitzers, and the 105 mm M101 and M192 howitzers. The M270 multiple long-range rocket launcher (MLRS) could hit a target twenty-five miles away. Each rocket launcher contained two canisters carrying six rockets apiece. Each rocket carried 644 "bomblets," which were released in midair. A single salvo of twelve rockets could saturate an area of approximately forty-five thousand square yards with "steel rain." The army also developed a tactical missile system (ATACMS), which could strike targets 100 miles away, such as antiaircraft emplacements, logistical sites, tactical bridges, and rocket and howitzer batteries, with 950 baseball-sized bomblets.

In the air the army operated two greatly improved aircraft; the AH-64B Apache attack helicopter and the UH-60 Black Hawk combat assault transport helicopter. Apache's cruised at 182

ABOVE: *The Apache AH-64 helicopter made its debut on the battlefield during Just Cause (Panama), firing AGM-114 Hellfire missiles, 2.75-inch rocket projectiles, and 30mm cannon shells. General Wesley Clark deployed 24 Apaches in Tirana, Albania, during the Kosovo intervention.*

knots per hour (227 max) with an operating range of 300 miles and a nine-ton load. The ship carried an M239 chain-gun 30 mm autocannon capable of firing 625 rounds per minute, and either sixteen Hellfire antitank missiles or seventy-six 2.75 folding-fin aerial rockets, or a combination of the two. The Sikorsky UH-60 Black Hawk replaced the Bell UH-1 Huey. The Black Hawk carried a crew of three and could transport eleven combat troops and a slung load of four tons at 150 knots. With eight seats removed, it carried four litters. Normally armed with two 7.62 mm machineguns, the UH-60 could be fitted with external "winglets" that carry, among other weapons and paraphernalia, up to sixteen Hellfire missiles.

The Patriot air defense system, a medium- and high-altitude surface-to-air missile (SAM), had both mobility and all-weather capability. A Patriot battery contained a radar set, and antenna-mast-group vehicle, a power plant, a control station, and eight

FAR LEFT: Truck-mounted surface-to-air antiaircraft missiles, usually in tubes of twelve rockets, can fire from one location, and to avoid detection, move to another location immediately after firing.

LEFT: Laser-guided Hellfire missiles, a key weapon on Apache helicopters, can also be fired from utility vehicles. Hellfires were first used in combat during the Persian Gulf War and could strike targets three miles away.

remote launching stations. The missile attained a speed of Mach-3 and carried a high-explosive warhead mounted on a rocket seventeen feet long. Though not intended as an anti-missile weapon, the Patriot performed reasonably well when used as such. The army continued to use a variety of missiles, including the Hawk, a medium-range surface-to-air missile; the Chaparral, a heat-seeking anti-aircraft missile; and the Stinger, a man-portable guided missile weighing thirty-five pounds.

The army's primary shoulder weapon, the M16A2, had a range of 500 meters. It served as a light, high-velocity, 5.56 mm caliber automatic rifle capable of firing 800 rounds per minute using twenty- or thirty-round detachable magazines. The M16A2 could also be fitted with a three-round burst device. The 9 mm Beretta became the standard hand weapon, replacing the old reliable Colt .45.

With a new unified command structure designed during the Reagan years, and a new army equipped with modern weapons, George H.W. Bush entered the first year of his presidency with the best military force in the world.

Chaos in the Persian Gulf

On September 9, 1980, Iraq invaded Iran in an effort to settle a long-standing border dispute. Saddam Hussein, who came to power in 1979, made the decision after establishing a dictatorship over 18 million people who were ethnically divided into one-half Shiite Muslims, one-forth Sunni Muslims, and one-fourth Kurds, all having their own language, culture, and separatist tribal societies. Anti-Western and anti-Israeli, Hussein went to war without an ally. When his offensive bogged down, he looked to the West for help. Because Iran's Ayatollah Khomeini posed a threat to American interests in the Middle East, the United States in 1982 removed Iraq from its list of countries supporting terrorism and two years later established diplomatic relations. The U.S. shared

ABOVE: M1A1 Abrams tanks of the 1st Armored Cavalry cruise across the desert during the Persian Gulf War. Armor-piercing projectiles from the Abrams 120mm gun easily penetrated Russian-built T-72 tanks.

intelligence information with Iraq until 1988, when a UN-sponsored ceasefire brought the conflict to an end.

Hussein came out of the war with military strength. He envisioned himself as the man destined to bring Arab nations back to power and by force, if necessary. He intended to take control of the region's oil reserves and to drive the Israelis out of the Middle East. He did not demobilize his million-man army at the end of the war with Iran but went on an enormous spending spree. His purchases included Soviet Scud missiles, T-72 tanks, and MiG-29 fighters. He also brought scientists into Iraq to develop chemical, biological, and nuclear weapons.

On July 17, 1990, Hussein began launching verbal attacks against the United Arab Emirates and Kuwait, acrimoniously accusing the latter of usurping Iraqi territory and stealing billions in oil from the massive Rumaila oil field that spans the joint border. He also wanted control of two Kuwaiti islands, concessions on loans made during the Iran-Iraq war, and a higher OPEC oil price to help pay for postwar

reconstruction. Aside from President Bush, few nations took Hussein's threats seriously. On July 25 Bush sent April Glaspie, U.S. ambassador to Iraq, to speak with Hussein. Although the Iraqi president promised not to invade Kuwait while talks with Egypt were underway, he continued to deploy an invasion force along the Kuwaiti border. On August 2 Hussein broke his promise to Ambassador Glaspie, sent troops across the border, and occupied Kuwait. Six days later Hussein announced that Kuwait had been annexed as the nineteenth province of Iraq.

Desert Shield

Hussein gave no heed to UN Security Council resolutions imposing sanctions on Iraq and demanding withdrawal from Kuwait. Much to Hussein's shock, almost every member-nation of the UN placed trade and financial embargoes on Iraq. Even the twelve Arab League nations, led by President Hosni Mubarak of Egypt, demanded that Iraq withdraw from Kuwait and pledged military forces for the defense of Saudi Arabia.

President Bush did not wait for Hussein to reply to UN demands and on August 9 began funneling the 82nd Airborne Division and FB-111 attack aircraft into Saudi Arabia as a tripwire if Iraqis advanced beyond Kuwait. Hussein had not counted on the United States taking a strong military stand against him, and threatened, "Yours is a society that cannot lose ten thousand dead in one battle." Baghdad's strongman was behind the times. Having learned harsh lessons from the Vietnam experience, U.S. forces no longer intended to fight high-casualty protracted wars of attrition.

On August 22 Bush called up fifty thousand reservists and three days later obtained authorization from the UN to blockade Iraq. By November 8 the United States had 225,000 combat-ready troops in and around Saudi Arabia, including the 82nd

Airborne, Twenty-fourth Mechanized Infantry, and 101st Airborne (Airmobile) division, plus elements from the navy, marines, and air force. Bush announced that he would send another two hundred thousand troops if Hussein refused to evacuate Kuwait.

Comparison of Forces

During Desert Shield, Hussein continued to build up his forces in Kuwait and southwestern Iraq. He sent about 550,000 troops, half his army, into the area. The Iraqi force consisted of forty-two divisions with forty-two hundred tanks (among them one thousand T-72 Russian tanks with 126 mm guns; 150 helicopters, six thousand personnel carriers; five thousand pieces of artillery; and some 550 combat-ready aircraft, including a number of MiG-25 and MiG-29 high-performance fighters and Su-24 and Su-25 attack planes. His weapons inventory included Soviet- and French-made surface-to-air missiles and Soviet Scud surface-to-surface missiles, the latter capable of carrying one thousand pounds of conventional explosives three hundred miles, which put Scuds in range of Israel. Hussein also had supplies of poison gas (mustard, tabun, and sarin) and binary chemical weapons that he had already used to kill

GENERAL H. NORMAN "THE BEAR" SCHWARZKOPF, JR.

Born in Trenton, New Jersey, on August 22, 1934, H. Norman Schwarzkopf grew up in a military family as the son of a German-American general having the same name. At the age of twelve, Schwarzkopf went to Iran during World War II when his father was sent to Tehran to train and reorganize the Iranian national police force in a diplomatic effort to help stabilize the regime of the shah. He spent a year in Iran, where he developed an interest and understanding of the Muslim culture. For the next several years, he followed his father through a series of assignments in Europe, attending schools in Germany and Switzerland before entering the Valley Forge Military Academy in Pennsylvania. Years later he admitted learning much about army life from his father.

In 1952 Schwarzkopf entered the U.S. Military Academy and four years later graduated forty-second in a class of 485. He earned his paratrooper's wings in 1957, and joined the 187th Infantry Regiment of the 101st Airborne Division as a platoon leader. In 1965, after earning a master's degree in mechanical and aerospace engineering at the University of Southern California, Captain Schwarzkopf volunteered to serve as a military adviser to the ARNV Airborne Division in Vietnam, where he earned two Silver Stars for bravery and a Purple Heart. He volunteered for a second tour in Vietnam and became commander of the First Battalion, Sixth Infantry, Twenty-third Infantry Division, earning a third Silver Star, three Bronze Stars, and another Purple Heart. Schwarzkopf also served as deputy commander of the Joint Task Force, which carried out the invasion of Grenada.

Promoted to major general in 1983, Schwarzkopf commanded the Twenty-fourth Mechanized Infantry Division. By 1986 Schwarzkopf, now a lieutenant general, had run the full gamut of army line and staff positions, including deputy chief of staff of Plans and Operations at army headquarters where he worked together with planners from all the armed services.

In 1998 Schwarzkopf received his fourth star, the highest rank offered in the army, and assumed the position of commander-in-chief of Central Command (CENTCOM). After Iraqi forces invaded Kuwait, he formulated the plans for Operation Desert Shield and Desert Storm and became the U.S. and UN commander of all troops during the Persian Gulf War. It would be the first battle test of the recently adopted AirLand Battle doctrine. Not surprisingly, the Twenty-fourth Infantry Division was an important part of Schwarzkopf's coalition order of battle.

ABOVE: General H. Norman Schwarzkopf, Jr. (1934–) thanks Scud-hunters, including members of the 1st Special Forces Operational Detachment—Delta, who had undertaken hazardous missions during the Gulf War.

ABOVE During the Persian Gulf War, a column of M113 APCs pause on the roadside.

Kurds living in Halabja. Intelligence also pointed to Hussein's effort to develop nuclear weapons, but no physical evidence had materialized.

While Hussein funneled forces into southwestern Iraq, President Bush began building an international coalition to oust the Iraqi army from Kuwait. He turned military matters over to General Colin L. Powell, chairman of the JCS, and burly CENTCOM commander, General Schwarzkopf. By December 1990 Schwarzkopf had more than 460,000 men and 40,000 women serving as the ground force in the Persian Gulf, plus six aircraft carrier battle groups. The U.S. force consisted of two marine divisions (the First and Second), seven army divisions (First Cavalry, First and Third Armored, First and Twenty-fourth Mechanized, and 82nd and 101st Airborne), the Second and Third Armored Cavalry Regiments, with some 380,000 ground troops, twenty-two hundred tanks, five hundred combat helicopters, and fifteen hundred combat aircraft. UN allied forces added another 110,000 combat troops in eight divisions, with about twelve hundred tanks, 150 helicopters, and 350 combat aircraft.

Hussein could have avoided a costly war had he obeyed instructions from the UN to withdraw his forces by January 15, 1991, from Kuwait. On January 12, after Hussein refused to budge, Congress gave President Bush authority to use military force to carry out UN Resolution 678 and free Kuwait. Hussein, commenting on the decision with unbridled confidence, bragged, "The mother of all battles has started."

Desert Storm

In the early morning darkness on January 17 (local time), U.S. Special Forces flying AH-64A helicopters slipped into Iraq and knocked out two Iraqi air defense systems. Moments later the first computerized war commenced as dozens of Tomahawk II land-attack cruise missiles fired from

the battleships *Missouri* and *Wisconsin* and other U.S. vessels in the Persian Gulf and the Red Sea began smashing into strategic Iraqi military and political installations. More surgical strikes by seventeen hundred American and allied aircraft followed from carriers and land bases in Saudi Arabia, damaging more than 160 sites throughout Iraq. Laser beam-guided bombs and preprogrammed missiles, aided by pinpoint satellite positioning and other electronic devices, homed on air bases; command and communications centers; chemical; biological and nuclear facilities; munitions works; bridges; oil refineries; and launchers for Soviet-made Scud-B ballistic missiles. Iraq was believed to have from thirty-two to thirty-six fixed and mobile Scud-launching platforms and from three hundred to three thousand Scuds in inventory, with which Hussein threatened to destroy Israel.

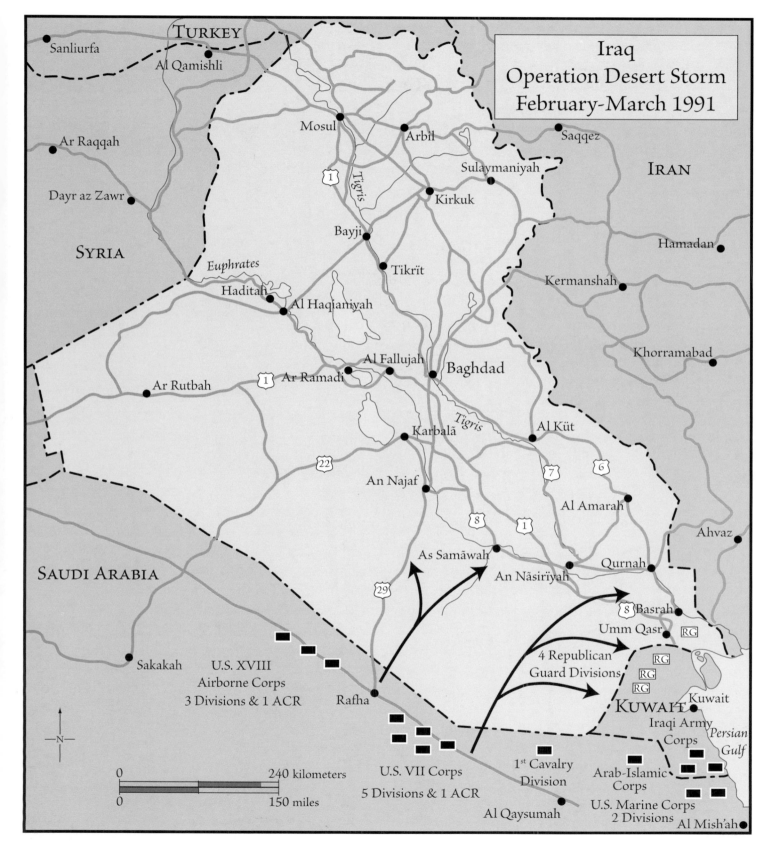

Iraq
Operation Desert Storm
February–March 1991

TURKEY

Sanliurfa

Al Qamishli

Mosul

Arbil

Saqqez

IRAN

Ar Raqqah

Sulaymaniyah

Kirkuk

Dayr az Zawr

Tigris

Bayji

SYRIA

Euphrates

Tikrit

Hamadan

Haditah

Kermanshah

Al Haqlaniyah

Ar Rutbah

Al Fallujah

Baghdad

Ar Ramadi

Khorramabad

Tigris

Karbalā

Al Küt

22

An Najaf

7

6

Al Amarah

Ahvaz

8

1

As Samāwah

Qurnah

SAUDI ARABIA

An Nāsirïyah

29

8 Basrah

Umm Qasr

RG

4 Republican
Guard Divisions

RG

RG

RG

Sakakah

U.S. XVIII
Airborne Corps
3 Divisions & 1 ACR

Rafha

KUWAIT

Kuwait

Iraqi Army
Corps

Persian
Gulf

N

U.S. VII Corps

1st Cavalry
Division

Arab-Islamic
Corps

0   240 kilometers

0   150 miles

5 Divisions & 1 ACR

U.S. Marine Corps
2 Divisions

Al Qaysumah

Al Mish'ah

During Operation Desert Storm (February–March 1991), eight army infantry divisions, two armored cavalry regiments (ACR), and the 1st Cavalry Division lunge across the Saudi border and into Iraq to strike the Republican Guard (RG) from the rear.

Twenty-four hours later, the first Scuds began landing in the vicinity of Tel Aviv. None contained chemical warheads. To keep Israelis out of the war and minimize damage from Scud attacks, the U.S. army based Patriot surface-to-air missiles around Tel Aviv to intercept and explode airborne Scuds. Iraq fired 39 Scuds at Israel, and most of those that landed did little damage. The worst Scud episode occurred at a barracks near Dharhan, where a wayward Scud struck and killed 24 National Guard personnel.

Air strikes, averaging three thousand sorties per day, continued against strategic targets. One week into the war, the Iraqi air force had either been destroyed or flown into and confiscated in Iran. Air attacks at night wiped out tanks, artillery, and trucks along the Kuwaiti border. Any attempt by Iraq military to forward reinforcements, food, water, and medicine were interdicted night and day by coalition air strikes. After pulverizing Iraq's infrastructure and military assets for five weeks and repulsing a futile enemy attempt to invade Saudi Arabia at Wafrah and Khafji, President Bush gave Hussein one final ultimatum: to withdraw from Kuwait by noon, February 23, or face further Allied action. Hussein called the ultimatum "shameful" and ordered his troops in Kuwait to begin dynamiting oil wells.

While the air show progressed over Iraq, most of which had been observed around the world on millions of TV sets, General Schwarzkopf's CENCOM staff refined the details of the ground offensive. Meanwhile, thirty-five thousand British, thirty-five thousand Egyptians, forty thousand Saudis, twenty thousand Syrians, ten thousand French, seven thousand Kuwaitis, and seventeen

RIGHT: At sunset in the Iraqi desert, half the squad in an APC takes turns watching for trouble in the front while the other half enjoys a little shut-eye in the sand.

thousand troops from other nations joined the coalition army, and CENTCOM fitted them all into the ground campaign.

On February 23 Schwarzkopf launched the ground assault. The main outflanking movement conducted by the XVIII Corps and the VII Corps swung into southern Iraq across a 150-mile front east of Kuwait. A second thrust led by U.S. Marines moved toward Kuwait City. A third force, composed mainly of Saudis, Egyptians, and Syrians, moved forward and swung eastward, moving on Kuwait City by the flank. By February 25–26 the vaunted Iraqi Republican Guard, overwhelmed by U.S. and British armor, began surrendering in droves. In a perfectly executed campaign based entirely on AirLand doctrine, Iraqi resistance collapsed. UN casualties in the 100-hour ground operation amounted to only 95 killed, 368 wounded, and 20 missing. Iraqis suffered immensely, losing more than thirty thousand killed, sixty thousand captured, and another fifty thousand-plus killed or wounded by air raids.

General Schwarzkopf attributed poor Iraqi performance to three factors: coalition air supremacy, the suddenness of the coordinated ground campaign, and the collapse of Iraqi morale, unit cohesion, and combat effectiveness due, in part, to intensive air attacks. Later a considerable number of army officers and enlisted men unofficially expressed regret that UN resolutions providing for the recovery of Kuwait did not include the removal of Saddam Hussein and his henchmen from control of the Iraqi government.

International Peacekeeping—Somalia

The UN left problems in Iraq unsettled but felt quite pleased that peace had been restored to the troubled Middle East. International peacekeeping had always been a UN initiative, and they believed that peace could be achieved so long as member countries like the United States and the United Kingdom maintained the armies necessary to achieve that goal.

Finding trouble spots in the world required no effort because civil war, political instability, genocide, and famine had made a home in Africa. Since gaining its independence in 1960, Somalia on the eastern horn of Africa had experienced nothing but political chaos. After years of bloodshed and forty thousand casualties, Mohammed Farah Aidid, a warlord who had fought his way to power, took control of Somalia's capital, Mogadishu, while the rest of the drought-ridden country starved.

In July 1992 the UN declared Somalia "without a government" and accepted President Bush's offer to provide peacekeeping troops to aid in the humanitarian distribution of food. The army sent ten thousand troops from the Tenth Mountain Division, never expecting to become involved in a situation requiring fifteen thousand more. In 1993, after General Aidid went into hiding, the UN took control of humanitarian responsibilities and initiated talks among the peace-minded warlords.

On January 20, 1993, William Jefferson Clinton of Arkansas became the forty-second president of the

BELOW: In 1993, after a brisk battle in the suburbs of Mogadishu, Somalia, men of the 10th Mountain Division stare down a street emptied by gunfire.

ABOVE: On January 8, 2002, Under Secretary of the Army Les Brownlee rides on a night motorized patrol with soldiers from the 10th Mountain Division at Camp McGovern near Brcko, Bosnia.

immediate and controversial move, he began a process that resulted in the Pentagon's policy toward gays as "Don't ask, don't tell." Clinton also initiated a "peace dividend," the downsizing of the military to reduce the national debt. This had an immediate impact on forces in Somalia and around the world. The only muffled objection to the president's downsizing policy came from the Pentagon. Clinton's controversial military policies eventually drove many competent career officers and enlisted men into retirement or civilian employment.

The U.S. Army—Bush/Clinton Years		
	1989	1997
Active Duty	770,000	495,000
Army Reserve	319,000	215,000
National Guard	457,000	367,000
Total	1,546,000	1,077,000

International Peacekeeping—Bosnia and Kosovo

One of the most troubling and controversial uses of the army occurred in 1995–1996 when President Clinton sent 18,500 men and women from the army to Bosnia-Herzegovina as part of a UN peacekeeping force of 21,000. The trouble began in 1991 when Croatia and Slovenia broke away from Yugoslavia and declared independence. An ethnic war ensued between Croats and Serbs that eventually expanded into Bosnia and Herzegovina. By 1995 two hundred thousand people had already been killed or wounded in the fighting when Yugoslav President Slobodan Milosevic's Serbian forces launched a campaign of "ethnic cleansing" against Muslims and other nationalities in Bosnia. To aid army peacekeepers, aircraft from navy carriers in the Adriatic Sea and USAF bases in Italy flew missions over UN-occupied areas to protect the troops on the ground. By August 1966 NATO had sixty thousand peacekeepers,

United States. He began withdrawing troops from Somalia, but he left too few behind: three thousand to handle humanitarian logistics and five thousand to protect the others while continuing the search for Aidid. With the U.S. force militarily weakened, Aidid's guerrillas soon became active in Mogadishu. On October 3–4, 1993, they ambushed American soldiers on the streets of the capital, killing eighteen and wounding seventy-eight. Special Forces Master Sergeant Gary I. Gordon and Sergeant First Class Randall D. Shugart earned the Medal of Honor by giving their lives while defending wounded members of a helicopter crew. The episode led to recall of all American forces in Somalia and was later detailed with vividness in the book *Black Hawk Down* and the Hollywood film of the same name.

"Don't ask, don't tell"

Soon after his inauguration, President Clinton confronted an issue that had been dangling for years, a policy toward gays in the military service. In an including twenty thousand U.S. Army personnel, policing disputed areas in Yugoslavia.

In March 1999 the bloodshed in Bosnia spilled into the Serbian province of Kosovo when ethnic Albanians revolted. The Serbian army swept into Kosovo on another ethnic-cleansing effort, this time against Albanians. For the first time in fifty years, American forces attached to NATO became involved in hostilities as well as peacekeeping.

Army General Wesley Clark, commanding NATO forces, organized Task Force Hawk and sent an expedition into Albania but failed to stop the fighting. Clark also attempted to bring three hundred aircraft to Albania, including twenty-four AH-64A Apache helicopters from the Eleventh Aviation Regiment in Germany, but the transfer required three thousand men and women to keep the planes serviced and in the air. The Pentagon disagreed with the use of helicopters, citing their vulnerability to ground fire, but Clark got his way. Clark's operation, once intended to include a few hundred soldiers and twenty-four helicopters, grew to a task force of five thousand. The operation accomplished nothing of tactical or strategic importance but lost two helicopters. Two soldiers were killed and two injured, the only American casualties in the Kosovo operation.

In 1995 President Clinton promised to keep U.S. troop involvement in the Balkans to one year. They are still there.

September 11, 2001

On January 20, 2001, Governor George W. Bush of Texas became the forty-third president of the United States after a close and hotly contested election. Nine months later, two jetliners flown by Osama bin Laden's al-Qaeda kamikaze imitators crashed into the twin towers of the World Trade Center in New York City. Another jet slammed into a section of the Pentagon building in Washington, D.C., and a fourth

jet, possibly heading for the White House, plummeted to the ground in Pennsylvania after its passengers rebelled against their captors. More than three thousand civilians died in the attacks.

Bush immediately targeted bin Laden's international terrorist organization operating out of Taliban-controlled Afghanistan. He demanded that the Taliban turn bin Laden over to the United States and destroy all of al-Qaeda's training camps. In October, after the Taliban refused to comply, Bush authorized Operation Enduring Freedom.

In October 2001 air strikes commenced against al-Qaeda and the Taliban, a radical Islamic organization providing shelter for bin Laden and his terrorist training camps. When the operation began, the Taliban controlled 80 percent of Afghanistan. By November 8 General Tommy Franks, commanding CENTCOM, had fifty thousand American soldiers deployed in the area along with full cooperation from the Northern Alliance and the Eastern Alliance, two Afghan opposition groups in perpetual conflict with the Taliban.

ABOVE: On September 11, 2001, a jumbo jet flown by al-Qaeda terrorists slammed into the Pentagon minutes after two airliners had crashed into the twin towers of the World Trade Center in New York City. The tragedy induced President George W. Bush to declare war on al-Qaeda and terrorism.

LEFT: In October 2001, Special Forces moved into Afghanistan to rally support against the Taliban and begin the search for Osama bin Laden. The first soldier killed in combat, Sergeant First Class Nathan R. Chapman, is brought home on January 8, 2003, his casket draped in the American flag and carried by an honor guard. More than 60 Green Berets joined the Chapman family at the Seattle-Tacoma International Airport to pay their respects.

Special Forces were already on the ground gathering intelligence and transmitting targeting information on Taliban and al Qaeda sites to carrier-based aircraft and missile ships in the Arabian Sea. Special Forces worked with the alliances and quickly mopped up the shattered al Qaeda and Taliban strongholds. In ten weeks Special Forces working with the alliances had toppled the ruling government, secured the Afghan capital of Kabul and several other cities, and chased bin Laden into the mountains near the Afghanistan-Pakistani borde—but never caught him. During operations around Kabul, a Marine Expeditionary Unit flew in from the Arabian Sea and captured the Kandahar airfield in southern Afghanistan. The U.S. Army assisted in setting up Afghanistan's interim government, and elements from the 101st Airborne remained for a while to keep the new nation safe from al Qaeda-Taliban incursions.

When President Bush sent forces into Afghanistan, he warned that the war on terror would be long, saying only, "It will take as long as it takes." On December 22, 2001, when the U.S. Army and the Northern Alliance installed Hamid Karzai as interim prime minister of Afghanistan, Secretary of Defense Donald Rumsfeld and Secretary of State Colin Powell informed the public that destroying the home base of al Qaeda was merely the first phase of a global war on terrorism.

On January 29, 2002, President Bush presented his state of the union address, declaring that Iraq, Iran, and North Korea constituted an "axis of evil," and that the United States would not permit them "to threaten us with the world's most destructive weapons." The words resonated around the world, and still do.

ABOVE: On May 28, 2004, while positioned on a ridge 1,500 feet above the Pesh Valley, Afghanistan, a Special Forces weapons sergeant trains an Afghan Security Forces soldier in the firing of a 75mm recoilless rife.

Weapons of Mass Destruction

Since Desert Storm, Iraq had persistently defied the terms of the agreement with the United Nations. Evidence existed that Hussein had diverted money from the sale of oil, intended for purchases of food and medicine, to rebuild an arsenal of weapons of mass destruction (WMD). WMDs fell into three categories of very different weapons. Iraqi's biological programs included the development of anthrax spores, the paralysis-causing toxin botulinum, and viral smallpox. Chemical weapons included nerve agents such as VX, sarin, tabun, and mustard gas, some of which had been experimentally used against Iraqi Kurds. Hussein had long sought a nuclear arsenal, and it appeared the program had been reinstated when he attempted to obtain yellowcake from Africa. Although UN inspections failed to find evidence of WMDs in Iraq, General Georges Sada, Hussein's top adviser and the number two man in the military, later explained that all WMDs had been transported in several jumbo jet shipments to Damascus, Syria, before doors were opened to UN inspectors. Bush believed the intelligence, as did Congress. He also knew that Hussein supported terrorism. After experiencing a diplomatic loggerhead in the UN, Bush decided the world organization could not be relied upon to protect America.

Iraqi Freedom

On March 17, 2003, Bush issued an ultimatum, warning Hussein and his two sons, Uday and Qusay, to leave Iraq in forty-eight hours or face a U.S.-led military invasion. After the time expired, Bush authorized Operation Iraqi Freedom, and U.S. forces,

ABOVE: On August 28, 2003, soldiers of the "Renegade" Platoon, Bravo Company, 2nd Battalion, 8th Infantry Regiment, conduct a raid in a village in Diyala Province during Operation Iraqi Freedom. A Bradley M3A3 Fighting Vehicle follows.

accompanied by Great Britain, Spain, and supported by thirty-three other countries, went to war.

In the early morning hours of March 20 the navy opened the campaign by launching dozens of Tomahawk cruise missiles armed with 1,000-pound warheads at Baghdad's command centers. Carrier and land-based aircraft followed with 2,000-pound "bunker-buster" bombs designed to destroy underground installations. Hussein survived the initial attack, but several of his top officials did not.

General Tommy Franks applied the same AirLand Battle doctrine used during Desert Storm with a U.S.-led coalition "Shock and Awe" bombing

ABOVE: On the night of July 22, 2004, as seen through an image intensifier, a Bradley Fighting Vehicle of the 1st Squadron, 9th Cavalry, 1st Cavalry Division, provides covering fire during a search operation in the Talaa Square area of Baghdad.

GENERAL TOMMY RAY FRANKS

Born on June 17, 1945, Tommy Franks grew up in Midland, Texas, and went to the same high school as President Bush and his wife, Laura. He spoke the same familiar dialect as all native-born Texans. Instead of taking the usual route of a professional soldier, Franks studied business administration at the University of Texas and later became involved in the military when he joined the U.S. Army to fight in Vietnam. After completing officer's training in 1967, he went to Vietnam as a second lieutenant and suffered three wounds while serving as a forward observer in the Ninth Infantry Division. Franks never went to West Point, but in 1984 he did attend the U.S. Army War College.

In 1990 Franks became involved in Iraq during the military buildup for Desert Shield and later served as assistant commander of the First Cavalry Division during Desert Storm. Three years after his promotion to lieutenant general in 1997, he took over CENTCOM, which is the unified command responsible for the Middle East. A year later, still as head of CENTCOM, Franks drew the assignment of removing the Taliban from Afghanistan and destroying al-Qaeda's terrorist training camps.

The dust had barely settled in Afghanistan when in 2002 President Bush put Franks in charge of Operation Iraqi Freedom. It appears that the general may not always have agreed with Secretary of Defense Rumsfeld on strategy, but the war plan for Iraqi Freedom was entirely designed by Franks and his staff. After the fall of Tikrit, Hussein's hometown, Franks declared the end of the Iraqi dictator's rule.

In May 2003, after major offensive combat operations ended in Iraq, Tommy Franks retired from active military service and wrote his memoir, *American Soldier*.

RIGHT: General Tommy Franks (r), CENTCOM commander, studies a weapons cache discovered by the First Brigade, 101st Airborne Division, in Najaf, Iraq. Behind him, Major General David H. Petraeus, division commander, looks on.

RIGHT: *Operation Iraqi Freedom (March–May 2003) launches out of Kuwait with the U.S. V Army Corps and the 1st Marine Expeditionary Force (MEF) leading the charge to Baghdad. Note the distribution of Special Forces (SOF) prior to and during the assault, and the 173rd Airborne striking from the north to protect the oil fields.*

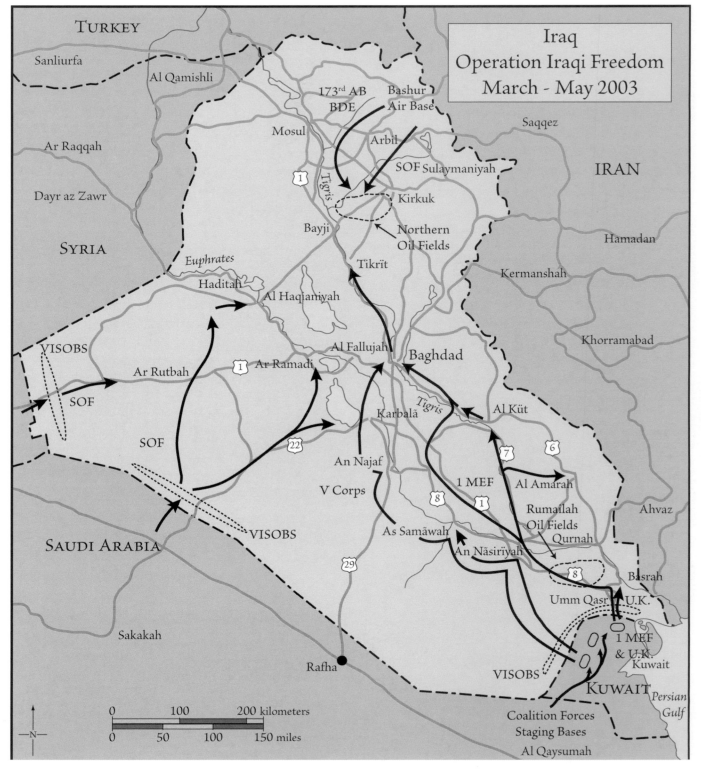

Iraq
Operation Iraqi Freedom
March - May 2003

campaign. Unlike Desert Storm, ground troops began moving into Iraq immediately. Very early in the action the 160th Special Operations Aviation

Regiment moved out of Saudi Arabia and Jordan and wiped out Iraqi observation posts along the southern border and moved toward the Euphrates. Another

LEFT: In November 2003, a Bradley Fighting Vehicle patrols the Abu Ghurayb market area of Baghdad to discourage terrorist acts. The turret is traversed to the rear, where the commander mans the 7.62mm machinegun for close defense.

BELOW LEFT: During Iraqi Freedom, an M3A3 Bradley Fighting Vehicle of Eagle Troop, 2nd Squadron, 3rd Armored Cavalry Regiment, races towards Fallujah in response to a call for armored support.

BELOW: On July 22, 2003, after being released from the hospital, Pfc. Jessica Lynch straps herself into a Blackhawk helicopter for her trip home to West Virginia.

Franks used only 242,000 American troops in Operation Iraqi Freedom, less than half the number deployed in Desert Storm. Most of the troops, about 130,000, were positioned in Kuwait along with 45,000 British and 18,000 Australian troops. Hussein no longer had his million-man army, but he did have 375,000 troops positioned in strategic cities.

Elements from the V Corps ran into opposition at Nasiriyah, where Iraqis had dug-in to check the American advance on Baghdad, now only 200 miles away. Nasiriyah had two bridges, and the V Corps needed one of them to get across the Euphrates. As part of the corps moved up the river to Najaf, the Third Infantry Division remained around Nasiriyah to root out the enemy and secure a bridge.

On March 23 during the fight at Nasiriyah, Private First Class Jessica Lynch, a supply clerk with the 507th Maintenance Company, became ambushed

Special Operations unit dropped into northern Iraq and with the 173rd Airborne Brigade began moving south in an effort to secure the northern oil fields.

In what General Franks called the "wave of steel," the U.S. V Corps with the Third Infantry Division began moving out of Kuwait and into southeastern Iraq as the First Marine Expeditionary Force and U.K. forces moved on Basra. Ben Rooney, in his book on the Iraqi War, called it "the fastest armored advance in the history of modern warfare."

ABOVE: On February 25, 2005, soldiers from U.S. Special Forces indoctrinate Albanian troops during a patrol in northern Iraq. Albania was one of the thirty-three countries that made up the coalition forces in Operation Iraqi Freedom.

and seriously wounded by Iraqi Fedayeen forces. After killing eleven and wounding five of the men riding in the same Humvee with a rocket-propelled grenade, Iraqis took Lynch to Saddam Hospital in Nasiriyah, which also served as Fedayeen command center. An Iraqi lawyer, whose wife worked at the hospital, informed U.S. troops of where Lynch was located. On April 1 U.S. Special Forces, consisting of Rangers, navy SEALs, marines, and air force pilots, entered the hospital in full battle gear and carried her out to a waiting helicopter. Lynch became the first POW to be rescued since World War II. Fully recovered and in college, she became an American hero, but being a modest women who grew up in the small town of Palestine, West Virginia, Lynch declared, "But I am not a hero…I'm just a survivor," and no doubt, happy to be one.

The Route to Baghdad

After the British captured Basra and the Third Infantry Division secured Nasiriyah and Karbala, the First Marine Expeditionary Force and the V Corps rolled through light resistance and a severe sand storm toward Baghdad.

On April 3 scouts from the Third Battalion of the Seventh Cavalry Regiment struck Highway 8 to Saddam International Airport, followed by the Third Infantry Division about twelve miles behind. Air strikes immediately followed, knocking out Republican Guard tanks and artillery guarding the airport. By morning, army forces had captured Saddam Hussein's last link to the outside world.

On the morning of April 5 the first U.S. tanks rolled through Baghdad on an information-gathering mission. Iraqi Information Minister Mohammed Said al-Sahhaf, better known as "Baghdad Bob," went on the air on April 8 to declare there were no American tanks near the city, although TV footage showed them running through the streets as he spoke. When Baghdad fell on April 9, the Iraqi people took to the streets and began tearing down the statues Hussein had erected of himself. About the same time, Special Forces entered the "Green Palace," one of Hussein's seventy-eight opulent homes. The elaborate palace occupied two square miles on the shore of Lake Tharthar, 150 miles north of Baghdad.

On April 10 Kurdish fighters secured the northern city of Kirkuk as U.S. forces moved on Tikrit, supposedly the last Iraqi stronghold. As troops entered Tikrit virtually unopposed, an Iraqi policemen approached an officer and told him where seven American POWs were being held in Samarra. As a detachment approached the building, Iraqi guards fled, leaving behind the five surviving members of Jessica Lynch's maintenance company and two crewmembers from a downed Apache helicopter.

On April 14 the Pentagon declared that major combat operations in Iraq had ended. In one of the quickest and decisive wars ever fought, only 126 American soldiers lost their lives, another 495 were wounded.

On April 15 the first meeting between coalition members and Iraqi opposition leaders took place in the ancient city of Ur. Soon afterwards, every American and British soldier received a pack of playing cards to help identify fifty-five of the most wanted members of the toppled regime. The printers saved the ace of spades for Saddam.

LEFT: The 1st Infantry Division (Big Red One) never missed a war. On January 16, 2004, men wearing the famous shoulder patch conduct a patrol with their M998 Humvees (High Mobility Multipurpose Wheeled Vehicles) near Ar Ramadia, Iraq. By the year 2000, more than 140,000 Humvees had been manufactured. The U.S. Army procured many of the armored M1114 versions.

SERGEANT FIRST CLASS PAUL R. SMITH

On April 4, 2005, President Bush presented Birgit Smith, the wife of Sergeant First Class Paul R. Smith, the first Medal of Honor to be awarded in Operation Iraqi Freedom. Accompanied by her eighteen-year-old daughter, Jessica, and her eleven-year-old son, David, Mrs. Smith received the medal during a White House ceremony. In an eloquent response, she said her husband was aware of the sacrifices he could be called upon to make in battle, and, "Even though he died, he would not have had it any other way."

Smith served with Company B, Eleventh Engineer Battalion, where he was a platoon sergeant. On April 4, 2003, while attached to the Second Battalion, Seventh Regiment, Third Infantry Division, he received orders to prepare a compound near the Baghdad airport for holding enemy prisoners. Smith's platoon knocked a hole in one of the nearby buildings and began converting it into a prisoner center. He did not know whether other buildings in the area had been cleared but commenced work. About one hundred Republican Guards came out of one of the buildings and attacked Smith's engineers.

After throwing two hand grenades, Smith obtained an AT-4 rocket launcher and fired into the advancing Iraqis. When his ammunition gave out, Smith grabbed a .50-caliber Browning machinegun from an M113 APC and proceeded to cover the withdrawal of the platoon and the injured from the compound. He fired three hundred rounds and stood off the brunt of the enemy attack before being killed.

Captain Brian Borkowski, then a lieutenant in the Eleventh Engineers, spoke of an earlier episode when the unit went through Karbala Gap. "Some of our vehicles went three rows deep into a minefield," Borkowski said. "Smith got down on his hands and knees and extracted mines to make a path out. He didn't tell the [drivers of the vehicles] to get out, he got them out."

This heroic deed never went into record books.

CHAPTER 9

INTO THE FUTURE

The U.S. Army has been faithfully protecting America's people for more than 230 years, and it is working hard today to address the challenges emanating from constantly evolving worldwide threats. The end of the Cold War in 1989 merely ushered in a new era of proliferating terrorism and insurgency. The army continues to perform its tasks by adapting to change and by developing the technology and techniques necessary to cope with wars having no discrete battlefields.

As the Afghan and Iraqi conflicts have demonstrated, the distinctions between conventional strategic, operational, and tactical levels of warfare are being transformed by acts of organized insurgency using weapons of terrorism having the potential for the mass destruction of civilians. At the strategic level, the president, secretary of defense, and the JCS determine political and military objectives. At the operational level, senior field commanders design

campaigns often composed of several battle plans to achieve strategic goals. Tactical wars once required soldiers to go into battle to destroy a specific enemy force or capture a slice of battlefield. Such slices often no longer exist. Some lay concealed in tiny urban pockets. Insurgency and terrorism have introduced a new equation into the process of warfighting, and this compels the army to create a more flexible and agile battle doctrine to meet the challenges of the future.

Lessons in Insurgency

The U.S. Army has taken a role in fighting insurgencies as far back as 1794, when George Washington sent fifteen thousand troops into Pennsylvania to suppress three thousand western Pennsylvanians rebelling against an excise tax imposed on whiskey. During the Whiskey Rebellion, nobody got hurt. During the twentieth century the army became involved in insurgencies in Haiti, the Dominican Republic, the Philippines, El Salvador, Nicaragua, Mexico, Lebanon, and many other locations, but the insurgencies usually stayed within the borders of the countries involved. The results varied, often becoming minor interventions and exercises in wheel spinning, but soldiers got killed. In most cases, U.S. officials concluded that outright military victory over insurgents would likely fail and that political settlements should be arranged when possible. Sometimes an infusion of military might is required. The army reached this conclusion long before nation-building began in Afghanistan and Iraq.

Having no government or legal standing as a nation, al Qaeda ushered in international terror and fostered multinational insurgency. Terrorists and insurgents wear no identifying uniforms or insignia. They have no official standing army, no ostensible political organization, and no apparent agenda other than to kill, kidnap, and terrorize Christians, Jews,

ABOVE: An M2A3 Bradley Fighting Vehicle comes fully loaded with various vision devices, a TOW (tube-launched, optically tracked, wire-guided) missile launcher on the left of the turret (right to viewer), and a three-man crew in fighting positions. The TOW increases the range of a Bradley's engagement options to 4,000 yards.

and peace-seeking Muslims who ignore the militant teachings in the *Quran* and the *Hadith*. The attack on the United States on September 11, 2001, fomented a new era of warfare against terrorism. Destroying al Qaeda operations in Afghanistan weakened but did not eliminate the widely distributed organization. The rapid military conquest of Iraq in 2003 merely attracted a new brand of terrorists from all over the Muslim world and attached them to al Qaeda's cause. Those terrorists also became insurgents, and the marriage of two complicated problems for U.S. forces attempting to bring peace and democracy to Iraq.

The question being studied today by the army is how to meet insurgency with counterinsurgency before the situation gets out of control. The American people naturally prefer that others fight and die when the conflict so obviously involves another country's vital interests. Terrorists and insurgents know our history. They read our newspapers, digest our disinformation, and misunderstand the political motives of our squabbling politicians.

The army understands the difference between insurgents and terrorists. Most insurgent groups want

RIGHT: During Operation Phantom Fury in November 2004, the crew of an M1 Abrams tank watches over a sector of Fallujah's streets after U.S. and Iraqi soldiers drove insurgents out of the city.

political control of a particular area and will use guerrilla war, terrorism, mercenaries, and political mobilization to achieve it. The objectives of al Qaeda terrorism do not include the creation of an alternative government capable of administering a political entity, but an overlap does exist between terrorism and insurgency.

In Iraq the army eventually got up to speed on counterinsurgency strategy and tactics. The AirLand Battle doctrine that worked so well getting coalition forces into Baghdad did not work at all pacifying a country overrun by Hussein's disaffected insurgents, Muslim militants, foreign terrorists, and rabble-rousing clerics. The army soon learned that insurgents could best be interdicted by training Iraqis to defend themselves and by creating a capable police force, a properly armed and trained military organization with intelligence gathering capabilities, and unity of effort. The success of the unification effort became

manifest during operations at Fallujah and marked the beginning of counterinsurgency tactics that will require perpetual refinement.

Terrorism, Insurgency, and Fallujah

Counterinsurgency, which requires a separate and different fighting doctrine, rarely involves a set-piece battle. It is a laborious flushing-out process performed by soldiers who depend upon intelligence, select paramilitary units, friendly forces, and help from local informants. The November 8, 2004, assault on Fallujah contained the elements of all. The combined operation with Iraqi troops provided a learning experience but not necessarily a one-way roadmap for all counterinsurgency operations.

Fallujah, a city of three hundred thousand people, is located in the Sunni triangle about fifty miles west of Baghdad. Everybody knew it was filled with five to six thousand insurgents, mostly of foreign extraction. Interim Prime Minister Ayad Allawi gave the U.S. and Iraqi forces a go-ahead to clean the enemy out of the city. The broadly advertised operation enabled fifty to sixty thousand people to leave Fallujah before

BELOW: During the fighting in Fallujah, Iraq, on November 15, 2004, a soldier from the 1st Cavalry Division takes cover behind a destroyed vehicle to scout the streets and the buildings that lay ahead.

insurgents halted the evacuation. Rumors quickly spread that insurgents intended to use the general population as human shields, and then claim the people were attacked by friendly forces. Iraqi informants also warned that the city had been tunneled to enable insurgents to relocate weapons and personnel from one point to another, and in many instances, from one mosque to another. International law protects mosques from attack, but religious and cultural sites lose legal protection when used as sanctuaries for military purposes.

On November 8 elements from the 1st Marine Expeditionary Force, armored units from the First Infantry Division, the Iraqi Thiry-sixth Commando Battalion, and the First Brigade of the Iraqi Intervention Force moved into Fallujah. The Second Battalion, Seventh Cavalry Regiment, known as the "Ghost Battalion," had previously performed counterinsurgency operations in Baghdad and Najaf and spearheaded the push into Fallujah with Bradley Armored Fighting Vehicles, Abrams tanks, and armored personnel carriers. "Our mission," said Major Scott Jackson, commanding the Ghost

Brigade, "was to penetrate the enemy defenses in Fallujah to allow for two Marine [regimental combat teams] to enter the city." The Second Battalion, wearing night-fighting gear, began the attack at dark. Iraqi battalions worked directly and effectively with U.S. combat teams.

By November 11 most insurgent strongholds in and around the city had been destroyed, but the enemy still had to be driven from mosques and civic buildings. Aircraft performing close air support destroyed most of the insurgent-infested sites. In the final mop-up, insurgents not killed or captured in the operation either escaped from the city or faded into the population, where many were later captured.

After combined forces secured the city, Prime Minister Allawi appointed Major General Abdul Qadar Mohammed Jassim, the Iraqi ground force commander, interim military governor of the province until elections could be held. During the roundup of prisoners, the general observed with understandable disgust, "Foreign fighters are the real terrorists here."

In Iraq the U.S. Army has gradually developed effective tactics for fighting counterinsurgency, and none too soon. Every mission uncovered weapons caches. Some were enormous cells filled with tons of rockets, missiles, mortars, artillery shells, grenades, small-arms ammunition, blasting caps, explosives, drums of weapons-grade fertilizer, and remote activation devices. Improvised explosive devices (IED) turned up in mosques, tunnels, schools, homes, spider holes, and buildings all over Iraq.

As one officer noted, "Iraqi Freedom is the first time the Army has ever conducted combat, peacekeeping, humanitarian relief, and ecological cleanup operations all at the same time."

Counterinsurgency and counterterrorism, however, will only be effective when all the nations of the world aid in the elimination of the threat.

LEFT: On November 28, 2005, a helicopter provides close air support for a squad of soldiers from the 7th Cavalry Regiment, 3rd Infantry Division, during a patrol of the Tigris River southeast of Baghdad.

The Future Soldier

In exchange for downsizing the military, the future soldier will virtually become, as today's advertising suggests, "An Army of One." As former army chief of staff General Eric Shinseki commented, "The army has to be small and smart." The "small" factor resonates from the American public's reluctance to wage war when their sons and daughters have to do it, especially when war is perceived as being somebody else's problem. The "smart" ingredient involves technology, but it also applies to the trained army soldier. An infantryman used to be a helmeted GI in a brown, green, or camo-colored uniform carrying a bayonet-tipped rifle in his hands and grenades in his belt. Today, when dressed in their full combat regalia, soldiers look more like creatures from outer space.

The next generation soldier will go into battle in a chameleon-like uniform that changes color to correspond with the environmental characteristics of the setting. He will carry medical body sensors to monitor physical condition, especially helpful if he has been wounded and requires medical attention. He will also have protective lightweight armor clothing and individual equipment, including a miniature computer and radio. Cables for the computer and radio connections will be built into the backpack frame. He will carry a light modular carbine that replaces the M16 rifle and the M4 carbine. The weapon will have optical components for delivering accurate targeting information and include a thermal sight, a multifunction laser sight, and a daylight video sight, thereby enabling a soldier to fire effectively day or night in all weather conditions. Tomorrow's soldier will also wear a new lightweight ballistic-resistant helmet with a see-through, heads-up display that can show video and thermal imaging integrated by sensory enhancements and networked with information from manned and unmanned ground and aerial machines for collaborative situational awareness.

The infantryman's computer will contain a radio and a Global Positioning System (GPS) locator. A handgrip wired to the pack and attached to the soldier's chest will serve as a computer mouse, allowing him to select screens, change radio frequencies, and transmit wireless digital information. A weapon-mounted miniature camera will enable the soldier to send video messages to squad, platoon, or company command posts. The computer's software includes tactical and mission support data, maps and tactical overlays, and dozens of other functions pertinent to guiding assaults and targeting enemy emplacements with artillery, mortars, missiles, and air assets.

A soldier will be able to sit at a desk in a command post or high mobility vehicle, collect information on a specialized portable computer, and using the Advanced Field Artillery Tactical Data System (AFATDS) home in and execute artillery attacks on targets of choice.

Many other weapons are in the pipeline for the future soldier. The twenty-five-year-old M82A3 sniper rifle will be replaced by the new .50-caliber

RIGHT: A soldier from the 82nd Airborne Division moves through terrain with a well-stuffed Modular Lightweight Load-Carrying Equipment (MOLLE) Rutsack on his back and an M-16 rifle under his arm.

XM107, which will be able to strike targets more than a mile away. As another replacement for the M16 and M4 infantry rifles, the soldier will carry an XM29 integrated airburst weapon equipped with two barrels, one firing 20 mm air-bursting munitions and the other firing a 5.56 mm rifle cartridge. The XM29 is accurate at one thousand yards, about three times the effective range of M16 and M4 rifles.

The Precision Guided Mortar Munition (PGMM) is also coming into the infantryman's arsenal: a laser-guided, lightweight, and accurate 120 mm mortar that makes it possible to directly strike an enemy position, causing less collateral damage. A Mortar Fire Control System (MFCS) integrates with a fire control computer and an inertial navigation and pointing system that will enable mortar crews to fire M120/M121 120 mm rounds in less than one minute, as compared to an eight- to ten-minute cycle between rounds.

A new future lightweight

OBJECTIVE COMBAT WEAPONS

On schedule for 2010 are several new weapons for the Objective Force Warrior (OFW). They consist of an assortment of technological improvements under the title Land Warrior Block 3.0. In addition to highly specialized protective gear and communications equipment, it is a completely new package of weapons.

The Objective Individual Combat weapon (OICW) truly makes the infantryman "An Army of One" once the highly specialized and versatile firearm becomes available for the battlefield. Taking cover will no longer help the enemy. Through the use of high explosive airburst ammunition, the OICW will increase lethality and double the infantryman's standoff range to one thousand meters.

The weapon looks like something out of Star Wars. In addition to operating like a rifle, it can also accurately lob a 20 mm grenade into a foxhole. The weapon contains its own mini-computer and can measure the exact distance from the firing point to the target. A soldier will use a built-in laser to aim and fire. The OICW system can track a moving target, calculate the speed, triangulate the angle, and fire with

accuracy. The system can also pick from a variety of possible targets the one closest or of the most immediate threat and eradicate it first. The greatest advantage is the weapon's ability to eliminate aiming errors caused by wobbling, windage guessing, and range of target. It is the ideal weapon for making every shot count.

The most significant argument against the weapon's deployment is its weight, eighteen pounds, which is twice the burden of a standard issue M16. It also has greater recoil than the M16, and some experts question whether the OICW meets the new army standard for lightweight shoulder weapons. Some experts suggest that to lighten the weapon the grenade-launcher should be separated from the rifle. At present the OICW is expected to become part of the soldier's arsenal on the battlefield by 2009.

The army is also planning on providing an Objective Crew Served Weapon (OCSW), a new and highly lethal heavy machinegun with all the capabilities of the OICW. It will be lightweight, easily carried by two men, and crew-served. The OCSW will have the accuracy and capability of taking out armor-protected enemy at a range of a mile.

Multirole Armament and Ammunition System (MRAAS) will be able to fire direct and indirect munitions up to forty miles using extended-range projectiles and a multipurpose smart warhead.

Heavier munitions systems will include the new Army Tactical Missile System (ATACMS), which is in the works to operate much like a ship-launched Tomahawk cruise missile. It is a surface-to-surface guided missile that is fired from a five-ton truck. The system will be able to launch an anti-personnel/anti-material warhead at strategic targets deep into enemy territory in any kind of weather.

A Line-of-Sight

FAR LEFT: The Air Warrior wears a Kevlar helmet with cover and with extra padding in the helmets to reduce head impact on landing. During daytime the men wear a desert camouflage uniform and lightweight jungle boots.

LEFT: The XM-107 semi-automatic sniper weapon is replacing most of the M-16s and M-24s used as sniper rifles during the war with Iraq.

FUTURE FORCE WARRIOR

The Future Force or Objective Force Warrior (FFW) is the U.S. Army's main initiative to develop and demonstrate revolutionary capabilities for future soldier systems. The basic concept is to create a lightweight, lethal, integrated combat system for each soldier that will include a weapon, head-to-toe individual protection, netted communications, portable power sources, and the enhancement of the individual soldier's performance. The key points can be summarized as:

LETHALITY—a family of lightweight weapons with advanced fire control, optimized for urban combat; synchronized direct and indirect fires as required.

SURVIVABILITY—lightweight, multifunctional, low-bulk body armor.

SENSORS & COMMUNICATIONS—Robust team communications; state-of-the-art distributed and fused sensors; organic tactical intelligence collection assets, all to be combined with better training leading to enhanced situational understanding, on-the-move planning, and close linkage to other force assets.

POWER—the modern army needs more power than ever before. The FFW will have a portable power supply to allow continuous autonomous team operations.

MOBILITY AND PERFORMANCE—the most important thing about all this equipment is that it does not restrict full movement during a mission. Additionally. an on-board physiological/medical sensor suite with enhanced prompt casualty care.

The Future Force Warrior system will be available to soldiers in 2010—but the development that started with the current Land Warrior does not stop there. The Vision 2020 Future Warrior system will be fielded 10 years later.

ABOVE: The Future Force Warrior will enjoy a reduced fighting load portable power source, and improved protection, lethality, and battlefield communications.

ABOVE. LEFT, and RIGHT: The current Land Warrior system includes PAS-13 Thermal Weapon Sights and Interceptor Body Armor providing protection against bullet and fragmentation wounds.

ABOVE: The Vision 2020 Future Warrior concept will be a completely integrated system which will be tailored to each individual, from an electro-spun combat uniform to a biomechanically engineered headgear subsystem.

TRAINING

Realistic training makes combat easier to handle. Today's training facilities are much more impressive than those of the past, with a full range of devices to ensure post-training analysis. Here, troops prepare to drop from a helicopter onto the roof of a training building. On entering (TOP), they begin clearing the building floor by floor. Outside (CENTER RIGHT), a team covers the building with a grenade launcher, while inside (BOTTOM RIGHT), soldiers secure the building room by room.

ABOVE: A soldier sights through the scope of an M249CB2 sniper rifle at a far distant target.

BELOW: A team spreads its tripod and sets up a XM307 25mm Advanced Crew Served Machine Gun. A soldier to the left of the machinegun covers the position with a standard M16A2 rifle.

During the next ten years, the future fighter will be all about mobility, equipment, and congressional funding.

The Army in the Air

During the next few years, the army will be fielding a new generation of fixed- and rotary-wing aircraft, some of which will be unmanned aerial vehicles.

The Guardrail/Common Sensor (GR/CS) is a fixed-wing RC-12 aircraft fitted with airborne signals intelligence (SIGINT) to provide signal intercept and targeting information on the location of enemy emitters. A system consists of six to twelve corps-based aircraft flying missions in groups of two or three day and night, around the clock, over areas of interest.

A new fixed-wing Tactical Unmanned Aerial Vehicle (TUAV) will soon come into operation for use in areas where real-time information is essential from areas where the risk of using piloted aircraft is too great. The TUAV will have an operating range of 200 kilometers and will be able to provide reconnaissance, surveillance, and target acquisition data at a range of 50 kilometers, day or night.

The RAH-66 Comanche is the army's next generation manned helicopter. It is designed to conduct reconnaissance and attack operations in all battlefield conditions, day or night, and in any weather condition. The Comanche will replace three helicopters (AH-1, OH-6, and the OH-58 Kiowa Warrior) now in the Army Aviation fleet, and by 2014 may itself be replaced by unmanned rotary-propelled aircraft.

Kiowa Warriors, however, will still be around as a rapidly deployable, lightly armed, reconnaissance helicopter. They have been retrofitted with advanced visionics, navigation, communications, weapons, and cockpit integration systems. The armament systems have also been improved to provide anti-armor, anti-personnel, and anti-aircraft capabilities.

Anti-Tank (LOSAT) missile will be launched from a highly specialized armored vehicle that can be sling-lifted and deployed by helicopter or airdropped by a C-130 transport. The missile is guided and fired horizontally from within the truck against heavy armor and field fortifications at ranges exceeding the main gun range of current tanks. The purpose of LOSAT is to reduce light infantry casualty rates when opposed by heavy armor.

The new Apache Longbow will be another addition to the Army Aviation fleet. The helicopter will have the ability to deliver deep precision strikes and provide armed reconnaissance and surveillance day or night. Capable of a speed of 167 knots, the Longbow can maneuver and use its rapid-fire weapons system to home on sixteen different targets in sixty seconds.

The new model Black Hawk (UH-60) can deploy a fully equipped eleven-man infantry squad to critical areas faster and anywhere within a 320-knot range. The helicopter is capable of carrying a sling-load of eight to nine thousand pounds. In a single lift, the L model can transport and reposition a 105 mm howitzer, its six-man crew, and thirty rounds of ammunition.

Future Combat Systems (FCS)

Future Combat Systems are about the twenty-first century soldier and originate from some of the lessons learned in Operation Iraqi Freedom and the war on terrorism: a conflict that has demonstrated that a joint, combined arms, network centric force has the capability of rapidly defeating an enemy in battle while acting as the key element in follow-on peacekeeping efforts. The experience is adding new dimensions to army doctrine.

The army's FCS-equipped Modular Force will be part of a joint team in any operation, against any level of threat, in any environment. The Modular Force's role is to balance the capabilities for battle space dominance, lethality, and survivability with agility, versatility, deployability, and sustainability. The force will be capable of developing situations of contact, engage the enemy in unexpected ways, maneuver to positions with speed and nimbleness, strike the enemy beyond the range of their weapons, and destroy enemy forces with enhanced fires and assault at times and places of the unit's choosing and with stamina against decisive points and centers of gravity.

The army's FCS network provides a family of systems that operate as a cohesive system-of-systems network where the whole of its capabilities is greater than the sum of its parts. The network, with its logistics and embedded training systems, is the key to

ABOVE LEFT: On November 3, 2004, an OH-58D Kiowa Warrior helicopter from the 1st Infantry Division takes off on a mission from Forward Operation Base MacKenzie in Iraq.

ABOVE: On December 5, 2005, an AH-64D Apache Longbow helicopter from the 1st Battalion, 101st Aviation Regiment, takes off from Forward Operating Base Speicher, Iraq, on an air support mission for troops on the ground.

RIGHT: *The graphic depicts how the many components of the Future Combat System (FCS) will integrate into an overall working and totally linked lethal system.*

ABOVE: *With its optical sensor package in the raised position, a Packbot climbs a debris mound during a Future Combat Systems (FCS) technologies demonstration, of which it is a component, during the autumn of 2005.*

BELOW: *In the Future Combat System, a soldier wears a Lightweight Video Reconnaissance System (LVRS), which enables him to see what is occurring near his sector but out of range of his sight.*

the army's transformation and enables the future force to employ revolutionary operational and organizational concepts. It enables the soldier to perceive, comprehend, shape, and dominate the future battlefield. The network is comprised of four overarching building blocks: a system of systems that define the operating environment; battle command software; communications and computers; and intelligence, reconnaissance, and surveillance systems. Technology, however, is rapidly changing. Weapons engineers have told General Peter Schoomaker, army chief of staff, that by 2010 computers will be replaced by electronics so tiny they can be embedded in clothing or eyeglasses and broadcast on the human retina.

Lieutenant General Joseph L. Yakovac, military deputy to the assistant secretary of the army for Acquisitions, Logistics, and Technology, said, "A lot of capability can be brought to a vehicle by software," adding that FCS vehicles will have digital command and control, automatic target acquisition, the Joint Tactical Radio System, and the Warfighter Information System-Tactical (WIN-T). The WIN-T system is the central part of LandWarNet, the army's

effort to integrate multiple systems into a joint, network-centric, knowledge-based warfare capability. WIN-T is designed to provide reliable, secure and seamless voice, video, and data communications to enable decisive combat actions by providing the operational picture for theater combat commanders on the move. WIN-T grew out of complaints from Lieutenant General William Wallace, commander of the V Corps during Operation Iraqi Freedom, who cited the difficulties he had experienced while trying to communicate over great distances to the spreading elements of his corps.

The core of a Future Combat System's building blocks is developed around a highly integrated structure of eighteen manned and unmanned air and ground systems and vehicles that provide maneuver, maneuver support, and sustainment systems, bound together by a distributed network supporting the soldier. The network is totally integrated, including reconnaissance and surveillance capabilities, and consists of special equipment, including everything the soldier wears, carries, and consumes. In the Modular Force, the soldier is an integral part of the network system.

Unattended Ground Sensors (UGS) are placed in combat areas or across a broad field to perform two major functions: intelligence, surveillance, and reconnaissance gathering; and, chemical, biological, radiological, and nuclear detection. The units can also be used for perimeter defense, target acquisition, and situational awareness. The units can be hand-deployed by soldiers or by robotic vehicles operating inside buildings or outdoors.

Non-Line-of-Sight Launch Systems (NLOS-LS) consist of a family of missiles in a highly deployable, platform-independent Container Launch Unit having self-contained tactical fire control electronics and software for remote and unmanned operations. Each launch unit contains fifteen missiles (Precision Attack

the system to dynamically update routes and target information. A single system consists of two UAVs and a control unit. It weighs forty pounds and is backpackable.

Class II Unarmed Aerial Vehicles (UAV) have twice the endurance and wider range than a Class I unit. Instead of communicating with the soldier on the ground, the UAV-II communicates with Mounted Combat System company commanders, providing reconnaissance, early warning, and target acquisition and designation. The aerial system is vehicle-mounted for vertical take-off and landing. The unit can remain aloft for two hours and has a working radius of sixteen kilometers.

Class III Unmanned Aerial Vehicles (UAV) perform multifunction aerial operations and have the range and endurance to support a battalion level force. Class III fixed-wing UAVs carry a payload in addition to communications links, mine detection, and chemical, biological, radiological, and nuclear detection. The vehicle also has the capability of performing meteorological surveys. Class III vehicles must have a take-off and landing area on a dedicated field. They operate within a forty-kilometer radius and can remain airborne for six hours.

Class IV Unmanned Aerial Vehicles (UAV) are rotary-wing aircraft designed with the range and endurance to serve a brigade and provide the Modular Force commander with communications relay over an area having a radius of seventy-five kilometers. The UAV will team with manned vehicles for emitter mapping and wide-band communications of 150 to 175 kilometers. The vehicle also carries on-board devices for processing chemical, biological, radiological, nuclear, and energy detection. Class IV UAVs will carry a payload, roam across an area of interest,

LEFT: A soldier in the 2nd Battalion, 5th Infantry Regiment, 25th Infantry Division, prepares to enter a cave in order to search for enemy fighters in the wilds of the Afghan mountains.

ABOVE: On September 21, 2005, an army technician prepares a Class I Unmanned Aerial Vehicle (UAV) for takeoff during a demonstration of the Future Combat Systems at Aberdeen Proving Ground, Maryland.

BELOW: An up-close look at the Future Combat Systems UAV shown above. The 15-pound vertical takeoff unit is man-portable and can be fitted with a variety of sensor packages for urban or jungle terrain.

Missiles (PAM) and Loitering Attack Missiles (LAM)) with its own computer and communications system capable of launching either a direct fire trajectory or a boost-glide trajectory. The missile will receive targeting information prior to launch, and mission data can be preprogrammed or changed in flight.

The **Intelligent Munitions System** (IMS) is an unattended munitions system that provides both offensive battle space shaping and defensive force protection capabilities. The system contains a combination of lethal and non-lethal munitions integrated with command and control features, communication devices, and sensors and seekers. The nonlethal capabilities are for controlling the movements of noncombatants. The system can be deposited anywhere, and once on the ground will report its GPS location for additional programming. The munitions system can be turned on and off to allow passage or to prevent it. The IMS can also be picked up and redeployed elsewhere.

Class I Unmanned Aerial Vehicles (UAV) provide dismounted soldiers with reconnaissance, surveillance, and target acquisition. The small air vehicle weighs less than fifteen pounds and, with a vertical take-off and landing capability, can operate in a city as well as in a jungle. Soldiers on the ground use

ABOVE: The Class IV Unmanned Aerial Vehicle (UAV) has a range and endurance appropriate for a brigade mission. It can operate in a fifty-mile radius, remain in flight for up to twenty-four hours, and perform emitter mapping and wide-band communications relay across a hundred miles.

conducts military operations in urban tunnels, sewers, and caves. The vehicle aids intensive or high-risk ground operations by providing urban intelligence, surveillance and reconnaissance, and is instrumental in detecting chemicals and toxic material, without exposing the soldier to the hazard. The unit weighs thirty pounds and is capable of carrying six pounds of explosives.

The **Multifunctional Utility/Logistics and Equipment (MULE) Vehicle** is a 2.5-ton Unmanned Ground Vehicle that supports dismounted operations. The MULE contains four major components: a common platform; an autonomous navigation system; an operator control unit; and three mission models. The vehicle is also sling-loadable under military rotary-wing aircraft. Mission models provide transport, countermining, or Assault-Light capabilities. The transport model carries up to twenty-four hundred pounds of equipment and supplies for dismounted squads in irregular terrain. The countermine vehicle detects, marks, and neutralizes mines. The Assault-Light Mule is used for reconnaissance, surveillance, and target acquisition and contains an integrated weapons system designed to aid dismounted infantry in locating and destroying enemy positions.

and operate day or night, even in adverse weather. Unlike the Class III, the UAV takes off vertically, requires no dedicated landing field, and can remain airborne for twenty-four hours.

Armed Robotic Vehicles (ARV) come in two models: the Assault variant and the Reconnaissance, Surveillance and Target Acquisition variant. The two models share a common chassis. The Assault robot can provide reconnaissance from remote locations; deploy sensors, direct-fire weapons, special munitions into buildings, bunkers, and other urban works; assess battle damage; act as a communication relay; support mounted and dismounted assault forces with direct fire and anti-tank weapons; and occupy key terrain and provide over-watching fires.

The Reconnaissance, Surveillance, and Target Acquisition model will perform most of the same operations in any urban or other battle space, and in addition locate and destroy or by-pass threat obstacles in buildings, bunkers, tunnels, and other urban works while acting as a communications relay.

The **Small Unmanned Ground Vehicle** (SUGV) is a lightweight, portable robotic ground vehicle that

The **Mounted Combat System** (MCS) is an assault vehicle with autoloading line-of-sight and beyond-line-of-sight firing capability up to eight kilometers. The MCS is built on a Manned Ground Vehicle chassis and manually operated. This mini-tank is highly mobile and maneuvers out of contact to positions of advantage. With its integrated sensor network, the MCS is capable of providing direct support to dismounted infantry and is capable of destroying bunkers and breaching walls during assault operations.

The **Infantry Carrier Vehicle** (ICV) is built in four versions, being either for a company

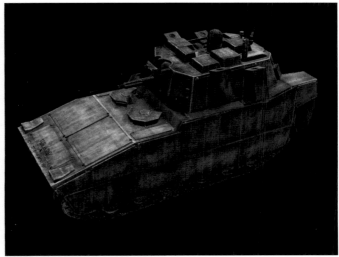

commander, a platoon leader, a rifle squad, or a weapons squad. The exterior of all four models are identical. Each platoon contains a platoon leader variant with three rifle squad variants and one weapons squad variant. The rifle squad variant and the weapons squad variant each carry a nine-person infantry squad to a location for close assault. Each ICV can maneuver day or night, blacked-out, in inclement weather, or during periods of limited visibility while effectively employing weapon systems. When delivering dismounted troops to close battle conditions, an ICV has the capability to aid the squad with self-defense and supporting 30 mm cannon fire while communicating battle conditions and threats to the Modular Force network. The Marine Corps and the navy also plan to use the vehicle.

The **Non-Line-of-Sight Cannon** (NLOS-C) is built on an aluminum armored Manned Ground Vehicle having a rubber-tracked platform and a combination diesel/hybrid engine. The cannon fires at targets in line-of-sight, beyond line-of-sight, and non-line-of-sight. The weapons system provides flexible support by its ability to change effects by using different ordnance round-by-round and mission-by mission. The system's primary objective is to support FCS combined arms battalions during assault operations. The cannon can move rapidly, stop quickly, and deliver first round effects on target in record time. The cannon is a one-of-a-kind artillery system with a two-man crew and an automatic ammunition handling system capable of firing a round every ten seconds and maintaining a rate of six rounds per minute at ranges of nearly fifteen miles. "It is light, but can handle recoil," said Daniel Pierson, who works for General Yakovac in Acquisition, Logistics, and Technology. The NLOS-C balances deployability and sustainability with responsiveness, lethality, survivability, agility, and versatility. The NLOS cannon vehicle with its 155

LEFT: The Non-Line-of-Sight Cannon (NLOS-C) provides the FCS Modular Force commander with unprecedented responsiveness and lethality because its networked communication system enables the cannon to accurately strike targets beyond the horizon.

CENTER: Three modular components of the FCS include a Small Unmanned Ground Vehicle (top), which is capable of performing tactical operations in urban terrain, tunnels, sewers, and caves.

The Multifunctional Utility/Logistics and Equipment (MULE) Vehicle (center) is a 2-1/2 ton Unmanned Ground Vehicle (UGV) which can carry more than two tons of supplies for dismounted infantry.

The Mounted Combat System (MCS) (bottom right) provides both direct and beyond-the-line-of-sight (BLOS) offensive firepower capability allowing unmanned components of the FCS to destroy enemy forces beyond the range of sight.

BELOW LEFT: The Infantry Carrier Vehicle (ICV) of the FCS comes in four platform versions: a company commander vehicle; a platoon leader vehicle; a rifle squad vehicle; and a weapons squad vehicle. Squad-carrying models transport nine fully equipped soldiers. ICVs can move, shoot, communicate, detect threats, and protect men under most terrain conditions.

ABOVE: The FCS Non-Line-of-Sight Mortar (NLOS-M) has a fire control system to conduct semi- to autonomous computation of technical fire direction, automatic gun lay, preparation of ammunition, and the firing the mortar the round.

ABOVE: The FCS Command and Control Vehicle (C2V) contains all the interfaces required to enable the commander to leverage the power of the FCS network and provide situational understanding to all the commanders in the area.

RIGHT: The FCS modular Medical Vehicle (MV) comes with two platforms: the Treatment (MV-T) model and the Evacuation (MV-E) model. Both vehicles provide trauma treatment. The MV-E maneuvers with the combat force where casualties occur.

mm weapon weighs less than twenty-four tons and fits easily into the cargo bay of a C-130 transport.

The **Non-Line-of-Sight Mortar** (NLOS-M) provides close support of tactical maneuvers that require both destructive fire and special purpose fire. The NLOS-M uses precision-guided 81 mm mortar rounds against high payoff and most dangerous targets and provides area suppression in support of Modular Force companies and platoons. The agile mortar vehicle can operate in all weather and terrain conditions at extended ranges and provide illumination ordnance on demand. The command and control system enables the NLOS-M to conduct semi- to autonomous computation of technical fire direction, automatic gun lay, preparation of the ammunition for firing, and mortar round firing.

The **Reconnaissance and Surveillance Vehicle** (RSV) is equipped with a suite of advanced sensors to detect, locate, track, classify, and automatically identify targets from increased standoff ranges in all climatic conditions, day or night. The suite includes a mast-mounted, long-range electro-optic infrared sensor; an emitter mapping sensor for radio frequency intercept and direction finding; remote chemical detection; and a multifunction radio frequency sensor. The system can also conduct automatic target detection and aided target recognition. The vehicles are equipped to distribute unattended ground sensors (UGS); deploy small, unmanned

ground vehicles (SUGV); carry two unmanned aerial vehicles (UAVs); and fire a variety of payloads.

The **Command and Control Vehicle** (C2V) is the hub of battlefield command and control. The platform provides for information management of the integrated network, using a range of communications and sensor capabilities within the Modular Force. The vehicle is located within the headquarters sections at each echelon of the Modular Force down to the company commander level and provides command and control to units on the move. The communications equipment can receive, analyze, and transmit tactical information via voice, video, and digital data inside and outside the Modular Force. C2V vehicles can also employ unmanned aerial vehicles to enhance situational awareness in areas where other deployed devices have been destroyed.

Medical Vehicle—Treatment (MV-T) and Evacuation (MV-E) provide advanced trauma life support within one hour to critically injured soldiers. The dual vehicles serve as the primary medical system within the Modular Force. The medical vehicles enable trauma specialists to maneuver with and be closer to combat operations, providing treatment and expeditious evacuation from the battle zone.

FCS Recovery and Maintenance Vehicles (FRMV) provide the means for recovering and repairing damaged assets in the field. Each Modular Force will have two to three combat repair teams within the forward support battalion to perform field maintenance and recovery operations. The vehicle holds three maintenance personnel with space to recover three crewmen from disabled vehicles. The FRMV also carries close combat support weapons and a MK-19 grenade launcher.

The Future Combat System is one of the most complex systems integration and development programs ever executed by the Department of Defense. Boeing and Science Applications

International Company were chosen to execute the systems integration and technical aspects of the program and to develop the expertise. The FCS program is currently on budget and on schedule for 2008, and will continue to spinout more of the eighteen elements of the core system through an incremental integration and evaluation process until the year 2014. The program, as defined through 2014, is expected to continue into 2025 and beyond. Immense training will be involved in weaning the soldier from today's conventional weapons to tomorrow's technological weapons. "Under the system of managing the Soldier as a system," said Brigadier General James Moran, commanding general, Soldier Systems Center, "two uniform systems are under development. The Future Force Warrior system will be available to Soldiers in 2010. The Vision 2020 Future Warrior system, which follows the concept of the 2010 Future Force Warrior system, will be fielded ten years later."

The army is particularly interested in making 2,131 FCS vehicles available for Stryker Interim Brigade Combat Teams by 2008. Stryker is the original designation for the Infantry Carrier Vehicle, named after two Medal of Honor recipients with the same surname: PFC Stuart Stryker, who served with the 513th Parachute Infantry in Germany during World War II, and Specialist Robert Stryker, who served with the First Infantry Division in Vietnam. The original ICV Stryker vehicle expanded into a series of ten variants and is still growing as part of the FCS. Among the units scheduled to receive FCS Stryker vehicles are the 172nd Infantry Brigade; the Second Armored Cavalry Regiment; the Second Brigade, 2=Twenty-fifth Infantry Division; and the Fifty-sixth Brigade, Twenty-eighth Infantry Division, of the Pennsylvania National Guard.

In addition to Stryker Interim Brigade Combat Teams, the FCS core program will use an Evaluation Brigade Combat Team throughout the development and spinout phase. This will eventually coalesce into a Current Force Brigade Combat Team equipped with the mix of refined FCS combat and tactical vehicles.

The design of Future Combat Systems as an approach to tactical fighting emanates from the sum of experiences encountered during the Afghan and Iraqi wars. The FCS is an answer to detecting and fighting insurgencies as well as performing rapid tactical ground movements when engaged in more conventional combat. The system is geared to effective fighting while giving the soldier the best weaponry, targeting tools, reconnaissance and surveillance, and protection that money and technology can provide. It also provides an early warning system against enemy incursions while detecting the presence of chemical, biological, and radiological weapons. With the global threat posed by

LEFT: The FCS Recovery and Maintenance Vehicle (FRMV) carries two or three technicians whose job is the repair and recovery of damaged equipment in the field. The FRMV carries sets of repair parts as well as an Mk-19mm grenade launcher.

LEFT: The army has also developed a highly capable Stryker force. In early 2006, the 172nd Stryker Brigade Combat Team rolled through Mosul, Iraq, in some of their newly refitted Stryker vehicles.

RIGHT: In February 2006, a Stryker team M1025A2 Humvee motors through the streets of Mosul, Iraq, with its Cupola Protective Ensemble (CPE) and equipment for designating targets for laser-guided ordnance.

Iran and North Korea's nuclear programs and potential nonnuclear programs of other prospective adversaries, the American soldier will need all the help he can get if and when preemptive action or defensive measures become necessary. Future wars will not follow the twentieth-century pattern.

Brigadier General Charles A. Cartwright is currently program manager for the army's Modular Force, and Dennis A. Muilenburg is Boeing Integrated Defense System's program manager for the Future Combat Systems. Fort Bliss, Texas, has been selected as the site for the thirty-five hundred soldiers of the Evaluation Brigade Combat Team (EBCT) to begin testing the Future Combat Systems program.

Until all the FCS vehicles become available, the army will continue to rely on conventional armored fighting vehicles with familiar names like Bradley and Abrams. Today's Bradley medium tanks come in different configurations designed for infantry and cavalry units. They have digital command and control capabilities, forward-looking infrared and independent sight targeting, and are armed with a 25 mm cannon and a tube-launched, optically tracked, wire-guided antitank (TOW) missile system. Abrams tanks, named for one of the great tank commanders of World War II, will continue to be the primary weapon in the arsenal of heavy armor through the transition to FCS. The modernized and specially armored Abrams M1A2 SEP tank is driven by a fifteen hundred horsepower turbine

BELOW: Army Reserve soldiers from the 357th, 366th, and 401st Chemical Companies practice nuclear, chemical, and biological decontamination and treatment procedures for simulated casualties at a joint civilian-military exercise at Fort McCoy, Wisconsin.

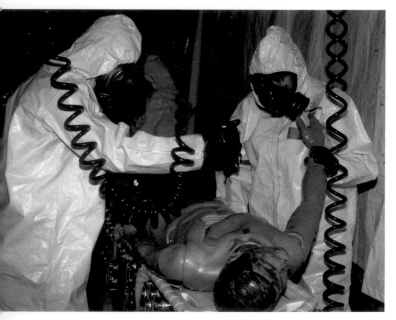

engine capable of 42 mph and carries a 120 mm main gun. New technology changes include the use of army common command and control software that gives the crew current time digital situational data and overlays.

Artillery munitions also continue to improve. The new 155 mm guided Excalibur round (XM982) can strike a target fifteen kilometers away with ten-meter accuracy, a capability that represents a huge improvement over existing munitions. Excalibur rounds will be used in army and Marine Corps howitzers, such as the Paladin 155 mm self-propelled howitzer (M109A6), the Lightweight 155 mm Howitzer (M777), as well as the future FCS Non-Line-of-Sight Cannon. During flight, the projectile "de-rolls," deploys canards, acquires GPS signals, calculates the navigation solution, and maneuvers itself to the target, which it then destroys. Excalibur is expected to be available in 2006.

Preparing for the Future—Irregular Warfare

Army planning revolves around the theory that the farther one projects from the present time, the more possibilities exist for changes to the future security of the United States, and any such planning must allow for unexpected and radical changes. Any option under study today requires a fundamental overhaul of existing defense policy and army and joint concepts, including changes in force structure and capabilities.

The probability of state-on-state warfare is considered low, while the likelihood of global instability and widespread irregular warfare is high. U.S. interests are routinely threatened at home and abroad. The demanding and admittedly unexpected requirements in Iraq have shown a need for manpower balanced between combat and nation-building tasks. Conditions in Iraq have also shown that the nation's complement of special operations forces have to be increased in size and capability. The spread of irregular warfare also suggests that army forces would likely be shifted from basing in the United States to trouble spots around the globe because of a growing importance to integrate U.S. military capabilities with forces from other countries where terrorists and insurgents operate.

Through the year 2011, the army will be studying operational concepts that will include:

- Expeditionary capability for rapid intervention with balanced forces.
- Emphasis on distributed operations, operations agility, distributed support and sustainment, and exploitation of maneuverability, thereby denying the enemy opportunities to exercise the initiative or develop sanctuaries.
- The need for a network-enabled battle command having full situational understanding.
- The stated goals of a full operational net assessment of the adversary and the ability to maintain a dominant decision cycle relevant to the adversary.
- Transition to a brigade-based force, with a resulting increase in the number of employable brigade combat teams.
- Reduced dependence on heavy forces, leading to a rebalancing of the force toward light- and medium-weight formations with higher manpower levels.
- Increase in civil-military and nation-building forces and capabilities through long-term integration of tactical forces.
- Fuller integration of military operations within the host government and military structure.

Fighting irregular warfare will require a major military effort devoted to nation-building not experienced since the Vietnam War, with the necessary shifts in capabilities and doctrine as conditions change. The future of the armed forces, and the army in particular, might very well require the force of the future to adopt nation-building as a new core competency. Under such a doctrine, soldiers could spend one-third to one-half of their military service in operational deployments where an understanding of the sources of conflict, local culture, and intricacies of civil-military relations are as important as individual combat skills..

Preparing for the Future—Weapons of Mass Destruction

Although the capability to use weapons of mass destruction (WMD) has spread globally, the threshold for their use has fallen, particularly in a few rogue nations having unstable and unpredictable governments. The army is developing a doctrine to address both state and non-state adversaries having or developing WMD capabilities, which includes the

ABOVE: A Cupola Protective Ensemble (CPE) gunner with a Stryker Combat Team stands alongside his vehicle.

elimination of the threat by negotiation or, as a last resort, preemptive military action.

While the proliferation of irregular warfare would seldom place U.S. national survival at risk, the increased threat of an enemy using WMDs to prevent U.S. intervention reduces the threshold for their use. Threats already exist as those state and non-state elements gain access and the ability to employ WMDs to deny U.S. intervention. The army's capability and willingness to influence regional conflicts under those conditions would be reduced. To obtain the cooperation of regional allies would require assurance that the U.S. could protect their country from WMD attack. The primary objective of a U.S. defensive policy must also evolve to reduce exposure of interventionary forces to WMD attacks. This requires the army be capable of detecting and destroying WMD arsenals and missiles at long range and preferably preemptively.

A future defense strategy that proposes low thresholds to intervention relies heavily on long-range engagement and endorses a "short war" perspective, which simultaneously reduces the conditions under which major land operations would be considered a desirable option. The U.S. Army is unlikely to conduct major land operations abroad in the face of expectations that an enemy would and could employ WMDs against American forces. Options would increase, however, if an adversary had limited WMD capabilities and limited operational reach. Under such conditions, U.S. forces would rapidly destroy WMD capabilities, close immediately with the enemy force, and employ highly mobile formations in distributed operations with decentralized forces targeting strategic sites to reduce the risk of catastrophic loss.

In the face of irregular warfare on one hand, and the enemy employment of WMDs on the other hand, the army must change and is changing. Future force fighting will require a new suite of capabilities, tactics, and techniques requiring shifts in investment to science, technology, and the acquisition of chemical, biological, radiological, nuclear, electro-magnetic-pulse, and explosive defense capabilities.

Changes must be made for the army to remain relevant and effective in future operational environments, and becoming merely marginally smarter, marginally more responsive, marginally more agile, and marginally more lethal, mobile, and survivable may not be enough.

A New Battle Doctrine

"We have to break free of the gravitational pull of our current doctrine, future concepts, and institutional biases," said U.S. Army Chief of Staff General Peter Schoomaker to a group of officers who have been tasked to refine a doctrine for irregular warfare.

The AirLand Battle doctrine of the late 1970s still applies to major land engagements and was a major

BELOW: Mounted on a M1025AR Stryker Humvee, a Common Remotely Operated Weapon Station (CROWS) can be articulated and accurately fired from in the vehicle or on the street.

factor in the success of the Persian Gulf wars. As insurgent forces and terrorists have demonstrated, AirLand is not an all-purpose doctrine. Traditional doctrine expected ground forces to make physical contact with enemy forces, assess the enemy's strength and capabilities, and then maneuver and apply the necessary power to achieve victory. With the technology being developed today, a fully digitized army will be able to assess the enemy's strength, deployment, weaponry, and communications capabilities before making physical contact. Having made that assessment, and having the ability to share all the information with joint forces, commanders will be able to maneuver into advantageous positions and make a series of lethal and decisive strikes without massed battalions ever coming in physical contact of the enemy.

When and how a new battle doctrine plays out depends on the availability of the new technology and learning how to use it through war-gaming. Army doctrinal changes will evolve between the current day and the year 2014, when all the new tools of communication, navigation, weaponry, aircraft, and space-based systems associated with current planning come together with Future Combat Systems and become realities. When a soldier can go to war, win battles without ever coming in physical contact with the enemy by using technology, and go home unharmed, conventional ground wars will become vestiges of the past.

Army Goals

The army budget continues to grow from $98.6 billion in fiscal years 2006 to $110 billion in 2007, plus supplemental funding to fight terrorism and insurgency. The current budget provides for an all-volunteer force of nineteen combat brigades with special consideration given to soldiers with families. The structure of the army consists of a regular strength of 482,400 actives, 350,000 Army National Guard, and 205,000 Army Reserve. The entire force of 1,037,400 men and women are part of the process to transform and improve army capabilities; restructure forces to a modular design; retain an all-volunteer force; generate and sustain a force to prevail in the global war on terrorism; and accelerate the use of promising technology to improve force protection and to enhance fighting capability.

As the U.S. Army moves into the twenty-first century, it is held in greater public trust, respect, and esteem than the Congress that funds it and the reporters who write about it. The men and women who serve in the army are becoming the peacekeepers of the world, and the process is just beginning. To keep the army technologically and physically capable and thoroughly trained requires a great deal of money and a constant infusion of career-minded young men and women. Today's army offers opportunities that transcend civilian pursuits and will continue to do so for decades to come. The tattered volunteer army that in 1775 began as an experiment in revolution and warfare has mightily matured into the caretaker of the world.

BELOW: The M109A6 Paladin tank looks more like a sophisticated laboratory from the inside. In a September 15, 2005 test with "Excaliber" smart 155mm guided rounds, the lightweight howitzer fired a shell ten miles that struck within twenty feet of the target.

BIBLIOGRAPHY

The Army Almanac: A Book of Facts Concerning the Army of the United States. Washington: Government Printing Office, 1950.

Bauer, K. Jack. *The Mexican War 1846-1848.* New York, Macmillan Publishing Company, 1974.

Boatner, Mark M., III. *Encyclopedia of the American Revolution.* New York: David McKay Company, 1966.

Boujnida, Cheryl, "Army Displays Latest Warfighting Innovations." http://www4.army.mil/ocpa/read.php?story_id-key=7481

Bragg, Rick. *I Am a Soldier, Too: The Jessica Lynch Story.* New York, Knopf, 2003.

Buckley, Kevin. "General Abrams Deserves a Better War." *New York Times,* 5 October 1969.

Byman, Daniel. "Going to War with the Allies You Have: Allies, Counterinsurgency, and the War on Terrorism." http://www.StrategicStudiesInstitute.army.mil/

Cartwright, Charles A., and Muilenburg, Dennis A. "Future Combats Systems—An Overview." http://www.army.mil/fcs/articles/index.html

Cosmas, Graham A. *An Army for Empire: The United States Army in the Spanish-American War.* Shippensburg, Penna.: White Mane, 1994.

Davidson, Philip B. *Vietnam at War, the History: 1946-1975.* Novato, Calif.: Presidio Press, 1988.

Dupuy, R. Ernest. *The Compact History of the United States Army.* New York: Hawthorn Books, Inc., 1964.

Dupuy, R. Earnest and Dupuy, Trevor N. *The Harper Encyclopedia of Military History.* 4th ed. New York: HarperCollins, 1993.

Dupuy, Trevor N., Johnson, Curt, and Bongard, David L. *The Harper Encyclopedia of Military Biography.* New York: HarperCollins, 1992.

Eisenhower, John S. *Yanks: The Epic Story of the American Army in World War I.* New York: The Free Press, 2001.

Faust, Patricia L., ed. *Historical Times Illustrated Encyclopedia of the Civil War.* New York: Harper & Row, 1986.

Franks, Tommy, with McConnell, Malcolm. *American Soldier.* New York: Regan Books, 2004.

Greene, John Robert. *The Limits of Power: The Nixon and Ford Administrations.* Bloomington: University of Indiana Press, 1992.

Harding, Steve, "Army Demonstrates Future Combat Systems." http://www4.army.mil/ocpa/read.php?story_id_key=7985

Heller, Charles E., and Stoft, William A., eds. *America's First Battles: 1776-1965.* Lawrence, Kan.: University Press of Kansas, 1986.

Herr, John K, and Wallace, Edward S. *The Story of the U.S. Cavalry: 1775-1942.* New York: Bonanza Books, 1984.

Hillstrom, Laurie Collier. *War in the Persian Gulf.* 3 vols. Detroit: Thomson Gale, 2004.

Jacobs, Bruce. *Heroes of the Army: The Medal of Honor and Its Winners.* New York: W.W. Norton & Company, 1956.

Keegan, John. *Fields of Battle: The Wars for North America*. New York: Vintage Books, 1997.

Kennett, Lee. *G. I.: The American Soldier in World War II*. New York: Charles Scribner's Sons, 1987.

Kent, Zachary. *The Persian Gulf War: The Mother of All Battles*. Hillside, N.J.: Enslow, 1994.

King, John. *The Gulf War*. New York: Dillon Press, 1991.

McNamara, Robert S., with VanDeMark, Brian. *In Retrospect: The Tragedy and Lessons of Vietnam*. New York: Times Books, 1995.

McPherson, James M. *Battle Cry of Freedom: The Civil War Era*. New York: Oxford University Press, 1988.

Marshall, S.L.A. *Men against Fire*. New York: William Morrow, 1947.

_____. *The Military History of the Korean War*. New York: 1963.

_____. *Vietnam: Three Battles*. New York: Da Capo Press, 1982.

Merrill, James M. *Spurs to Glory: The Story of the United States Cavalry*. Chicago: Rand McNally & Company, 1966.

Murphy, Audie. *To Hell and Back: The Epic Combat Journal of World War II's Most Decorated G.I.* New York: MJF Books, 1977.

Palmer, Bruce, Jr. *The 25-Year War: America's Military Role in Vietnam*. Lexington: University Press of Kentucky, 1984.

Peers, William R. *The My Lai Inquiry*. New York: W. W. Norton, 1979.

Peterson, Harold L., ed. *Encyclopedia of Firearms*. New York: E.P. Dutton, 1964.

Pritchard, Russ A., Jr. *Civil War Weapons and Equipment*. London: Salamander Books, 2003.

Rivera, Sheila. *Operation Iraqi Freedom*. Edina, Minn.: Abdo Press, 2004.

Rooney, Ben. *The Daily Telegraph War on Saddam: The Complete Story of the Iraqi Campaign*. London, Robinson, 2003.

Schwartz, Richard Alan. *Encyclopedia of the Persian Gulf War*. Jefferson, N.C.: McFarland & Company, 1998.

Sheftick, Gary, "Army Moves Up Fielding of Future Combat Systems." http://www4.army.mil/ocpa/read.php?story_id_key=6189

Simpson, Charles M, III. *Inside the Green Berets: The First Thirty Years*. Novato, Calif.: Presidio Press, 1983.

Sorley, Lewis. *Thunderbolt: General Creighton Abrams and the Army of His Times*. New York: Simon & Schuster, 1992.

Stanton, Shelby L. *The Rise and Fall of an American Army: U.S. Army Ground Forces in Vietnam, 1965-1973*. Novato, Calif.: Presidio Press,1985.

U.S. Army, "Army Tests 'Excalibur' Smart Artillery Munition." http://www4.army.mil/ocpa/read.php?story_id_key=7983

U.S. Army, "FCS Overview," (and related documents). http://www.army.mil/fcs/factfiles/overview.html

U.S. Army, "Ghost Battalion Leads Fight in Fallujah." http://www4.army.mil/soldiers/view_story.php?story_id_key=6573

U.S. Army, "The Army Budget—Fiscal Years 2006 and 2007." http://www4.army.mil?ocpa/read.php?story_id_key=6828

Ward, Christopher. *The War of the Revolution*. 2 vols. New York: The Macmillan Company, 1952.

Weigley, Russell F. *The American Way of War: A History of United States Military Strategy and Policy*. Bloomington, Ind.: Indiana University Press, 1977.

_____. *History of the United States Army*. New York: The Macmillan Company, 1967.

Wright, Robert K. *The Continental Army*. Army Lineage Series by the Center for Military History, United States Army: Washington, D.C., 1983.

Zwier, Lawrence J. and Weltig, Matthew S. *The Persian Gulf and Iraqi Wars: Chronicle of America's Wars*. Minneapolis: Lerner Publications Company, 2005.

INDEX